THE INVOCATION OF THE NAME OF JESUS

Eileen,
with much love
oremus pro invicem

Raul C+

THE
INVOCATION
OF THE
NAME
OF JESUS

As Practiced in the

Western Church

RAMA COOMARASWAMY

FONS VITAE

1999

This edition printed and distributed by
Fons Vitae, Louisville, KY

Printed in the United States of America

Library of Congress Catalog Card Number: 99-67570

ISBN-1-887752-26-9

This edition published by
Fons Vitae
49 Mockingbird Valley Drive
Louisville, KY 40207-1366
email: Grayh101@aol.com
website: www.fonsvitae.com

The author has consciously chosen to retain the use of "he" to represent
both sexes and refers to the following, found in the Summa, 1.46.1 ad 3,
"The image of God belongs to both sexes, since it is in the mind wherein
is no sexual distinction."

CONTENTS

Deus humilium celsitudo, qui beatissimum Joannem Columbinum, confessorem tuum dilectissimum, tantae charitatis in te ardore inflammasti, ut Jesu nomen desideratissimum Filii tui in suo vivido corde et ore semper habere meruerit: concede quaesumus, ut ejus meretis et precibus ita in tuo nomine amore incendamur, ut mente et corde te unice super omnia diligamus et promissa humilibus praemia conseqamur, Per Dominum nostrum Jesum Christum.

(O God, with that great humility which the blessed John Columbinus, your confessor, manifested, in whom you greatly delighted, who was inflamed with such love towards your great charity, that the Name of Jesus, your most delectable Son, was constantly invoked both in his beating heart and in his mouth; grant we beseech you, that by his merits and prayers, that the same love of this Name will be ignited in our minds and hearts, and that we might love You alone above all things and as a result be granted the gift of humility. Through Jesus Christ our Lord.)

FROM THE MASS OF ST. JOHN COLUMBINO
(Acta Sanctorum)

On the Name of Jesus

Recent years have seen a revival of interest in the Prayer of Jesus. Various individuals and groups have embraced this form of prayer without any solid foundation in its theology, and without the "protection" that adherence to traditional and orthodox forms provide. Moreover, many Christians assume that this method of prayer—often referred to as Hesychast—is the exclusive property of the Eastern Orthodox Churches, and hence foreign to Catholic practice. The net result is that this most efficacious form of prayer is decried and neglected by many for whom it would and should provide a powerful and secure *viaticum* through the perils of the modern world.

It is not my intention to concentrate on the Prayer of Jesus as practiced in the Orthodox Church. The reader who is interested will however find much benefit—the principles involved are universal—from reading *The Way of the Pilgrim* (Seabury Press, New York); *Writings from the Philokalia on Prayer of the Heart, Early Fathers from the Philokalia*, and *The Complete Philokalia* (Faber and Faber), *On the Invocation of the Name of Jesus* (Fellowship of St. Alban and St. Sergius, London), *On the Invocation of the Name of Jesus* by Lev Gillet (Templegate) and *On the Prayer of Jesus* by Bishop I. Brianchaninov (Watkins, London), all of which are readily available. Appended at the end of this study is a current essay by the Archmandrite Plaucide Deseille on the Hesychast prayer in the Orthodox Church.

What I hope to show is that this form of prayer is deeply rooted in the traditions of the Western Church and that such has been the case from time immemorial. Even more, I hope to provide a theological basis for its use and to show that it is a prayer eminently suitable to contemporary man and the present times.

7

I

1) To speak of prayer as being "contemporary," apart from the fact that it is said at a given time, is almost a contradiction in terms—rather like the catch phrase of "atheistic Christianity." The essence of prayer, as St. John of Damascene and many other saints have said, is to "elevate the soul to God." Now prayer is directed towards God, who being present in the "everlasting 'now'," is neither ancient nor modern, but essentially eternal. Thus it is that St. Hilary of Poitiers says: "It is a pious saying that the Father is not limited by time," and the Council of Ancyra states: "If anyone says that the Father is older in time than His Only-Begotten Son, and that the Son is younger than the Father, let him be anathema." To fix the "heart" in a given time or place, in any specific historical situation, is to imprison it in the "coils of time" from which (thanks to habitual grace) it by its very nature seeks to escape. As St. Augustine says: God has created us for Himself and "our heart cannot be content until it finds repose in Him" (*Confessions* I). If prayer is communicating with the Father (*cum-union*), it is communicating with what is eternal, and when effective, "lifts one out of time." Thus it is, as Eckhart says, that "the intellect's object and sustenance is essence, not accident," and again, "the life that is, wherein a man is born God's son, born into the eternal life . . . is a-temporal, and un-extended."

2) What in man partakes of eternity? It is his entire being. While we profess the resurrection of the body, it is the soul which most directly participates in the divine life.[1] According to Catholic teaching, "the soul is the spiritual part of man, by which he lives, understands, and is free; hence is able to know, love, and serve God" (*Catechism of Pius X*). It follows that prayer that does not partake of knowledge and love—the former being of the intellect and the later of the will—is hardly prayer. St. Thomas Aquinas instructs us

---

1. The body has its role to play. It assumes appropriate positions in prayer, attitudes which both reflect and support the soul in its activity.

that "our intellect in understanding is extended to infinity," (*Summa contra gent.* 1–43); that "truth is the good of the intellect," (ibid., I–79); and that "man's beatitude consists in the knowledge of God" (*Quest. disput. de veritate* XX-3 ad 5). The very concept of enlightenment (as when one turns a light on in a room) implies instantaneity. He also tells us that "love resides in the will" and that "the movements of the free-will are not successive, but instanta-neous" (*Summa* I-II, CXIII, 7). Thus it is that every "lover," be he an ancient Roman or a modern lothario, trows his love to be eter-nal. Every act of loving and of knowing is timeless, though its object may vary and even be temporal. However, in prayer, it is both the object and the act which are timeless, and hence it is that Rúmí says "the journey of the soul is unconditioned with respect to time and space" (*Mathnawi*).

3) The reality of the eternal present is also bound up with the action of the Holy Ghost whose operation is immediate: *"and sud-denly there came a sound from heaven as of a rushing mighty wind"* (Acts 2:2). Moreover, God has loved us since eternity, and if we say that He loves us "now," we must again turn to St. Thomas Aquinas where he cites Boethius with approval as saying that "God is 'ever'" (*semper*) because "'ever' is with Him a term of present time, and there is in this a great difference between the 'now' which is our pre-sent and [the 'now' which is] the divine present; our 'now' connotes changing time and sempiternity, while God's 'now,' abiding, unmoving, and self-subsistent, makes eternity" (*de Trin.* I, 4).

4) Individual prayer (as opposed to canonical) has as its aim, not only to obtain particular favors, but also the purification of the soul: it loosens psychological knots or, in other words, dissolves subcon-scious coagulations and drains away many secret poisons; it external-izes before God the difficulties, failures, and distortions of the soul, always supposing the prayer to be humble and genuine, and this externalization—carried out in relation to the Absolute (another timeless word) has the virtue (strength) of re-establishing equilibri-um and restoring peace, in a word, of opening us up to grace.

5) The only contemporary problem in prayer is the inability of contemporary man to pray. A normal man prays, for if man is not a metaphysical animal, he is only an animal. The medieval description of Antichrist as a man whose knee-joints are formed "backwards," thus one who cannot kneel, is a paradigm of modern man. If Christ's words have no meaning for modern man, this is because modern man is sick (an illness, one might add, primarily of the visual and auditory organs). It is not prayer, tradition, and the Gospels that have lost their "relevance," but modern man who has become in his way of life irrelevant. Surely the cure of the disease is never to be achieved by the patient giving his physician the virus! St. Alphonsus Liguori tells us that "the man who prays is saved; the man who does not pray is lost. The saints are in Heaven because they made use of prayer; the damned are in Hell because they refused to pray."

6) If one considers the nature of prayer, be it individual or canonical, it must contain the following elements: it is not enough for man to formulate his petition; he must also express his gratitude, resignation, regret, resolution, and praise (Cassian, *Conferences*). In his petition man is concerned to look for some favor, provided it is of a nature agreeable to God, and so to the Universal Norm; thankfulness is the consciousness that every favor of destiny is a grace which might not have been given; and if it be true that man has always something to ask, it is just as true, to say the least, that he has always grounds for gratitude; without this, no prayer is possible. Resignation is the acceptance in advance of the non-fulfillment of some request; regret, or contrition—the asking of pardon—implies consciousness of what puts us in opposition to the divine will; resolution is the desire to remedy transgression, for our weakness must not make us forget that we are free; finally, praise signifies not only that we relate every value to its ultimate source, but also that we see every trial in terms of its usefulness.

7) But none of the concepts in the preceding paragraph can be expressed in an exclusively contemporaneous manner. One may ask

for a Cadillac instead of a chariot, but one must still ask with resignation, gratitude, regret, resolution, and praise. Moreover, the very words that one is forced to use in all these categories are not new, but have existed from all time, for they are innate (*in-natus*) in the soul that raises its heart and mind to God. Sadly, much of current liturgical prayer is just noise precisely because it fails to incorporate in its expression these very attitudes that have been with man since his creation. To void prayer of its volitive and intellectual content is to reduce it to mere "feeling" and to make it subject to the sins of pride, ignorance, and intellectual sloth, qualities which, as Hillaire Belloc has shown, are the principle characteristics of the modern mind (*Survivals and New Arrivals*).

8) If the invocation makes the divine Logos present in man, man must respond in prayer by placing himself in the divine presence—and hence in the divine present. Man must live and pray in this "now," rather than become distracted in some vanished past or elusive future. The past is "dead," as is the separative ego's involvement in it. It is the motionless present which is the gate to eternity. Thus man must become a "son of the moment," and "die before he dies"(Angelus Silesius). "Pray for us sinners now and at the hour of our death."

9) Let us then pray to God that we may be lifted out of time and that our minds and hearts be raised to what is eternal and timeless: "*Munda quoque cor nostram ab omnibus vanis, perversis et alienis cogitationibus; intellectum illumina, affectum inflamma . . . in saecula saeculorum, Amen.*—Cleanse our hearts from all vanity, from all perverse and alienating thoughts. Illuminate our intellect, inflame our will . . . for ever and ever, Amen" (taken from the traditional prayer said before reciting the divine office of the Roman Church). In our life of prayer, says St. John Climacus, rather than looking for new forms of expression, "we should constantly be examining and comparing ourselves to the holy fathers and the lights who lived before us" (*Ladder of Divine Assent*). Let us not invent new ways to pray lest "*we bubble out folly*" (Prov. 15:2) and

"inherit the winds" (Prov. 11:28). Let us not, as Eusebius says, seek to "cut out for ourselves a new kind of tract in a pathless desert" (*Preparation for the Gospels*). Let us make our prayer partake of the eternal and seek not to conform ourselves to the present times— *"nolite conformari huic saeculo"* (St. Paul's words in Rom. 12:2).

10) In the prayer of the Name, as we shall see, all these require-ments are fulfilled. It is no wonder then that the Church has advo-cated its use throughout her history.

II

11) It would seem axiomatic that any teaching on the spiritual life must satisfy the needs both of the intellect and the will, or to phrase it in more traditional terms, must provide both a Doctrine and a Method. The "why" and "how" of our existence must be answered. On a more mundane level, before starting out on a jour-ney, we must provide ourselves with both a directing map and a means of travel. In the Middle East they tell the story of a blind man and a lame man who set out for the "heavenly city." They could make no progress until they joined forces, the lame man climbing on the back of the blind one and directing his footsteps. Thus a marriage of forces is essential. As St. Thomas teaches, the will must adhere with all its strength to the good that the intellect perceives, "the will and the intellect must act reciprocally upon each other" (*Summa* I XVI, 4). Thus we have "joined in one flesh," Christ Himself, who says *"I am the Truth and the Way"* (John 14:6).

12) The will is, as the Schoolmen were fond of saying, "essen-tially a blind faculty"; it needs direction, formation, and perfection. If St. Paul could ask *"Lord, what wilt thou have me do?"* (Acts 9:6), how much more must we pose the same question. The Cistercian Abbot Lehodey tells us that to be effective, the spiritual life "requires our active co-operation, our personal exertions" (*Holy Abandonment*). As St. Thomas teaches, "man is united with God through his will"

(*Summa* I-II, 87, 6). Now this blind and unruly will must like a wild stallion, be bridled lest as St. Paul said: *"the things that I will, I do not."* Methodology can be likened to the reins. Thus it is that St. Bridget of Sweden asked Christ to assist her in "bridling" her will and early Christian iconography portrays Christ as the Driver of the Chariot.[2]

13) To embark upon a method without a doctrinal basis is like a horse whose reins are not in the hands of a capable rider; it is like attempting to cross unknown waters without a map, a course which is always possible, but one fraught with the dangers of shipwreck. Such an attempt not only deprecates the intellectual component of the spiritual life, it also denies the role of Revelation which the source we seek to discover has provided for us. It is to cut off the infinite which, as St. Thomas teaches, can be comprehended only by the intellect. On the practical level. Doctrine and Method, like the Intellect and the Will, can never be divorced. This is why in Buddhist symbolism Doctrine and Method are pictured as being in a tight conjugal embrace.[3] The sanctified soul is the "Bride of Christ."

14) All this is not to deny the role of grace which both initiates the spiritual pilgrimage and sustains it through its many stormy difficulties, but rather to stress that we must prepare ourselves to accept the graces that God always desires to pour forth. To argue that the *"Holy Spirit bloweth where it will"* in no way obviates what we have

---

2. In Eastern spiritual writings the emphasis is on "concentration" rather than the "will." This is because, to quote *The Catholic Encyclopedia*, "the control of attention is the vital point in the education of the will."

3. Hindu writers speak of a "way of knowledge" (*jnana*) and a "way of love" (*bhakti*). They are careful however to point out that these "ways" represent tendencies rather than absolute separables. One cannot love what one does not know, nor fail to know what one loves. Reference to other religious cultures should not be interpreted as fostering any false syncretism. The author, of mixed cultural background, uses such references only in order to cast clearer light on Catholic principles. Justice requires that their source be identified.

said, for we must admit that it is within our power to turn away from the light—the light which shines forth from the Paraclete. Grace, as the saints teach, "does not replace nature, but rather perfects it." Thus Eckhart teaches, "God is bound to act, to pour Himself out into thee, as soon as ever He shall find thee ready."

15) All these principles are brought together in the invocation of the Name. One cannot pronounce this Name with the lips or in the heart without conceiving it ("conception" as we shall see is no idle term) in the Intellect and without "bending" the Will to the task. It is both a Doctrine and a Method. This is born witness to by the prophet Zechariah who said, "I will strengthen them in the Lord, and they shall walk up and down in His Name" (10:2). It is simultaneously a most efficacious channel for the outpouring of grace, for as St. Paul tells us, "no man can say that Jesus is Lord, but by the *Holy Ghost*" (1 Cor. 12:3).

III

16) If we are not bound by time and contemporaneity, we are free to examine the writers who throughout all times have spoken to the issues under consideration. The *lex orandi* being an expression of the *lex credendi*—our prayers reflect and give expression to doctrines of the Church that are universal in time and place. However, it must be clearly understood that doctrines cannot change or evolve. As St. John of the Cross said in the sixteenth century, after the Apostles passed away, "there are no more articles to be revealed to the Church about the substance of our faith" (*Ascent of Mount Carmel*).[4] What is doctrine is true, and Truth cannot change. To believe that we can be better theologians than St. Paul, or know more than the Church Fathers is one of the great fallacies of our age.

---

4. The Church teaches that Revelation comes to us primarily from Christ, but also through the Apostles.

One of two things must be accepted. Either there is theological progress, and then theology is not important, or theology is important, and then there is no such thing as theological progress. Let us have the humility to say with Origen who declared in the second century that "Paul understood what Moses wrote much better than we do . . ." (*Prologue to his Commentary on the Song of Songs*). Let us remember that, as St. Augustine says, "the true and right Catholic faith" is culled, "not from the opinions of private judgement, but from the witness of the Scriptures; it is not subject to the fluctuations of heretical rashness, but grounded upon Apostolic truth" (*Sermon* XXXIV). And so it follows that "the object we have in view is not, in any way, to publish some favorite and clever method of our own" (Gueranger, *Sermon on Advent*), but rather to cull from the writings of the saints—from those men "whose words are an extension of the Word of God" (Pius X)—statements that can "enlighten our intellects and inflame our wills"—which is to say, true doctrine and an effective methodology of prayer.[5] We will find that Father Schwertner is right when he says in his paper on *Devotion to the Adorable Name of Jesus* that "there is no devotion to our Lord—except the Blessed Sacrament itself—that has better Scriptural guarantees, none more rigidly dogmatic, none richer in its patristic sanctions and supports" (*Holy Name Society Publication*).

IV

17) *"And the Word was made flesh"* (John 1:14). These words can be most aptly applied to the Name which is, as it were, the auditory aspect or primordial manifestation of the divine essence. Indeed, St. Bernardine of Sienna teaches us this in his sermon on *The Glorious Name of Jesus Christ*, and the Apostle John witnesses to

---

5. St. Albert the Great makes this clear: "Development is the progress of the faithful in the faith, not of the faith within the faithful."

this in the Apocalypse saying *"His Name is called the Word of God"* (19:13). Our Lord Himself says *"I have manifested Thy Name to the men who Thou hast given me . . . because the words which Thou hast given me, I have given to them"* (John 17:6). Origen tells us in his *Commentary on the Canticle of Canticles* that "God emptied Himself, that His Name might be as ointment poured out, that he might no longer dwell in light unapproachable and abide in the form of God, but that the Word might be made flesh."

18) Let there be no confusion as to what Name is meant. He is given a *"Name which is above all names."* It is a Name *"above all principality, and power and virtue, and dominion, and above every name that is named, not only in this world, but in that which is to come."* Now this is not only to imply that "Jesus" is a more appropriate Name for God than any other—though such it is—but also to instruct us that this Name signifies the "entire economy of the Incarnation and the Redemption . . . the Wisdom, the Power, the Goodness, the Majesty and all the attributes of God" (Augustine). As Father Thomas of Jesus says: "Isaiah called Him by the names of Wonderful, Counselor, God the Mighty, the Father of the world to come, the Prince of Peace and many other things, all of which are encompassed in the Name of Jesus of which these others are only explanations" (*Sufferings of Jesus Christ*)[6]. St. Thomas of Aquinas tells us that "we cannot name an object except as we understand it, we cannot give names to God except in terms of perfections perceived in other things that have their origin in Him" (*Compendium*). However He is *"named the Word of God"* (Apoc. [Rev.] 19:13) and St. Thomas also tells us that "the unique Word of God expresses as

---

6. Everything in creation reflects in some manner one or the other of the divine qualities or "names" of God. But only man, being made in the divine image, is capable of reflecting them all. To do so however, he must make real or realize what is divine in him. The Name which contains all the names "virtualizes" this potential to the degree that the individual unites himself with this Name.

it were in a single instant, all that is in God" (*de diff. divini Verbi et humani*). Dionysius the Areopagite says that many names are attributed to God in a "symbolic revelation of His beneficent emanations" and lists the perfusion of these including "Truth," "Wisdom," "Word," "Ancient of Days," "Sun," "Breeze," but above all he says, this sacred Name is now made manifest in "that Name which is above all names." Thus it follows that the Name of Jesus is a revealed Name, a Name existent in the mind and bosom of the Father before all time, a Name of Power, a "Marvelous Name" as David the Psalmist says, and an "Inexplicable Name" as St. Thomas says in his Commentary on *The Our Father*. St. Bernardine of Sienna says, "the Name of Jesus is itself God through which God the Father and the Holy Spirit communicate in the Divine Unity" (*Sermon on the Name*). Both Jeremias and Amos clearly state *"Dominus nomen eius—the Lord is His Name"* (Jer. 33:2; Amos 9:6). Thus Cornelius Lapide in his *Commentary on Paul's Letter to the Philippians* says, "*Nomen ergo Dei, est ipse Deus et divinitas*—indeed the Name of God is itself God and divine." More recently Father Prat S.J. has said in his *Life of Christ* that "in Holy Scripture the 'Name' of God is God Himself, made manifest to man in the voice of creation, revealed to Christians through the instrumentality of Christ." And so, *"The Word was Made Flesh."*

V

19) *"And it came to pass . . . and she brought forth her firstborn son . . . and His Name was called Jesus, that given Him by the angel before He was conceived in the womb"* (Luke 2). St. Athanasius says, "the Word was made manifest" in creation, and goes on to say that "the renewal of creation has been wrought by the self-same Word who made it in the beginning" (*De Incarnatione Verbi Dei*). Now, "in the beginning" does not imply an origin in time, but an origin in the First Principle, and from this the theological deduction follows that

God (the Eternal) is creating the world *now*, as much as He ever was. Thus Eckhart says: "God's beginning is primary, not proceeding" and again "the eternal Word is being born within the soul, its very self, no less, unceasingly." He says further, quoting St. Augustine, that "this birth is always happening. But if it happen not in me what does it profit me?" And if this happens in the fullness of time, we must remember that "time is fulfilled when it is finished, that is, in eternity . . . here there is not before nor after; everything is present . . . . May we attain to this fullness of time so help us God" (Eckhart again).

20) But this birth can only "be consummated in the virtuous soul for it is in the perfect soul that God speaks His Word" (Eckhart). He goes on further and says: "It is more worth to God His being brought forth ghostly in the individual virgin or good soul than that He be born of Mary bodily," for "God created the soul according to His most perfect nature that she might be bride of His Only-Begotten Son . . . so lifting up the tent of His eternal glory, the Son proceeded out of the Most High to go and fetch His Lady whom His Father had eternally given to Him to wife and to restore her to her former high estate." Thus it is that our Co-redemptrix is at one and the same time His Mother, His Daughter, and His Bride, crowned in heaven as His Queen. And all this is possible for us![7] Indeed, it is our soul that can become His mother, daughter, bride, and be crowned with Him in heaven. This is why St. Bonaventure says: "O devout soul, if you would rejoice in the happy birth, remember that first you must be Mary" (*Opuscula* II). This is why Angelus Silesius says: "I must be Mary and give birth to God" (*Cerubinic Wanderer*). This is why St. Louis de Montfort says: "the more the Holy Spirit . . . finds Mary, His dear and inseparable spouse in any soul, the more active and mighty He becomes in

---

7. As Abbot William of St. Thierry said, "when the faithful soul is joined to the Word of God, the bride meeteth the bridgroom" (*The Golden Epistle*). Christ Himself said that "whosoever shall do the will of my Father that is in heaven, he is my brother and sister and mother" (Matt. 12:50).

producing Jesus Christ in that soul," and again, "God the Father wishes to have children by Mary till the consummation of the world" (*True Devotion to Mary*). Thus our Lady embodies in her all those virtues in their plenitude that we must make our own, if like her we are also to be Christ-bearers. Like her, we must be able to say *"Be it done unto me according to Thy Word"* (*Magnificat*). For, as Eckhart says, when "the Father speaks the Word into the soul, and when the 'son' is born, the soul becomes Mary."

> Let the soul of Mary be in each of us to magnify
> the Lord,
> Let the spirit of Mary be in each of us to rejoice in
> God.
>
> —*Prayer of St. Ambrose.*

VI

21) Now the "Bride of Christ is a virgin." This is most strange, for as Theophylact says after Chrysostom: "brides do not remain virgins after marriage. But Christ's brides, as before marriage they were not virgins, so after marriage they become virgins, most pure in faith, whole, and uncorrupt in life" (quoted by Cornelius Lapide). "The soul's virginity," says Augustine, "consists in perfect faith, well-grounded hope and unfeigned love" (*Tract. on John* XIII). It is pertinent that the Feast of the Holy Name of Jesus is established on the Sunday before Epiphany which also recalls the Marriage Feast of Cana. This is because "it is on the wedding day that the Bridegroom gives His Name to the bride, and it is a sign from that day forward that she belongs to Him alone" (Guaranger, *The Liturgical Year*). As Cornelius Lapide says: "those whose souls are on fire with charity, and who are ever exercising themselves in it, enjoy the bliss of betrothal to God and the possession of His nuptial gifts of divine joys. For charity is a marriage-union, the welding of two

wills, the Divine and the human, into one, whereby God and man mutually agree in all things." May we then *"be virginized"* as St. Therese of Lisiaux says in a letter to her sister Celine, "so that we may become pregnant." "I am not chaste unless Thou ravish me" (John Dunne).

> Of pure Virgins none
> is fairer seen,
> Save one
> Than Mary Magdalene.
>
> *—John Cordelier*

22) Do not ask whether the soul must be virginal before it can become pregnant with the Divine Word, nor yet again pose the question if it is possible for the soul to be virginal unless it is so impregnated. This is the same question that Augustine posed in his *Confessions:* "Which ought to be first, to know Thee or to call upon thee?" This is to ask which partner is more active in the conjugal embrace. The answer is simple, for all this happens in the fullness of that time which has been discussed above. But what has all this to do with the invocation of the Name? The answer is that the Name is given to the betrothed soul by the Bridegoom. It is the cry of the virginal soul and the means by which the soul is virginalized. "Jesus, Thou glorious Name, Thou hidden bridge that carrieth over from death to life, at Thee have I arrived and stand still! . . . Be a bridge to my speech that I may pass over to thy Truth" (St. Ephrem, *Rhythm* VI). The Divine Name resides as a "jewel in the lotus," the latter being the perfect symbol of divine receptivity.

VII

23) There is an intimate relationship between the invocation of the Divine Name and the Eucharistic Sacrifice. If the Eucharist

represents "the unbloody sacrifice of the cross," the Name can be said to represent "the unbloody sacrifice of the Circumcision." St. Bernard tells us that "we read about the first effusion of the Blood of Christ at the time of His Circumcision, when our Lord Jesus Christ received the Name of Jesus, a mystery that already indicated that by His pouring forth of His Blood, He would become for us a veritable Jesus, a Saviour."[8] St. Bonaventure tells us: "This Name of Jesus was fittingly applied at the first shedding of the blood of the Lamb most pure. It was for our salvation that the first drop of blood was shed," for "the crucifixion of Jesus actually began at His birth" (*The Mystical Vine*). Further testimony to this is given by the Blessed Mary of Agreda, who in her visions saw the Angels Michael and Gabriel instructing our Lady prior to the rite of Circumcision, saying: "Lady, this is the Name of thy Son, which is written in the mind of God from all eternity and which the blessed Trinity has given to thy Only-Begotten Son and our Lord as the signal of salvation for the whole human race; establishing Him at the same time on the throne of David. He shall reign upon it, chastise His enemies and triumph over them, making them his footstool and passing judgement upon them; He shall raise His friends to the Glory of His right hand. But all this is to happen at the cost of suffering and blood, and even now He is to shed it in receiving this Name, since it is that of Savior and Redeemer; it shall be the beginning of His sufferings in obedience to the will of the Eternal Father" (*City of God*). Thus He who is *"named the Word of God"* wears *"a garment sprinkled with blood"* (Apoc. 19). And we must also be *"sprinkled with the blood of the Lamb"* if we are to be included among the *"one hundred and forty-four thousand having His Name and the Name of His Father written on their foreheads"* (Apoc. 14). This is why St. Bernard instructs us in the *Book of Sentences* that "there are three circumcisions, that of the flesh among the Jews, that of the heart as

---

8. The literal meaning of "Jesus" is "Saviour."

among the Christians, and that of the tongue in the perfect." With the New Dispensation there is no need for bodily circumcision. As Gilbert of Tournay teaches us, "Jesus is the spiritual minister of our circumcision." It is the invocation of His Name that can purify our hearts and our lips like a burning coal. The circumcision of "the tongue among the perfect" reminds us that Isaiah only announced the Virginal birth and the coming of the Messiah after his lips had been touched by the burning coal. It also brings to mind the statement of St. Thomas of Villenova to the effect that "in heaven one always repeats, always invokes and always honors the Name of Jesus . . . in heaven one knows all the truth and all the strength of this Name" (*Sermon for the Feast of the Circumcision*). No wonder that St. Bernardine of Sienna felt that the vision of St. Paul *"in the third heaven"* was of the Name in glory. Thus it is that a Muslim saint has said: "The lights of some people precede their invocations, while the invocations of some people precede their lights. There is the invoker who invokes so that his heart may be illuminated, and there is the invoker whose heart has been illuminated and therefore he invokes" (Ibn 'Ata'illah).

24) The saints repeatedly tell us that "God became man that man might become God," or to use the Greek phrase, "divinized."[9] While modern man has little trouble in accepting the historical birth of a man called Jesus, it requires the eyes of faith to see this individual as God incarnate. There is even greater difficulty in believing in the Real Presence in the Eucharist—but this also is an "In-carnation." Thus it is that stories of saints like Hugh of Lincoln or Père Lamy[10] in the present century, who were seen to hold the

---

9. See Father Deseille's discussion of divinization in the Appendix.

10. The Mass can also be envisioned as the calling down onto the altar (in this world) of the "Perpetual Sacrifice" of heaven. As M. Olier, the saintly founder of St. Sulpice said: "in order to present the mystery of the holy Sacrifice of the Mass, one must know that this sacrifice is the Sacrifice of Heaven. . . . A Sacrifice is offered up in Paradise which, at the same time, is

infant Jesus in their hands at the moment of Consecration are dismissed as pious exaggerations. The Name also "In-carnates" the Divine Presence in the soul of the person who invokes. If there have been many saints who went into ecstasy on seeing the exposition of the Sacred Sacrament, there have been others such as John Capistrano who went not only into ecstasy, but into a state of levitation, simply on hearing the Name of Jesus pronounced.

25) The current disbelief in the possibility and the reality of God's incarnational nature extends beyond the rejection of His historical Messiahship, the Real Presence and in the power of His Name. Having rejected Christ in his Merciful manifestation, we are even more prone to reject him in his capacity of Judge. Hence it is that almost no one believes in the final coming (except perhaps in some sort of vague "Omega" tied to the concept of the evolutionary perfecting of man and God), for to do so is to be filled with fear, and *"fear of the Lord is the beginning of wisdom."* Those who think that fear is out of style would do well to remember that St. Francis prayed in his dying blessing for this fear to be given to his brothers. And thus it is that if we "do not fear His glorious and fearful Name," the Lord "will bring back all the afflictions of Egypt" (Deut. 28:58), a warning repeated in Chapter 11 of the Apocalypse.

---

offered up here on earth, and they differ only in that here on earth the sacrifice occurs unseen." What M. Olier is referring to is explained in the Apocalyptic vision of St. John the Apostle in which he describes the sacrifice of the Lamb, slain but alive and seated on the throne, with the twenty-four ancients adoring Him with melodies on the harp (Apoc. 5:6–14). As Scripture teaches, "the Lamb was slain from the beginning of the world" (Apoc. XIII:8), the "Lamb, unspotted and undefiled, foreknown indeed before the foundation of the world, but manifested in the last times for you" (1 Pet. 1:19–20). Thus in the Mass we see the Celestial Sacrifice of the Lamb brought down from Heaven and present on the altar before our eyes. One can envision the Divine Name of Jesus in similar terms—with the difference that every man, not just a priest, is empowered with the capacity of calling this Name down in his own heart—of making Jesus present within his soul.

26) The Eucharistic character of the Divine Name is further stressed within the traditional Roman liturgical rite. When the priest communicates he says: "I shall take the bread of life and call upon the Name of the Lord; I shall drink the cup of salvation and call upon the Name of the Lord." Thus it is that the "passive" reception of the Sacred Species calls forth the "active" response of the invocation. Thus it happens that the priest—and those who join themselves to the sacrifice, prolong their communion in a continuous prayer, potentially fulfilling the Scriptural command to "Pray without ceasing."

27) So powerful is this Name that it provides us with graces not unlike those of the Eucharist itself. Thomas à Kempis, author of *The Imitation of Christ*,[11] tells us that "just as when the devout communicate, or when the priest celebrates Mass with devotion and reverence, so also when a person blesses Jesus and His Mother by calling on their Names, do they partake of the sacred bread and wine" (*Valley of the Lilies*). There is a medieval rosary of thirty-three beads used with the Name of Jesus which in the absence of the Mass is said to provide one with all the graces that attending Mass would provide.[12] The Desert Fathers of the early centuries who lived as solitary hermits in the Egyptian desert were deprived of sacramental sustenance for prolonged periods of time. They are said to have been sustained by the invocation of the Names of Jesus and Mary. Tradition holds that the Byzantine Rosary of knotted wool was "invented" by St. Anthony the Great. One can further say that the Invocation of the Name has the same relationship to other forms of prayer that the Eucharist has to the other sacraments. Thus it was that St. Bernardine of Sienna gave to his cypher of the Name of Jesus the form of a monstrance; the Divine Name carried in thought

---

11. The attribution of authorship to Thomas à Kempis has been disputed, an academic issue of relatively little interest.

12. Not in the sense of replacing the obligation of attending Mass, but when for some reason it is impossible to fulfill that obligation.

and in the heart and through life is like the Holy Eucharist carried in procession. Thus Meister Eckhart says the following of the Name which could also be said of the Blessed Sacrament: "The Father neither sees, nor hears, nor speaks, nor wishes anything but His own Name. It is by means of His Name that the Father sees, hears and manifests Himself. The Father gives thee His eternal Name, and it is His own life, His being and His divinity that He gives thee in one single instant by His Name" (*Comm. on St. John*). Similarly what the Blessed Eymard says of the Holy Eucharist could also be said of the Name: "The Eucharist is the Kingdom of God on earth. My body becomes Its temple, my heart Its throne, my will Its happy and humble servant, my life Its victory"(*Eucharistic Retreats*).[13]

28) *"Do this in memory of me"* (Luke 22:19). Like the Mass, the invocation of the Name is an offering and hence a sacrifice. Not only a sacrifice "of praise and thanksgiving," but also one of "propitiation" (appeasing God's anger) and "petition" offered for the "living and the dead." Finally, it is also "immolative," for we can inwardly offer Jesus to His Father as victim slain and triumphant. It is further immolative because "prayer is a torture chamber" (St. Chrysostom) in which our ego and self will is immolated. "Our soul is an Upper Room where an invisible Lord's Supper may be celebrated at any time" (Gillet). Having prepared this "Upper Room," and having offered up the Divine Name therein, we recognize that we are "temples of the Holy Ghost." The Holy Name is of course, not a new sacrifice of the cross, but when sacrificially used is a means to apply to us here and now, the fruits of that oblation. "It helps us in the exercise of the universal priesthood, to make spiritually actual and present the eternal sacrifice of Christ" (Gillet). During the time of the Old Dispensation, it was forbidden—except for prophets—to pronounce the Name of God. Even in writing it was only represented by the Tetragrammaton—the four consonants

---

13. The Eucharist remains the primary source of grace and the central act of worship in Christendom.

JHVW representing for them the "incommunicable Name." "The Name of Jesus is the true manifestation and full expression of the holy Tetragrammaton: out of the ineffable, hidden Name of YHVH, the Name of YHSVH has been revealed, with its inserted S (*shin*) representing the "mercy" of the inexpressible Divinity who has willed to manifest himself" (Private correspondence, Hugh Urban, Jr.). This prohibition and protection against potential profanation was lifted once the long-awaited Messiah was born and the *"Word became flesh."* Just as He allowed His Body to be abused and profaned, once His Name became manifest, it too was subject to abuse and profanation. *"It must needs be that offenses come, but woe unto those through whom they come"* (Matt. 18:7).

30) St. Bernard instructs us in his fifth sermon for the season of Advent regarding the Incarnation that: "In the first coming, He comes in the flesh and in weakness; in the second, He comes in spirit and in power; in the third He comes in glory and in majesty; and the second coming is the means whereby we pass from the first to the third."

The Venerable Peter of Blois says: "We are now in the second coming, provided that we are such that He may come to us; for He has said that if we love Him, He will come into us and take up His abode with us. This second coming is full of uncertainty for us" (*Sermon on Advent*).

The Abbot Gueranger (so highly recommended as a spiritual writer by St. Thérèse of Lisieux) says:

> We must remember that, since we can be pleasing
> to our heavenly Father only inasmuch as He sees
> within us His son, Jesus Christ, this amiable Savior
> deigns to come into each one of us, and transform
> us, if we will but consent unto Himself, so that
> henceforth we may live, not we, but He in us. This
> in reality is the one grand aim of the Christian reli-
> gion, to make men divine through Jesus Christ: It

is the task which God has given to His Church to do, and why she says to the faithful what St. Peter said to his Galatians: My little children, of whom I am in labor again, until Christ be born within you *(Sermon on Advent).*

John of Ruysbroeck says: "The second coming of Christ our Bridegroom takes place every day within good men; often and many times, with new graces and gifts, in all those who make themselves ready for it, each according to his power" *(Adornment of Spiritual Marriage).*

St. Louis de Montfort says: "God the Son wishes to form Himself and so to speak incarnate Himself in His members every day" (*True Devotion to Mary*).

Finally, Angelus Silesius says: "It is in you that God should be born, for if Christ were to be born a thousand times in Bethlehem, and not be born in you, you would be lost forever" *(Cerubinic Wanderer).*

And what better way can we bring about this birth than by invoking the name of Jesus, of asking Him with each repetition of the Divine Name to dwell in our hearts? And ultimately, who is it that invokes this Divine Name in our hearts if not other than He who dwells there calling forth His own Name eternally?

31) Clearly one can call the invocation of the Name the "Prayer of the Incarnation" for the *"Word made flesh"* is manifest in a most singular manner in this Name. This explains why St. Paul taught that *"in the name of Jesus all [creation] bows down, in heaven, on earth, and in hell"* (Phil. 2:10). *"Let us offer the sacrifice of praise to God continually, that is the fruit of our lips giving thanks to His Name"* (Heb. 13:15). *"Let the desire of our souls be Thy Name and the remembrance of Thee"* (Isa. 26:8). *"Let us rise up and walk in the Name of Jesus Christ of Nazareth"* (Acts 3:6), that *"believing, we might have life through His Name"* (John 20:31). Are we not told that *"if we ask the Father anything in His Name, He will give to us"* (John 14:14)? Let us then *"praise His great and terrible Name, and give glory to Him with*

the voice of our lips, and with canticles in our mouths, and with harps" (Eccles. 39:20) for His Name is *"as oil poured forth"* (Song of Sol.. 1:3). *"And when two or three are gathered together in my Name, there am I in the midst of them"* (Matt. 18:20). And who are these *"two or three"*? According to St. Catherine of Sienna (*Dialogues*) and St. John of the Cross (*Ascent of Mount Carmel*), they are the "intelligence, the will and the memory."

VIII

32) In the Old Testament we are told that if the Divine Name is invoked upon a country or person, it belongs henceforth to God; it becomes strictly His and enters into intimate relations with Him (Gen. 48:16; Deut. 28:10; Amos 9:12). Thus it is that in the office of Compline[14] this dedication is repeated every night *"Tu autem in nobis es, domine, et Nomen sanctum tuum invocatum est super nos—* You indeed are in us O Lord, and your Holy Name is invoked over us." In Genesis 4:26 we read *"and to Seth, in turn, a son was born and he named him Enoch. It was then that men began to invoke the Lord by name, and Enoch walked with God"* (*Jewish Publication Soc. Trans.*). The Psalms tell us that *"Moses and Aaron invoked the Name of God."* Aggeus the Prophet spoke *"in the Name of the Lord"* and Job *"blessed His Holy Name."* Abraham *"called upon the Name"* as did Isaiah, Ezekiel, Daniel, and Jeremiah. Michah and Zechariah *"walked up and down in His Name."* As James the Apostle said, *"all the prophets have spoken in the Name of the Lord"* (James 5:10). And is not all this most reasonable, for as David the Psalmist sings: *"Bonum est celebrare domine, et psallere Nomini tuo Altissime—For it is good to celebrate, O Lord, and to sing your Name, O most high."*

---

14. The Divine Office was once said by every priest, most nuns and monks, and innumerable laymen. Compline is the part of this Office said before retiring.

33) New Testament theology is based primarily on the writings of St. Paul who literally mentions the Name of Jesus hundreds of times. St Jerome complains that he so loved this Name that he could not keep it out of his speech and even used it where it obscured his meaning. When Paul was martyred by decapitation, it is said that each time his head struck the pavement it uttered the name of Jesus. Such is most understandable, for Christ Himself called Paul *"a vessel of election to carry My Name"* (Acts 9, 15). And he it was who taught us to *"do all whatsoever you do in word or in work, do all in the Name of the Lord Jesus Christ"* (Col. 3:17), because *"whosoever shall call upon the Name of the Lord shall be saved"* (Rom. 10:13). And Peter concurred, telling us *"there is no other Name under heaven given men whereby we might be saved"* (Acts 4:12). Now this last promise reiterates what *"the word of the Lord"* spoke through the mouth of the prophet Joel (Joel 2:32) and is again confirmed by Christ Himself when He says, *"if you ask the Father anything in my Name, He will give it to you"* (John 16:24). It is not surprising then, that, as St. Thomas Aquinas informs us: "St. Paul bore the name of Jesus on his forehead because he glorified in proclaiming it to all men, he bore it on his lips because he loved to invoke it, on his hands for he loved to write it, in his heart for his heart burned with love of it" (quoted in *Wonders of the Holy Name* by Father Paul O'Sullivan). St. Paul not only lived with this sacred Name on his lips and in his heart, according to tradition he also died repeating with his parting breath the Name JESUS, JESUS, JESUS!

34) In the early Church, it was not necessary to organize devotion to the adorable Name of Jesus in a systemic way, for it was an age when, as St. Jerome says, "the blood of Christ was still warm in the hearts of the faithful." That it was in common use is well demonstrated by the fact that so many martyrs, faced with horrendous forms of torture, died with the Name of Jesus on their lips and in their heart (*Gesta Martyrum*). Its use by the Desert Fathers is well known; its inclusion in the prefaces and other liturgical formulas of the early centuries is well documented. Ancient ecclesiastical writers such as St.

Justin, Tertullian, Origen, St. Cyprian, and St. Clement of Rome take every opportunity to praise it in the most glowing terms.

35) St. Ignatius of Antioch who succeeded St. Peter to this see, went to his martyrdom invoking the Divine Name: "When his executioners asked him why he repeated this name so often, he answered: 'It is because I bear this name written in my heart!'And in fact, after his death his heart was opened, and there the name of Jesus Christ was found written in letters of gold. And at the sight of this miracle, many pagans were converted" (*Golden Legend*). This so impressed St. Ignatius of Loyola that he changed his name from Inigo to Ignatius (Father Laturia's *Biography*). Similar statements are made about the hearts of St. Camillus de Lellis and the Blessed Henry Suso. Hermes the Shepherd (c. 150 A.D.) says: "to receive the Name of the Son of God is to escape death and give way to life." He says no one can enter the Kingdom of God except through the Name of the Son." He goes further and says: "the Name of the Son of God is great and immense, and this is what supports the entire world" (*Pasteur* III). St. Irenaeus (202) tells us that "we cannot number the graces which the Church throughout the world receives in the Name of Jesus Christ" (*Adversus Haereses*). Origen (c. 215) says: "the Name of Jesus calms troubled souls, puts devils to flight, cures the sick; its use infuses a kind of wonderful sweetness; it assures purity of morals; it inspires kindness, generosity, mildness" (*Contra Celsum* I). Constantine (312) is said to have placed the Greek monogram of the Name upon the shields of all his soldiers. St. Ambrose (c. 370) greatly loved the Name and felt that while it was "contained in Israel like a perfume in a closed vessel, the New Covenant was a vessel opened from which it poured forth *ex abundantia superfluit quidquid effunditur*—poured forth from its abundance almost like a flood" (*de Spiritu Sancto* I:8). St. Paulinus of Nola (354–431) referred to it as "a living ambrosia . . . if one tasted it just once, one would not be able to be separated from it . . . it is for the eyes a serene light, for the ears the very sound of life" (*Carmina* IV). St. John Chrysostom (c. 370) instructs us to "thus

abide constantly with the Name of our Lord Jesus Christ, so that the heart swallows the Lord and the Lord the heart, and the two become one." St. Augustine says of this Name that it is *"quod est nobis amicius et dulcius nominare—it is so pleasant and sweet to pronounce"* (*City of God*). St. Peter Chrysologus (450) tells us in one of his sermons on the Annunciation that "in this Name we adore the entire majesty of the Godhead." St. John Climacus (sixth century) tells us to "strike our adversaries with the Name of Jesus, there being no weapon more powerful on earth or in heaven" (*Ladder of Divine Ascent*). St. Patrick advocated the use of the prayer of Jesus as is reported in the Golden Legend[15]—and this in the Hesychast form: "Lord Jesus Christ, have mercy on me, a sinner."

36) There was in the thirteenth century a certain falling apart of the medieval synthesis. It was a period in which the Church and society at large were faced with problems of internal decay, many external threats, and above all the attacks of the Albigensians. It was an era however which produced such saints as Thomas Aquinas, Dominic, and St. Francis. It was also an era which once again reaffirmed the power of the Name of Jesus. Pope Urban IV is said to have added the Name of Jesus to the Angelic Salutation. It was the Council of Lyons in 1274 that Pope Gregory X, perhaps urged on by St. Bonaventure (Longpre), passed the legislation that started our hallowed custom of bowing the head at the Name of Jesus. Here it was decreed that since the Name of Jesus is the Name above all names, we should "extol it by showing a special reverence," and since every knee should bow at that Name, we are held "especially during Mass, or other sacred functions, to bend the knee of our hearts, which we can indicate by an inclination of the head, when we hear that Name." Immediately after the Council Pope Gregory X wrote to Blessed John of Vercelli, the then master of the newly founded Dominican order, asking him to spread devotion to this

---

15. See Chapter 6

Name. He in turn wrote to all the Dominican priories and ordered that every church should have an altar dedicated to the Holy Name of Jesus and that societies and confraternities should be formed under the title of INVOCATION of the Holy Name of Jesus. Thus it was that the various Holy Name Societies were established—societies which in diluted form exist even to our own times—thus giving rise to the tradition that it was St. Dominic who established the practice of saying the Rosary as we know it today.[16]

37) As we come to late medieval times, we find an even greater profusion of devotion to the Name. Thus it was that the Name of Jesus was in the mouth of St. Francis "like honey and the honeycomb" (Thomas of Celano's *Biography*); and St. Francis himself wrote "no man is worthy to speak Thy Name" (*Praises composed when the Lord assured him of His Kingdom*). St. Bernard wrote whole sermons on the Name filled with such phrases as "Jesus is honey in the mouth, melody in the ear, a song of delight in the heart" (*Commentary on the Song of Songs*). St. Bernardine of Sienna travelled throughout Italy preaching the prayer of the Name—it is said that when he spoke the Name would appear as if in a monstrance on his fingertip. St. Bonaventure cries out: "O soul, whether you write, read, teach, or do anything else, may nothing have any taste for you, may nothing please you, besides the Name of Jesus" (*Opuscula*). St. Ignatius of Loyola made the Name in its symbolic form "IHS" the seal of his order.[17] Another order, now defunct, called the Jesuates was established for the sole purpose of spreading

---

16. St. Dominic is credited with converting the Albigensians by means of the Rosary. Regardless of the historical accuracy of such a claim, it is of interest to note that one of the essential characteristics of the Albigensian heresy was the denial of the Incarnation. The Rosary, as is discussed in paragraph 28, is the prayer of the Incarnation *par excellence*.

17. For a discussion of the origin of the symbol IHS see Peter Biasiotto, O.F.M.'s *History of the Development of Devotion to the Holy Name*, St. Bonaventure College and Seminary, St. Bonaventure, N.Y., 1943.

this devotion. In England Richard Rolle cried out: "O good Jesu, Thou hast bound my heart in the thought of Thy Name, and now I can not but sing it; therefore have mercy upon me, making perfect that which Thou hast ordained" (*Fire of Love*). In Germany Angelus Silesius says: "the sweet Name of Jesus is honey on the tongue: to the ear a nuptial chant, in the heart a leap of joy" (*Wandering Pilgrim*). Meister Eckhart says that "believing in the Name of God, we are God's sons." In France St. Joan of Arc placed the Name upon her standard and Richard of St. Victor taught that "the invocation of the Name is the possession of salvation, the receiving of kisses, the communion of the bed, the union of the Word with the soul in which every man is saved. For with such light no one can be blind, with such power no one can be weak, with such salvation none can perish" (*Selected Writings*). In the Netherlands Thomas à Kempis, author of the *Imitation of Christ*, instructs us that "as you travel on this earthly pilgrimage, take for yourself as provision (*viaticum*), like a shepherd's staff held firmly in the hand, this short prayer, "JESUS-MARIA" . . . wherever you go, wherever you walk or stand or rest, invoke Jesus and invoke Mary" (*Valley of the Lilies*).

IX

38) The Name of our Co-redemptrix Mary is also "divine." St. Alphonsus Liguori assures us that it "came from heaven and was given us by divine ordinance." The Venerable Mary of Agreda tells us that shortly after our Lady's birth, she was transported to Heaven and presented before the throne of the Most High. It was then that:

> His Majesty wished himself to give and impose the name in heaven. He thereby made known to the angelic spirits that the three divine Persons had decreed and formed the sweet names of Jesus and Mary for the Son and Mother from the beginning

before the ages, and that they had been delighted with them and had engraved them on their eternal memories to be as it were the Objects for whose service They should create all things. Being informed of these and many other mysteries, the holy angels heard a voice from the throne speaking in the person of the Father: 'Our chosen One shall be called MARY, and this name is to be powerful and magnificent. Those that shall invoke it with devout affection shall receive most abundant graces; those that shall honor it and pronounce it with reverence shall be consoled and vivified, and will find in it the remedy of their evils, the treasures for their enrichment, the light which shall guide them to heaven. It shall be terrible against the power of hell, it shall crush the head of the serpent and it shall win glorious victories over the princes of hell.' The Lord commanded the angelic spirits to announce this glorious name to saint Anne so that what was decreed in heaven might be executed on earth (*City Of God*).

39) It is not surprising then that many saints have invoked her name in conjunction with that of Jesus, as well as in isolation (St. Thomas of Villenova). And even on the level of human reason such a practice commends itself. The Blessed Virgin, this most perfect soul, this individual who is wisdom incarnate, cannot be conceived of apart from Jesus. To say "Mary" is to say "Jesus"—for she was in every sense full of the Holy Trinity. If one says pitcher, one must also imply, if not say, content. But one cannot conceive of the content without the container. Mary—the perfect soul in a state of grace— is Mother, Daughter, and Bride to Christ—crowned with Him in heaven as his Queen. The "Marian virtues"—purity, beauty, goodness, and humility—are precisely those required to support the more

adamantine "Christic virtues." In seeing her, says St. Louis de Montfort, "we see our pure nature" (*True Devotion to Mary*). The blessing of the Virgin is on him who purifies his soul for God, for this purity of the Marial state is the essential condition for the spiritual actualization of the Real Presence of the Word. By greeting the Blessed Virgin, the soul conforms itself to her perfections while at the same time imploring the help of Mary who personifies these perfections. Hence it is that the saints have blended her Name with that of Jesus. St. Anthony of Padua invoked her Name constantly. Henry Suso said of it: "O sweet Name! What must thou be in heaven, when thy Name is so love-inspiring on earth!" The Abbot Franconus said that next to the Holy Name of Jesus, "the Name of Mary is so rich in grace and sweetness that neither in Heaven, nor on earth, is there any other Name that so fills the soul of man with grace, hope and sweetness." St. Anselm says: "The most sweet Name of Mary is a precious ointment which breathes forth the odor of divine grace; let this ointment of salvation enter the inmost recesses of our souls." St. Alphonsus Liguori sang forth: "Gladly shall my lips repeat, every moment, thy dear Name" (*Glories of Mary*). He who says Jesus says God, and equally, he who says Mary, says Jesus. Hence it is that Dante wrote in the *Paradiso*:

> There is the rose wherein the Word divine made Itself flesh
> The Name of the beauteous flower which I ever
>   invoke, Morning and Night.

40) The Angelic Greeting embodies the Divine Name of Jesus as a "jewel in the lotus." It has rightly been called "the Hesychast prayer of the Western Church." It is of interest that the Rosary only came into common use in the Church in its present form after Pope Urban ordered that "the adorable name of Jesus" be added to the Angelic Salutation in the year 1262. Both St. Gertrude and the Blessed Jane of France were assured by our Lady that this was her favorite prayer. Thomas à Kempis states that whenever one says the

"Hail Mary"—"Heaven rejoices, the earth wonders, the devil shudders, hell trembles, sadness disappears, joy returns, the heart smiles in charity and is penetrated with a holy fervor, compunction is awakened and hope is revived." This Angelic Greeting embodies the entire economy of the spiritual life within its confines. It embraces within a single breath both the Divine Names of Jesus and Mary, and as it were summarizes all that has been said above. The Name of Jesus resides in the virginal womb, a womb that has been called by the saints both a "furnace" and a "bridal chamber." For those who would slight the Rosary, the words of our Lady to the Blessed Alan de la Roche (quoted in St. Louis de Montfort's *True Devotion to Mary*) should act as a most powerful deterrent. "Know, my son," she said, "and make all others know that it is a probable and proximate sign of eternal damnation to have an aversion, a lukewarmness, or negligence in saying the Angelic Salutation which has reformed the whole world." To consider this a pious exaggeration is to hide one's disbelief under a cloak of hypocrisy, and as Pius XI says in his encyclical, *Ingravescentibus malis*, "to wander from the path of truth."

X

41) One must ask why Doctors of the Church like Saints Augustine, Bernard, and Dominic were so devoted to Invocation of the Name of Jesus? Why, also, were saints like Francis of Assisi, the Blessed Suso, St. Edmund, the king of England, St. Camillus de Lellis, St. Jogues, the Jesuit martyred by the Hurons in Canada, St. Joan of Arc, St. Louis de Montfort, Thomas à Kempis, St. Ignatius of Loyola, St. Vincent Ferrer, Francis de Sales. And why are others in our own times, like Sister Consolata Betrone and Father Pio the Stigmatist, to mention only a few and to say nothing of the entire Hesychast tradition on Mount Athos down to the

present day?[18] Why is it that St. Jane de Chantal and others have actually branded this Name with a red-hot poker over their hearts? The answer lies in the fact that only man, being made in the Image of God in a direct and integral manner, has the gift of speech. This being so, speech as well as intelligence and will must play a part in salvation and deliverance. Indeed, both Intelligence and Will are actualized by prayer which is speech, both divine and human, the act relating to the will and its content to intelligence. Speech is, as it were, the immaterial though sensory body of our will and of our understanding. But speech is not necessarily exteriorized, for articulated thought also involves language. Now, if this is so, apart from the canonical prayers imposed on the Universal Church, nothing can be more important than the repetition of the Name of God. Eckhart says: "God is the Word which pronounces Itself. Where God exists, He is saying this Word; where He does not exist, He says nothing. God is spoken and unspoken. . . . Father and Son expire their holy breath, and once this sacred breath inspires a man, it remains in him, for he is essential and pneumatic." *"For the Word of God is quick and powerful, and sharper than any two-edged sword, piercing even to the dividing asunder of soul and spirit, and of the joints and marrow, and is a discerner of thoughts and intents of the heart"* (Heb. 4:12). Does not Joel in the Old Testament assure us as did Paul that *"whosoever shall call upon the Name of the Lord shall*

------

18. Father Pio spent the last hours of his life constantly invoking "Jesu-Maria" (Dorothy Gaudiose, *Prophet of the People*, (Alba House, N.Y., 1973); Sister Consolata Betrone (1903–1947) used the formula "Jesus, Mary, I love you—Save souls" and her writings are best presented in *Jesus Appeals to the World* by Lorenze Sales, (Alba House, N.Y., 1955). For St. Isaac Jogues, see *Saint Among Savages* by Father F. Talbot (Image, N.Y., 1961). The works of St. Louis de Montfort are available from Montfort Publications, Bayside, N.Y. Other references are found in *The Wonders of the Holy Name*, a small pamphlet by Father Paul O'Sullivan (The Catholic Printing Press, Lisbon and Dublin, Portugal).

be delivered" (2:32)? We have already seen that the prophets and the saints consider the Name to be one with God; that the saints in heaven, as St. Thomas of Villenova tells us, invoke it constantly, and now Eckhart tells us that "the eternal Word is spoken in the virgin soul by God Himself." Thus the invocation of the Name in the heart *incarnates* into us the fullness of the Trinity in so far as we can bear it.[19]

42) Consider how many people in the Gospels were healed *"in the Name of Jesus."* Now "healing" in the Scriptures always has a two-fold meaning. It always refers to both physical and spiritual healing. As Richard Rolle says: "every man who lives in this wretched life is ghostly sick, for there is no man who lives without sin, which is ghostly sickness. . . . This Name Jesus is nought else but to say in English Healer or Health." Thus it is that the invocation of this Name exerts a healing quality on our souls. But it does far more, for it slowly transforms us till at last, through the grace of God, we and the Name become as one. If part of the mystery of the Incarnation resides in the statement of St. Irenaeus (and many others) that "God became man that man might become God," surely we can say that God gave us His Name that we might incorporate it into our hearts, and with our memory, intelligence, and will absorbed in the Name be able to say with the Blessed Angela of Foligno: "Thou art I, and I am Thou" (*Visions and Instructions*); and with St. Paul: *"I live, not I, but Christ in me"* (Gal. 2:20).

43) God in naming Himself, firstly determined Himself as being and secondly, starting from Being manifests Himself as Creation—that is to say, He manifests Himself "within the framework of nothing" or "outside Himself." Man for his part describes

---

19. The Name of the Son is not distinct from that of the Father, for just as the Son is the carnate manifestation of the Father, so is His Name the audible manifestation of the Word. As it says in the Apocalypse, *"one hundred and forty four thousand having His Name and the Name of His Father written on their foreheads"* (Apoc. 14).

the inverse movement when he pronounces the same Name, for this Name is not only Being and Creation, but also Mercy and Redemption. In man, it does not create, but on the contrary "undoes," and that in a divine manner, since it brings man back to the Principle. If God "pours Himself out in His Name" (St. Bernard), a man in invoking this Name reaches the "fullness of plenitude." As seen by God, the Divine Name is a determination, a limitation and a "sacrifice." As seen by man, it is a liberation, limitlessness, and plenitude. The Name, when invoked by man, is nonetheless always pronounced by God, for human invocation is only the "external" effect of the eternal and "internal" invocation by the Divinity. What is sacrificial for the divine is liberating for man. All revelation, whatsoever may be its mode or form, is a "descent" or "incarnation" for the Creator, and an "ascent" or "ex-carnation" for the creature.

XI

44) The invocation of the Names of Jesus and Mary is our surest protection against evil. It was in this Name that the Apostles cast out devils. Contemporary exorcists tell us that nothing is more powerful in defeating the enemy, nothing more frightening to his minions, than the repetition of this Name. But evil is not only to be found outside us in the possessed; it is also present in our own souls. And hence it follows that there is no greater protection available to us against the temptations and snares of the Devil than the invocation of the Names of Jesus and Mary.

45) The Church promises us that should we say the Divine Names of Jesus or Mary at the time of our death—providing it is said with a proper attitude—our salvation is assured. To quote the Raccolta or source of indulged prayers:

A plenary indulgence[20] at the hour of death, if they
have been accustomed to invoke the holy Name
frequently during life, provided that, after confession and Communion, or at least an act of contrition, they devoutly invoke the holy Name of Jesus
(Mary) with their lips if possible, otherwise in their
hearts, and accept death with resignation from the
hand of God as the wages of [original] sin.

The practice of facing death with the support of the Divine Name
dates back to the time of the early martyrs. Not only St. Ignatius
whom we have mentioned, but also St. Lawrence, St. Agatha, and
innumerable others. It is no wonder then that St. John Eudes used
to pray to the Blessed Virgin, saying: "Let me die with these divine
words in my heart and on my lips—'JESUS-MARIA'—and let me
pronounce them in union with all the love which ever has been, is
now, and ever shall be in all hearts which love Jesus and Mary"
(*Life*). It is no wonder then that so many saints, not only those of
the early centuries, but men and women close to our own times like
St. Francis Xavier, St. Vincent de Paul, St. Margaret Mary (through
whom God revealed the devotion of His Sacred Heart), and Father
Pio died with the Name of Jesus on their lips. Every time we invoke
the Name of Jesus we make an act of Faith, Hope, and Charity. For,

---

20. A "plenary indulgence" implies the forgiveness of all our sins and the
entire temporal punishment due to these sins—hence a guarantee of direct
entrance into heaven. An act of contrition involves sincerely saying audibly or
internally the prayer once said by every Catholic in Confession: "O my God,
I am heartily sorry for having offended Thee, not only because I fear the loss
of heaven and pains of hell [this would be incomplete though adequate con-
trition], but also because I have offended Thee my God who art infinitely good
and worthy of all our love. [This added phrase constitutes perfect contrition.]
I resolve with the help of Thy grace, to amend my life, to confess my sins, and
to do penance." How readily such important and oft-repeated prayers come to
mind in times of crisis.

as St. Bonaventure says, the Name is "full of Grace, for in it faith is founded, hope is confirmed, love increased and justice brought to perfection" (*Opuscula*). It is not an accident that the principal prayers of the Church repeatedly advocate this form of prayer. The first petition of the Our Father asks *"Hallowed be Thy Name"*, that is, as St. Thomas Aquinas explains, "to manifest and make His Name known among us" (*Comm. on the Pater Noster*). The soul in a state of grace answers in the words of the Magnificat: *"Holy is His Name"*; and the faithful cry out in their loving prayer: *"Hail Mary, full of grace, blessed art thou among women, and blessed is the fruit of thy womb JESUS. Holy Mary, Mother of God, pray for us sinners now and at the hour of our death."*

XII

46) It is impossible to say the Names of Jesus and Mary without the soul assuming an attitude that is at once resigned, regretful, resolved, and full of praise. And if we invoke the Name worthily, it will come to pass that our hearts will be His Kingdom, that our will slowly be transformed into His will; it will be for us as St. Bernard says, a constant nourishment; it will cancel debts to both God and man—as St. Ephram says: "the King came forth to us, Who blotted out our bills and wrote another bill in His own Name that He might be our debtor" (*Rhythm* IV); and finally, it will be for us a protection against temptation, for "the demons fly at the sound of this Name." No wonder then that St. Bonaventure said: "O how fruitful and blessed is this Name endowed with so great a power and efficacy!" (*Opuscula*).

47) For those who are called to this form of prayer—and no claim is made that this is the only path to God—every necessary act, be it professional or social, partakes of and is an aspect of the invocation. God wishes us to call upon Him not only with our tongues, but with our entire body—with every member—and with all our being; indeed with our total life and our very existence. If God

wishes us to invoke His Name, or rather, wishes to invoke His Name in us, then every necessary (and needless to say, honorable) act—reflecting as it does a conforming on our part to His will for us, becomes of its very nature an invoking of the Supreme Principle. The Invocation is a form of "recollection," a way of practicing the "remembrance of the presence of God" along the lines advocated by the Blessed Brother Lawrence. *"Let the desire of our souls be Thy Name and the remembrance of Thee"* (Isa. 26:8). And if God invokes His Name in us, our allowing the faculties of our soul to conform to this Divine Presence in us is precisely what transforms us—both our nature and our actions—into a "manifestation" of the Divine Name. That which formerly was central to our lives—our attachment to the ego and the world—no longer exists. That which formerly has hardly a reality for us—the Divine Presence—now becomes a reality. The "remembrance of God" is at the same time a "forgetting of self," for the ego is the seat of pride, crystallization (that is, hardness of heart), and of the forgetfulness of God. In the invocation the ego, as it were, no longer exists, for the Name has "absorbed" it into its own reality, into its own purity, absoluteness, and essence.[21] As Christ said to Sister Consolata Betrone: "Sanctity consists in the forgetting of yourself, in your thoughts, your acts, your words, indeed in all things" (*La Toute Petite Voie d'Amour*). As Christ said to St. Catherine of Sienna: "You are she who is not, whereas I am HE WHO IS" (*Life,* Blessed Raymond of Capua). In the same way, the person who invokes the Divine Name will arrive at a point where he can say "I (ego) do not exist, only the Name exists, for He and His Name are One." In the last analysis it is God Himself who pronounces His Name in us, or who causes us to pronounce it, for as Scripture says, we can do nothing without Him. God became incarnate in His Name so that we could become incarnate in God by means of His Name.

---

21. Strictly speaking the ego is not "destroyed" but perfected by becoming its true self. It is "annihilated" in its "separateness," but not in its "union."

XIII

48) The invoking of the Name is not *per se* a mechanical guarantee of salvation, for not everyone *"who calls Lord, Lord, will be saved."* A donkey carrying perfume on his back will still remain a donkey, though even then it is possible for some of the perfume to rub off on him. The Divine Names are not immune from misuse or even profanation. A spiritual means can only be effective within the framework of the tradition that offers it, and only when utilized with the proper intention. *"Thou shalt not take the Name of thy God in vain"* (Exod. 20:7; Deut. 5:11). If it holds true for the Eucharist that *"whosoever shall eat this [divine] Bread . . . unworthily . . . eateth . . . damnation to himself"* (1 Cor. 11:27–29), it is also true that he who uses the Divine Names in a presumptuous manner risks losing all. One must invoke the Name for the proper purposes and in a proper state of soul. One must be in a state of grace (or at least desire so to be) for to "call upon the Lord" while obstinately clinging to what the Lord forbids is absurd (*ab-surd us*).[22] If we have a loving Christ, we also have a wrathful God. Without justice, there can be no mercy. If we have a Name of Love, we also have a Name that is "terrible." If we invoke the Name, we must do so within the womb of the Bride of Christ, within the framework of the Christian tradition. *"And Thy wrath is come, and the time of the dead, that they should be judged, and that Thou shouldest render reward to thy servants, the prophets and the saints, and TO THEM THAT FEAR THY NAME"* (Apoc. 11:18).

---

22. From a Catholic point of view, a priest who falls into a state of mortal sin can give communion or confect the sacrament (say Mass) if no other priest is available to whom he can go for confession, and he is under obligation to communicate or celebrate Mass. He must however make a perfect act of contrition and go to confession as soon as it is possible. Similarly, a person in a state of mortal sin should not invoke the Divine Name without going to confession, but if a priest is not available, he can do so providing he makes a sincere act of contrition and intends to go to Confession as soon as ever it is possible.

49) The question of intention is essential. Acts are nothing outside the intentions that give them their meaning. One may invoke with a view to salvation; one may invoke because one loves the climate of the sacred—the perfume of the divine presence; one may invoke because one loves the invocation; one may invoke because the Name is the only reality; but one cannot invoke to satisfy some profane and worldly desire.[23] One cannot misuse the Divine Name to satisfy the needs of the separative ego. One cannot pray for that which is not in conformity with the Divine Equilibrium. All prayer to Heaven must incorporate or express, apart from legitimate petition, gratitude, resignation, regret, resolution, and praise. This is why the Divine Name is usually incorporated in an appropriate formula such as "Lord JESUS Christ, have mercy on me a sinner." It is the setting that provides the intention. When the Name is invoked in isolation—a methodology which should not be undertaken without appropriate spiritual direction—it becomes a heady wine, but even then it embraces intentions—indeed, all the possible correct intentions, for it intends what Christ Himself intends.

50) Just as in the Rosary where one is free to meditate either upon the meaning of the words of the Angelic Greeting in themselves, or upon the various Mysteries recapitulating the Life of Christ and Mary; so also with the invocation, one is free to meditate upon the essence of the Name, or upon appropriate themes which can be considered as concomitant with the Name. Thus, for example, the invocation carries with it of necessity abstaining from anything that distances us from God—not only from gross sin, but also from dissipation and vanity—attachments to our ego or the world. Again, the Name by its nature is Action. It is like a sword by means of which we slay the enemy within and without. As St. Thérèsa of Liseaux said, "salvation is won on the point of a sword."

---

23. It is of course legitimate to pray for our legitimate needs—"give us this day our daily bread."

The Name which is Beauty manifest is also Peace and Contentment. What more can we desire than to rest in its perfume? It can also be envisioned as the source of our Confidence and Trust. Given all that has been said of its use, and above all the very meaning of the word Jesus which is Salvation, it becomes the strongest means by which we can assure our salvation. Beyond this the Name is Truth and Objective Reality which when it resounds in our hearts becomes as it were the Subjective Reality of our true self. In uniting ourselves to the Name we unite ourselves to Christ. The first two themes relate to the Way of Purgation, the second two to that of Illumination, and the third pair to that of Union.

XIV

51) Man is born in both space and time. To avoid being lost in space he must seek a fixed point in reality or a center. To avoid being caught up in the coils of passing time he must seek a fixed point in eternity. The Divine Name provides access to both. Centrality: The Name is one with what is named. It is the form in the formless. In so far as it is He who invokes the Name within us, the Name provides man with a centrality that is both immanent and transcendent. The Kingdom of God is within. Eternity: the Name is actuality within duration. Being one with what is named, it is eternal and atemporal by its very nature. Every invocation brings man back to the everpresent "now." The Name is so powerful that a single invocation is capable of liberating man. But if the Name is eternal, man finds himself embroiled in passing time. The present "moment" constantly eludes him. By repeatedly invoking the Divine Name, he repeatedly brings himself back to the center and back to the present moment. This is why the Divine Name must be continually repeated. It is now, at this very moment, that we must invoke the Name which makes the present moment the gate to eternity.

XV

52) In the Old Testament we are instructed to *"let nothing hinder you from praying always"* (Sirach 18:22), and in the New, St. Luke tells us *"keep watch, praying at all times"* (Luke 21:36). Now this evangelical council can be fulfilled in many ways according to the manner in which the soul is called by God, for as Christ says, *"I have chosen you."*—it is always God who calls us, and not we who call Him. For those who are called to invoke the Name either in isolation or within a formula, no form of prayer is more simple, more direct, and more suitable to the present times than this. Thus we read in Zechariah (13:8–9): *"Two parts in all the earth shall be scattered, and I will bring the third part through the fire, and will refine them as silver is refined: and I will try them as gold is tried. They shall call on my Name and I will hear them. I will say 'thou art my people' and they shall say 'the Lord is my God.'"* This passage is part of the prophecies pertaining to the end of times. And who are the third part that are to be brought through the fire? They are, according to Cornelius Lapide that portion of mankind that in the "final days" remains faithful to God and invokes His holy Name (*Commentaria in Scripturam Sacram*).

XV

52) Sufficient has been said about the sacred character of the Divine Names for us to comprehend with clarity the sin of blasphemy. "All sins are hateful in the sight of God but the sin of blasphemy ought more properly to be called an abomination to the Lord" (St. Alphonsus Liguori). As St. Gregory of Nazianus says, "the devil trembles at the Name of Jesus and we are not afraid to profane it" (*Orat.* XXI). "He who blasphemes," says St. Athanasius, "acts against the very Deity itself." The blasphemer, says St. Bernardine of Sienna, makes of his tongue "a sword to pierce the heart of God." He

continues, "all other sins proceed from frailty or ignorance; but the sin of blasphemy proceeds from malice." St. Chrysostom says, "there is no sin worse than blasphemy" because, as St. Jerome says, "every sin compared to blasphemy is small." St. Thomas Aquinas says that just as the saints in Heaven, after the Resurrection, shall praise God with their tongues, so also the reprobates in Hell will blaspheme Him with their tongues (*Summa* II-II, 13), and St. Antonine says that he who indulges in the vice of blasphemy already belongs to the number of the damned, because he practices their art. (Mostly taken from a sermon by St. Alphonsus Liguori).

XVI

53) The very idea of methodology in the spiritual life offends the "modern mind" which is in revolt against reason, discipline, and indeed, against all authority. The modern mind above all wants to "feel," for in feeling it makes itself—its own egoity—the criterion of its own state of soul, and feeling requires neither thinking nor discipline. The modernist forgets that John the Baptist cried (as in the wilderness of the modern world), *"prepare ye the way of the Lord."* He forgets that Advent must precede Christmas and that Advent is a penitential season. He may admit to the need for methodology in science, in business, or even in madness, but denies its role in religion. Love and faith are reduced to "feeling" and feeling can never be methodological. What then is this preparation that must precede the coming of Christ? It is the training of the will which requires obedience, discipline, and virtue. It is the training of the intellect which requires the abandoning of Pride, Ignorance, and Intellectual Sloth. And if there is to be no method, there is to be no direction. Everyone becomes his own spiritual director, and it is a fact that a person who is his own lawyer, both in this world and the next, "has a fool for his advocate." (A Sufi adage holds that a person who is his own spiritual director "has the

Devil for his guide.") To enter the spiritual life without a guide is to ignore the words of Christ—the blind cannot lead the blind—it is to ignore the repeated warnings of almost all the saints including John of the Cross and St. Teresa of Ávila. It is to ignore the evangelical councils embodied in all the traditional catechisms. It results, as Philo says, in a person "wandering around in the maze of his own personal opinions." Indeed, it is to play the role of Eve in the garden of Eden and, in every sense of the phrase, to "play with fire." "Whatever is done without the approval of your spiritual father," as St. Bernard says, "must be imputed to vainglory and therefore has no merit" (*Comm. on the Song of Songs*).

All this being so, a word of warning must be given against the use of this form of prayer (or for that matter, any serious endeavor in the spiritual life) outside of a traditional framework. Accepting the disciplines of the Church trains the will; accepting its doctrinal formulations trains the intellect. It is precisely submission to such a framework that provides the basis for spiritual growth and protects one against self delusion. Moreover, every effort should be made to find a spiritual director—preferably one familiar with the way of the Name. In the absence of such, those who feel called and desire with all their hearts to "invoke," should throw themselves on the Mercy of Jesus and Mary while consulting the writings of saints and authoritative texts dealing with the subject.[24] It is ever a fundamental principle of the spiritual life that God never abandons us and never tries us beyond our feeble capacities. *"When the Spirit of Truth is come, he will guide you unto all truth"* (John 16:13).

XVII

Let us in conclusion join St. Anselm in his prayer of the Name of Jesus taken from his Second Meditation:

---

24. A brief bibliography is provided at the end of the book.

Be free of fear then, O sinner, breath freely and do not despair. Hope in Him whom you fear. Fly to Him from whom you have flown. Invoke Him assiduously whom you have sinned against in your pride O Jesus, Jesus, do unto me according to your Name. O Jesus, that you might forgive this proud sinner, have pity on this miserable person who calls upon your sweet Name; O delectable Name, Name of blessed hope, Name that is the comforter of sinners. For what is Jesus, if He is not a Savior? Therefore, O Jesus, know yourself for what you are and be to me a Savior. You did not make me that I should perish; You did not redeem me that I should be condemned; You did not create me out of Your infinite goodness that Your work might be destroyed by my iniquity. I pray You O most bountiful One that You do not allow me to perish on account of my sins. Know Yourself, O most benign Jesus, for what You are and obliterate in me whatever is foreign to You. O Jesus, Jesus, have pity on us while there is still time for mercy so that we will not be condemned on the day of judgement. Of what use to You is my blood? Of what use to You is my being condemned to eternal damnation? *'The dead shall not praise Thee O Lord, nor any of them that go down into hell'* (Psalm 93). If You admit me to the fullness of Your merciful bosom, it will not become less capacious because of me. Therefore, admit me, O most desirable Jesus, admit me to the company of Your elect so that I may praise You, enjoy You, and give glory to you along with those who love your Name. You, O Jesus who with the Father and the Holy Spirit, reign for ever and ever, Amen.

JESUS-MARIA

St. Bernardine of Sienna

INTRODUCTION

Anyone familiar with the Scriptures, and especially with the Psalms, cannot fail to be impressed with the number of references to the Name of God. It has been incorporated into the liturgical formulae and prayers of the Church since the time of St. Paul. It is recommended to us in both the *Pater Noster* and the *Magnificat* and has been joined to the prayer of the publican—"Lord Jesus Christ, have mercy on me a sinner"—since the time of the Apostles. The following sermon of St. Bernardine of Sienna, often referred to as the "Apostle of the Name," is probably the most complete discussion on the subject by any single author in the Roman Church.

St. Bernardine was born at Massa, near Sienna (Italy) on September 8 (the birthday of the Blessed Virgin) in 1380. Both his parents died before he reached the age of eight and he was brought up by a devout aunt named Dianna. Encouraged by her, he grew in grace and virtue, and from childhood demonstrated a tremendous love of the poor. He interrupted his studies as a young man in order to care for the victims of the plague which struck Sienna, and actually became the director of the La Scala Hospital which still stands and functions today across the street from the cathedral of this city. At the age of twenty-two he entered the Franciscan order and during the course of his life is said to have preached in almost every city of Italy. He was pressed to accept three different Bishoprics but managed to evade them. In 1438 he was made Vicar-General of the Franciscan order and worked to reestablish the rule of strict observance. At the time of his taking this position, there were only twenty houses and two hundred religious under this rule. When he died, there were over three hundred houses and at least five thousand religious. He died in 1444 during the singing of vespers. As he breathed his last, the monks were chanting the antiphon: *"My Father, I have made Thy Name known to the people that Thou hast given me."* He was sixty-four years old.

St. Bernadine is of course most famous for his love of the Name of Jesus. While the Chrismon (the letters used to symbolize the Name of Christ) can be traced back as far as the Epistle of Barnabas, the particular form of this emblem that St. Bernadine preached is said to have appeared miraculously at his fingertips during a sermon on the subject. This symbol was adopted for his order by St. Ignatius of Loyola, was carried on the standard of St. Joan of Arc, and variants to this day can be seen to adorn both Catholic altars and Protestant "tables." The Feast of the Holy Name was promoted by St. Bernadine and was appropriately established to coincide with that of the Marriage at Cana, for it is, as Gueranger says, "on the wedding day that the Bridegroom gives His Name to the bride."[1] This symbol is appropriately painted in gold on a blue background, blue being the color of faith, hope, and charity. It can be seen to this day placed over the entrances of many homes and churches in Tuscany, and is also placed over the entrance to the hermitage of St. Francis of Assisi, a place hallowed in memory to St. Bernadine as well as to the founder of his order.

Though St. Bernadine must have given many sermons on the Holy Name of Jesus and is said to have ended all his sermons with an exhortation to this devotion, it is of interest that in his *Opera Omnia,* only one is listed that is exclusively devoted to this subject. A second one, more recently discovered, has been published in a Siennese historical journal. However, if we have only one or two, the length and completeness more than compensate for the paucity.

---

1. Due to liturgical reasons, the feast is often celebrated on January 1, the Feast Of the Circumcision

Lest anyone should feel that St. Bernadine's teaching is exaggerated, or not truly Catholic, they should know that in his lifetime he was accused of heresy for these very teachings, and silenced. He was however ably defended by St. John of Capistrano (who wrote his life), and a thorough Papal investigation followed. Pope Martin V declared Bernadine's conduct, doctrine, and teaching on the Holy Name as orthodox and offered him the Bishopric of Sienna. This confirmation was again made by Pope Eugene IV. In the centuries since his death, innumerable saints have spoken in praise of it.

The sermon itself, after an introductory discussion, is divided into three sections. Each section in turn is divided into four chapters. Each chapter discusses the meaning of one of the twelve rays that surround the emblem of the Name. This translation is offered, not as an exercise in scholarship, but rather as a work of devotion. biblical passages in the sermon often depart slightly from the Vulgate, as is understandable when one realizes that they were quoted from memory. Whenever possible, the translations are taken from the Douay-Rheims version. They are italicized as in the original. To my knowledge, no previous complete translation in English exists. Any errors are of course my own.

JESUS MARIA

St. Bernadine of Sienna

PALM SUNDAY

"At the Name of Jesus every knee shall bow, of those that are in heaven, on earth and under the earth"—
taken from the second chapter of Paul's letter to the Philippians and read in the lesson for today.

When the human mind makes bold to speak of the Name of Jesus, and of its praise, it finds itself deficient; the tongue cleaves to the palate of the mouth and all speech dries up. Indeed, this Name is so great, so much more profound than the very oceans, that no human intellect is fully capable of expounding it; this is why St. Isidore says "the spoken Name is like a well of wisdom that makes things known to us." Now it is the nature of names to specify that which is named, and the Name of Jesus instructs us in an incomprehensible manner. Who is able to explain the incomprehensible? Is it possible to reveal the infinite? And what man can possibly express in mere words the meaning of the Incarnation—God-man? This is what David the prophet expresses when he says to the Lord in Psalm 47: "According to Thy Name O Lord is Thy Praise," which is to say that the very Name itself is Thou, a giving praise O Lord. But who is able to explain this—The Name—which thing in and of itself gives praise to God? Who can be found so full of grace and virtue as to proclaim this praise in an appropriate manner? Absolutely no one, unless his lips be "circumcised." Thus it was that when Isaiah (6) was raised up in the contemplation of the vision of the King of Glory, before speaking of Jesus whom he referred to as Emmanuel, and before speaking of the Virginal Conception, acknowledged his speech to be unworthy. It was only after he experienced the mystery of the Seraphim, after he felt the burning coal upon his lips and was purged and spiritually circumcised, that he announced the Virginal Conception and the Name of the Son, disclosing to us in these two things, a most sacred mystery. Come, therefore, O Jesus Christ, minister of our spiritual circumcision, touch my lips, take away my iniquity, purge my affections, illuminate my mind, eliminate my imperfections, move my tongue and make my speech and action such that, for the glory of Thy Name, it may burst forth with the burning heat of Thy charity, mixed with the flame of Thy piety. Grant that I might taste the great sweetness of Thy Name not merely on my lips, but even more that I might find refreshment and delight from it in my interior soul. For just as water gushing forth from a fountain forms at first a gentle and narrow stream that murmurs softly and sweetly, but later grows into a broad and deep river, so also the Name of Jesus seems at first to be a small sound, a phrase easily spoken, but is at the same time pregnant with meaning and overflows with a superabundance of ineffable grace. All that God has ordained for the salvation of mankind is encompassed and comprehended in the Name of Jesus. The Name is variously translated by St. Jerome as "Savior," "Deliverer," "Benefactor," "Salvation," and "He who saves us from sin, delivers us from evil, and confers on us both grace and an abundance of glory." He is proclaimed "Savior" first of all because it is He who saves us from sin: as the angel declared unto Joseph (Matt. 2): *"and His Name shall be called Jesus, and He shall save His people from their sins."* Second, He is so proclaimed because He frees us from our enemies to whom we are subject; as Zacharias says (Luke 1): *"He saves us from our enemies and from the hand of those who hate us."* Third, He is called the "fullness of salvation" because He confers on us grace. Thus it is that David, who had lost that salvation by sinning, says in Psalm 50: *"give us the joy of Thy salvation."* Fourth, He is called "Salvator" because of the abundance of His glory, and hence Jacob says in Genesis 40: *"I await thy salvation O Lord,"* which is to say, the glory already promised. All this and much more that is lofty and stupendous is encompassed mysteriously in the blessed Name of Jesus.

Because of its great excellence, this Name was first revealed by the Father; second, it was prefigured many times in the Old Testament; third, it was spoken forth by the prophets; fourth, it was announced by the Angel Gabriel; fifth, it was revealed to the Virgin; sixth, it was proclaimed by the Apostles, and seventh, it is venerated and adored by all creation.

Truly this Name was first given forth by the Father, for the entire Trinity was written in the book of life in the beginning and for all eternity. And indeed, who else would dare to impose a Name on the Eternal Word unless it were God the Father Himself? Certainly He who settled the Name of Jesus on the Eternal Word acknowledges this when He says in Isaiah 45: *"I the Lord who calls forth Thy Name,"* and again in the same place: *"I have called forth Thy Name."* Also in Isaiah 62 God says: *"and thou shalt be called by a new name which the mouth of the Lord shall name.*" Indeed, this Name was given Him from the beginning of time, when as the Apostle says in Romans 2: "*the Son of God was predestined in excellence.*" In the same vein Isaiah says in Chapter 63: "*O Lord, everlasting is Thy Name,*" and again elsewhere: "*may Thy Name be blessed for ever, which Name was from eternity, before the sun shone forth.*" Even more is written about this Name in the book of life, concerning which book Moses said in Exodus 32: "*either deliver the people from this evil, or if Thou canst not, strike me out of the book of life that Thou hast written.*" Now the Lord said to the Apostle in Luke 10: "*rejoice, because thy name is written in heaven*"; and Daniel (12) saw that in this book of life are written all the names of the elect that are to be revealed on the day of judgement. And on the top of this book, as well as on the foreheads of all the saved, is placed this Name of Jesus, for the Lord said, speaking through the prophet: "*on top of the book it is written of me.*"

Second, the Name of Jesus is prefigured many times in the Old Testament. Indeed there were many Jesuses in Judea, who as St. Bernard said, anteceded the real Jesus. But these prefigured names were empty of glory, for they did not shine forth; they did not nourish, nor did they heal. The Synagogue was at that time laboring in darkness, hungry, unable to be healed, unable to be satiated, until she knew Jesus to rule over Jacob and over all the world. Indeed, we read of three Jesuses that came to Israel. First of all there was Jesus, son of Nun, or Josue, and he is called "Savior" because he led the Jews out of their exile in the desert and apportioned up to them the promised land. Second, there was Jesus, son of Josedech, and he is called "Savior" because he was a most holy priest and he rebuilt the temple where he officiated. Zechariah 3 spoke of this saying "*the Lord showed me Jesus the high priest.*" Third, there was Jesus, the son of Syrach; he was a prophet, priest and most wise teacher, whence it is said of him in Ecclesiasticus 5 that "*he renewed Wisdom from his heart.*" But how very great is the difference between these prefigured Jesuses, and the real Jesus! The first Jesus, that is Joshua, having broken and dispersed the seven kings of Canaan, led the children of

Israel into the promised land; but our Jesus, having broken the powers of hell led all the saints into eternal glory. Second: Jesus, son of Joshua, rebuilt the temple Jerusalem even more gloriously than the initial one built by Solomon, as it says in Haggais 2, and which temple is also a prefiguring of Christ, but our sweet Jesus rebuilt the temple in grace and in truth—verily rebuilding a nature which was inclined to ruin, one which in fact was (by original sin) brought to ruin, and in this rebuilding he made a most complete holocaust of his body and of his heart. The third Jesus was a prophet, a priest renewing Wisdom from his heart rather than from his own strength. Over and above this he taught in many obscure words, symbols, and figures of the Old Testament. But our loving Jesus was a prophet great in works and in speech, explaining the symbols and figures, clarifying what is obscure, and also renewing Wisdom in the New Testament. Moreover he teaches the doctrines of the Father and the Holy Spirit as one having power, and not like the scribes and pharisees. Indeed, He was the priest of priests, as the prophet says: *"Thou art a priest forever, according to the order of Melchisedech."* From all this you can clearly see that these Jesuses were not the true Jesus. Nor do we preach about their name when we announce and extol the Name of Jesus, for we preach Jesus Christ, Son of the living God, who is the true Savior of the world. Just as the daystar goes before the sun, as darkness goes before light, as heralds go before a king, so do these figures go before the mystical Truth. These aforesaid Jesuses were sent forth like the staff of Hilesius (the servant of Elijah), going before the prophet to bring the dead to life (2 Kings 4). Nor were these Jesuses able to give meaning to their own names, for their names were empty of true salvation. And just as the staff of Hilesius, when it was laid upon the dead person, failed to resuscitate him until the man who sent the staff came down himself, so also it was not until the true Jesus, who had sent these other Jesuses before Him, assumed our nature and proved Himself to be the real Jesus by saving His people from their sins, that there was life—not as before which is only an image empty of salvation.

But listen to what He did. Whence came our voice and feeling and return of life back to us as St. Bernard asks. The prophet Jesus, powerful in action and in speech, descending from the mountain on high somewhat like Elijah from Mount Carmel, deigned to visit the dead human race, which was dust and ashes; deigned to abase Himself, and to lie over mankind as Elijah lay over the dead body; to place Himself on the same footing as the least; to impart the light of His eyes to the blind; to loosen the mouth of the dead with the kiss of His own mouth; to strengthen human weakness with the strength of His hands; to replenish with His breath the spirit of man which was dead. O what a delight it is to think on these things! How wonderfully my very bowels are replenished! How satiated is my heart with spiritual sweetness! My very bones burst forth in praise.

Now the boy that Eliseus lay on "gasped" seven times, which "gasping" is recapitulated in the Church, which seven times each day (in the Divine Office) gives praise to the Savior. And you, O sinner will also gasp seven times if you conform and return your five exterior senses and two interior senses to the inspiration of the prophesy of Jesus—rejoicing and singing *"my heart and my flesh exult in the living God."* The coming of Jesus was foretold on three occasions in the past. Thus in Habakkuk 3 it says *"I will rejoice in the Lord: and I will joy in God my Jesus."* Also in Esdras 4, admittedly non-canonical, God says *"and it shall come to pass after many years that My Son Jesus shall be killed and the world shall be converted."* Lastly the Sybil Erithrea pronounced the Name of Jesus in a wondrous manner as St. Augustine tells us in *de civitate Dei* (lib. 18, c.23) where he speaks of the Sybillian verses concerning the last end of the world, which verses had been translated from Greek into Latin. Now the translation, because of the rhythm of the verses, was not able to conform in all things to the original—and this was especially true of the first letters of the lines. If however we take the first letters of all the lines in the original Greek, they spell out "Lord Jesus Christ, Son of God and Savior."

Fourth, this Name of Jesus was announced by the angel—we read in Luke I that the Angel Gabriel said to Mary *"do not be afraid, Mary, thou hast found grace with God,"* that is to say, that very thing which Eve had lost; *"behold thou wilt conceive in the womb,"* which is to say, you will receive Him completely in your self; *"and thou shalt bring forth a son and thou shalt call His Name Jesus,"* from which it is clear that Jesus is his personal Name and Christ is a title or surname. It is as if the angel said "thou art that soul, so full of grace, on which account it was conceded to thee by God that thou shouldst give to the world the Savior, and that thou shouldst announce to the whole world, before all men and all women, the saving and glorious Name of Jesus. Hence it is that in the second chapter of Luke it is said: *"and His Name was called Jesus, which [He] was called by the angel before He was conceived in the womb"*— and hence it is that this Word is the appropriate theme for the Feast Day of the Circumcision.

Fifth, the Name was revealed to the world by the Virgin, and over and above this, by her holy husband Joseph—for only these two were given this duty by God through an angel, the duty of naming Christ Jesus the Son of God. Concerning the Virgin, Scriptural authority has already been given above. Concerning Joseph, we read in Matthew II that the angel said to him: *"do not fear to accept Mary for thy wife, for that which is Conceived in her is of the Holy Ghost and she shall bring forth a son and thou shalt call his name Jesus."* These two, Joseph and Mary, first revealed to us on the day of His Circumcision, that He who had been born was Jesus, that is, the Savior of the world; and concerning the manner in which this Name was imposed, Isaiah (55) said *"and the Lord shall be named for an everlasting sign that shall not be taken away"*—that is, to say, from those that believe in Him.

Sixth, this Name was taught by the Apostles to the entire world starting first in Judea as is written in Acts 5: *"and every day they ceased not in the temple, and from house to house, to teach and preach*

Christ Jesus." See then, how sweet the Gospel of Christ is—from whence it comes about that Jesus is the Savior. *"He takes away all sin. He who mixes together what is useful and what is sweet."*

And from Judea the Apostles went to Greece, and from there finally to Italy, and in this we see mystically fulfilled all that Pilate wrote in the triumphal title placed on the cross: *"Jesus of Nazareth, King of the Jews"* which title was written in Hebrew, Greek, and Latin. In this way the Apostles taught the glory of the Name of Jesus in all languages, fulfilling the words of the prophet Isaiah (18): *"the sound of them shall go out into all the lands."* And what else can this be than the preaching of this *Name which is above all names,* as that vessel of election about which St. Paul teaches. For Paul is like the holy candelabrum of the Apocalypse over which this Name shines like a bright star, its brilliance illuminating the entire world—as God says in Acts 9: *"for this man is to Me a vessel of election to carry My Name before the gentiles, and before the kings and the children of Israel."* Indeed, how greatly did Paul show his own glory when he said *"for I judged not myself to know anything among you but Jesus Christ, and Him crucified."*

Seventh, truly this Name is venerated and adored by all creation. Indeed, does not every knee bend before this Name, and do not people even today perform miracles through this same Name? This is why Origen says: "the Name of Jesus is a glorious Name and worthy of all worship." It seems reasonable then, and certainly it is not improper to say and to believe with a pious devotion, that when St. Paul was caught up into paradise—as he himself testifies in 2 Corinthians 2, and *"heard secret words which it is not granted to man to utter,"* that he then learned perfectly in just what manner the Name of Jesus is adored by all—for in the state of rapture the meaning of "to hear" is the same as "to see" or "to learn."

Now we can find evidence for the above statement on three planes, for the knowledge of God is threefold. First by nature; second by grace, and third through glory. The first is by nature, for the human intellect is able to know God by nature as the philosophers do; for according to Boethius, the knowledge of God is by nature inborn in all men. Second, we can know God by grace; that is by the living faith after the fashion of the faithful who know Him in this life. Third, we may know Him by glory, which is to see God in His Essence as the blessed see Him in heaven. It is of course impossible for us to achieve this state during our pilgrimage in this world unless divine and supernatural power operates miraculously to elevate us to it, as it did with the Blessed Paul—for this is the third heaven into which Paul was raised up insofar as he saw the Divine Essence. St. Augustine (*de videndo Deum*) says that Paul heard hidden words because he was enlightened and instructed in such high mysteries that it was not permitted that he should speak of them to men, for the human tongue was not fit to explain, nor the human nature able to comprehend those things which pertain to the Spirit of God. Now in the vision discussed above, we can piously meditate that Paul saw the most great glory of God which is contained in the glory of God the Father. *"In the highest heavens, above all principalities and powers and virtues and dominions, and above every name that is named, not only in this world, but also in the world which is to come. And all things He made subject under His feet,"* as written in Paul's letter to the Ephesians 1.

Now when Paul saw God in such sublime glory, being spiritually inflamed and bursting with love, he gave forth with a loud cry saying "Jesus my love!" On hearing this Name cried out, all the saints in heaven bowed down and adored Jesus in His Name. Paul understood that the bowing down was before the Name of Jesus because before this Name all the spirits in hell bend their knee, and we, as wayfarers in this world have a similar obligation. Returning to our subject however, and recalling what we have said above, Paul, instructed with the Spirit of God, writes universally concerning the Name in his Letter to the Philippians 51 saying: *"at the Name of Jesus every knee should bow, of those who are in heaven, on earth and under the earth."* On heaven through glory, on earth through grace and in hell through eternal justice. For the Name of Jesus is poured forth like oil, not only perfuming heaven, but also flooding the earth and even seeping down into hell. Herein it is that the Church wishes all to be satiated, stating in *de immunitate Ecciesia* (in the sixth chapter entitled "holiness is appropriate to the house of the Lord") that:

1) This Name is above all names and no other Name is given to man in which he should place his trust for salvation—the Name being referred to is clearly that of Jesus Christ who saves His people from their sins.

2) It is appropriate for the members of the Church, on hearing this Name, to publicly demonstrate some sign of spiritual reverence. If one does not genuflect, it is because the command is generally fulfilled in an inward manner (especially when one partakes of the sacred mystery of the Mass), that is to say that as often as this glorious Name is mentioned, the head is bowed—which is as it were, a bending of the knee in one's heart. And it is most useful that this devotion be observed with fervor, and that we increase this fervor, because the Name of Jesus should always be contemplated in a most loving manner. Just as the sun with its power and splendor and warmth stimulates growth and gives life to material things, and thus serves all of creation, so also does the Name of Jesus initiate and sustain the life of grace in those wandering through the pilgrimage of this world. This is why Zechariah 6 says: *"the rising sun is His name"*—that is to say, like the sun rising in the east. And again, this is why Psalm 18 says: *"he has set His tabernacle in the sun"*—that is in the mystical sun which is radiating faithfully the tabernacle of His Name. We distinguish therefore the flames of this burning Name in twelve different rays, so that we can discuss the subject under twelve chapter headings—like the twelve Apostles. We hope to expound the fullness of the meaning of these rays of the Name of Jesus to the faithful so that—as it says in Ecclesiasticus 42: *"the light of the sun is seen by all."*

SECTION I
THE FOUR PRINCIPAL RAYS:
THE "POWERS" OF THE NAME
OF GOD, OUR JESUS CHRIST
THAT REACH OUT TO THOSE
IN NEED

The Name of Jesus has four principal rays that represent its four powers, like beams of strength, for the Name by its very nature is opposed to four evils. First it is opposed to sin; second, to strife; third, to concupiscence; and fourth to affliction. The Name of Jesus is opposed to these four evils because first of all, it is the refuge of sinners; second, it is a standard (flag) in battle; third, it is a remedy for those who are spiritually or physically sick; and fourth, it is a solace to sufferers.

CHAPTER I

Concerning the First Ray of the Name of Jesus in
which is clearly demonstrated how great is the mercy
of this Name extended towards sinners.

First of all, this Name is a refuge of sinners, that is to say, against the evil of sin—for who is the sinner that does not fear this powerful Name? Who is it that does not quake before the Name of divine anger, and who is not terrified before the Name of the furious God, and who is it that does not tremble when he hears the Name of the God of vengeance? Yet, behold how the Name of Jesus is a sweet refuge into which is poured forth the power and the majesty of God, for it is sweet with piety and shows forth the great mercy of God. Formerly, in the Old Testament, in the law of fear, it was a terrible Name, whence Isaiah says (30): *"behold, the Name of God cometh from afar, His wrath burneth and is heavy to bear."* See how terrible was the Name of God in those times, giving forth fire and wrath and heavy burdens that scourged and scalded and overburdened us; but now it has been tempered in the fountain of mercy and piety, that is to say, in the womb of the Virgin Mary, through our most loving Jesus Christ. Now this fire is changed and cooled; the wrath is sweetened and the burden lightened. Just as the word *filius* can be said to be derived from *philos*—which means love—so also is the immense love of God made clearly manifest to us in the New Testament. Thus it is that the Angel said to Mary in Luke 1: *The Holy Ghost shall come upon thee and the power of the most High shall overshadow thee, and therefore also the holy thing which shall be born of thee shall be called the Son of God."* O most loving and most gracious Name! O Holy Name! O Pious Name, full of sweetness, so greatly desired by the ancient fathers, so anxiously awaited and with such prolonged weariness, called on with so much yearning and with so many tears of desire! But at last the time of grace has mercifully arrived—that time which the prophet desired when he said: *"say to my soul: I am thy Salvation."* It is almost as if the prophet said: O Lord thou hast said enough, *"for thus spoke the Lord, God of hosts, the God of vengeance, our just God."* It is as if he said: I beseech Thee O Lord, hide Thy Name of power from us; let us not hear Thy Name of vengeance; may Thy Name of justice not be spoken;—rather give us Thy Name of mercy. And now *"The Name of Jesus rings in my ears, because now Thy voice is sweet, and truly Thy face is beautiful."* Behold, what a sweet solace is the Name of Jesus! Without this Name both the ancient fathers and even the men of the New Testament hoped in vain to find salvation. It is because of this that it says in Matthew 2, *"the angel said to Joseph, thou shalt call His Name Jesus, for He will save His people from their sins."* And again, Peter says in Acts 10: *"to Him all the prophets give testimony, that by His Name all receive remission of sins, who believe in Him,"* that is to say, believe with faith operating through love. And again, in I John II is said: *"I write to you, little children, because your sins are forgiven you for His Name's sake,"* and in Acts 4 Peter says: *"there is no other Name under heaven given to men, whereby we might be saved."*

Now this Name of Jesus is prefigured in Exodus 28 by the Tetragrammaton. Nicholas of Lyra in his gloss on this passage says that the sixth ornament of the high priest was a plate of purest gold hanging over his forehead and tied with a violet string, and on this plate was written the Name of God—Tetragrammaton. This ornament was somewhat like a crown, but an imperfect crown, for according to Josephus and Rabbi Solomonem, it passed from ear to ear over the forehead forming a semicircle; however, if one ignored the back part of the head it appeared to be made like a perfect crown. Now God instructed Moses that, across this ornament, *"thou shalt grave with engraver's work HOLY TO THE LORD,"* which is according to Nicholas of Lyra, the Name of God—Tetragrammaton. Also, the same author in his *questiones contra Judaeos* makes the following comment on these words of Jeremiah (23): *"you have perverted the words of the living God, the Lord of hosts"*: he says, wherein do we have God? In Hebrew it is expressed by the Tetragrammaton, the Name of God, which signifies the Divine Nature in its intrinsic essence, and without respect to anything external. And if indeed this Name was written on the golden plaque that was placed on the forehead of the high priest when he entered into the Holy of Holies, it was because this signified that no soul could enter into the temple of the kingdom of heaven to make a sacrifice of praise unless he carried the Name of Jesus written on his forehead.

Now this Name is written on the forehead of the soul at the time of Baptism. Though it can be washed away by mortal sin, it is again written on the forehead through the power of absolution in confession. Thus it is that it says in Apocalypse 3: *"and I shall write on him the Name of my God,"* for indeed, that Name is only given to one whose nature the Name expresses. This is shown from Genesis 2 where Adam named all things because he knew the nature of all things. The Name therefore is only written on the forehead of sinners when by true contrition they merit it, in order that by means of this Name they might be raised to the true knowledge of Christ. And this is what the Apostle implies when he says in 2 Corinthians 3: *"Ye are our letter,"* that is, the Epistle of Jesus Christ *"written on the fleshy tables of the heart."* From all this we can understand that a person who has profaned himself with the guilt of sin, has in the last analysis, no power to help himself, and no way to be forgiven, except by means of a contrite heart. If however he invokes this Name of Jesus in his heart, and murmurs this Name in his mouth, it follows that the remission of all his sins occurs, for as the prophet Joel (2) testifies: *"whoever invokes the Name of God shall be saved."* However, he must invoke it with a pure heart that is full of devotion, and not just with polluted lips, for such a real invocation includes in it true contrition. Now if true contrition is necessary for salvation, and if invoking the Name of God reflects this contrition, then the words of the prophet Joel are indeed most important. Certainly invoking the Name in the heart and with the lips and in the proper frame of mind greatly increases the guarantee of salvation. However, it is possible for a person to fall into sin unexpectedly, or to be exposed to the danger of sin. Hence it is necessary to invoke the Name of Jesus frequently as a protection, and then, no matter what ill fortune the heart falls prey to, the Name of Jesus which is the Name of Salvation comes to its help. This is why the Apostle says in his letter to the Colossians 3: *"all whatsoever you do, in word or in work, do all in the Name of the Lord Jesus Christ."* Moreover, experience clearly teaches us that just as one who frequently invokes the devil from out of an evil heart, when something unexpected happens to him, calls upon the devil with his lips—so also it happens that a person who is in the habit of invoking the Name of Jesus, when he stumbles, will also quickly pronounce with his mouth this sacred Name. God is our witness to this, for he says in Matthew 12: *"out of the abundance of the heart the mouth speaketh. A good man out of a good treasure bringeth forth good things: and an evil man out of an evil treasure bringeth forth evil things."* In all of the sacred Scriptures, and throughout the entire Gospels, no one who invoked the Name of Jesus was ever cast down. And now we pass on to the second ray.

CHAPTER II

Concerning the second Ray of the Name of Jesus, that
in no matter what battle a devout man undertakes
for himself, the Name of Jesus triumphs.

The Name of Jesus is a standard in battle, that is to say, in the fight against evil. For even though the contempt of Pharo and his like should rise to the point of being scandalous, even then, if we but recollect the Name of Jesus, it is to fight with confidence—for this Name subjects all the fury of our enemies to us. Truly we have three adversaries in this life; the devil, the flesh, and the world. First of all the devil is our adversary because when anyone seeks and tries to abandon a life of depravity, and to change himself into a new man, the devil opposes him with all his strength and cunning. Hence it says in Ecclesiastes 2: *"son, when thou comest to the service of God, stand in justice and in fear, and prepare thy soul for temptation."* Elsewhere St. Gregory says, that to draw near to the Savior is to draw near to temptation, for the light of righteousness follows upon the shadow of temptation. In the same manner, should the devil rise up against you, do not be afraid, but raise up against him the banner of salvation which is Jesus, and invoke His Name. Listen and have faith in what God says in the Gospel of St. Matthew: *"In my Name devils are cast out"*; and this power He gave to his disciples saying in Matthew 10: *"cast out devils."* Now the disciples found this to be true, for it says in Luke 10: *"and the seventy-two returned with joy saying: 'Lord, the devils also are subject to us in Thy Name.'"* And note well Christ's response: *"I saw Satan falling from heaven like lightning"*—which is as if He said: do not be surprised if the devils are afraid of My name, and are cast down through the power of My Name, for after all, Satan and all his angels were ejected from heaven by the strength of this Name and fell like lightning. Hence, we read in Apocalypse 12 that after the battle in heaven between St. Michael and the dragon, and after the dragon had been defeated and sent into eternal punishment, all the saints and angels in heaven rejoiced and cried out saying *"now is come salvation and strength,"* that is, the power of salvation through the Name of Jesus, *"and the power of His Christ,"* which is amply discussed in the book *de Circumcisione Domini.* Nor should we be surprised if by this Name demons are cast out, for, truly, they cannot stand its power and its terror, for as Jeremiah (10) says: *"Thou art great"* (that is to say, Lord Jesus), *"and great is Thy Name in might."* And again, the prophet says in Psalm 110: *"holy and terrible is Thy Name,"* holy that is, to the good angels and to just men, but terrible to demons and to impious souls. And this can be demonstrated from an example.

When St. Bernard Papius of Modiolone was visiting in this area, a certain person whose wife was under the influence of an evil spirit brought her to the saint and the devil began to speak to him from out of her mouth saying: "do not drive me out from this little old lady." To this the servant of God replied: "not I, Bernard, but our Lord Jesus Christ will drive you out!" after which he began to pour forth in prayer. Then the evil spirit said: "no matter how willing I am to leave this woman," for he was greatly vexed with her, "it is not possible, for the great God does not wish it." The saint said to him: "and who is the great God?" to which he answered "Jesus of Nazareth." To this the man of God asked: "Have you ever seen Him?" and the evil one answered: "even so." So he asked him where and he answered: "in glory." The saint asked: "were you then in glory?" to which the devil answered: "certainly." The saint then asked "In what manner did you forsake this glory?" and the evil one answered: "with Lucifer many of us fell." Now all this was spoken from out of the mouth of the little old lady with a sorrowful voice, but loud enough for all to hear. The saint then asked: "can you ever gain back that glory?" to which the evil one answered laughing in a strange way: "it is too late for that." There followed an argument between the saint and the evil spirit, after which the devil departed from her. But as soon as St. Bernard had left and gone a short distance, the evil one returned into the old woman and her husband ran after the saint and informed him what had happened. The saint then gave him a talisman, a folded piece of paper on which was written "In the Name of God, Jesus Christ, I admonish you, O devil, never to presume to disturb this woman again," and this she hung around her neck. And when this had been done, the devil made no further attempt to bother her.

Our second adversary is the flesh, for it is full of filth and evil, whence St. Bernard says in his fifteenth sermon on the Song of Songs: "Does one of us feel sad?[1] Let the Name of Jesus come into his heart, from there let it spring to his mouth, so that shining like the dawn it may dispel all darkness and make a cloudless sky. Does someone fall into sin? Does his despair even urge him to suicide? Let him but invoke this life-giving Name and his will to live will be at once renewed. The hardness of heart that is our common experience, the apathy bred of indolence, bitterness of mind, repugnance for the things of the spirit—have they ever failed to yield in presence of that Saving Name'? The tears dammed up by the barrier of our pride—how have they not burst forth again with sweeter abundance at the thought of Jesus' Name? And where is the man, who, terrified and trembling before impending peril, has not been suddenly filled with courage and rid of fear by calling on the strength of that Name? Where is the man who, tossed on the rolling seas of doubt, did not quickly find certitude by recourse to the clarity of Jesus' Name? Was ever a man so discouraged, so beaten down by afflictions, to whom the sound of this Name did not bring new resolve? In short, for all the ills and disorders to which flesh is heir, this Name is medicine. For proof we have no less than His own promise: '*Call upon me in the day of trouble; I will deliver you, and you shall glorify me.*' Nothing so curbs the onset of anger, so allays the upsurge of pride. It cures the wound of envy, controls unbridled extravagance, and quenches the flame of lust; it cools the thirst of covetousness and banishes the itch of unclean desire. For when I name Jesus, I set before me a man who is meek and humble of heart, kind, prudent, chaste, merciful, flawlessly upright and holy in the eyes of all; and this same man is the all-powerful God whose way of life heals me, whose support is my strength. All these re-echo for me at the hearing of Jesus' Name. Because He is man I strive to imitate Him; because of His divine power, I lean upon Him. The examples of His human life I gather like medicinal herbs; with the aid of His power I blend them, and the result is a compound like no pharmacist can produce. Hidden as in a vase is this Name of Jesus. You, my soul, possess a salutary remedy against which no spiritual illness can hold out."

Third, the world is an adversary. When you are, by the judgement of God, allowed to be shipwrecked on the seas, or to fall into similar dangers, and the buffs of your enemies rush against you like threatening waves; when you are a victim of treachery, or to the terrors of thunder and lightning; when calamities strike, such as earthquake, or the destruction of one's home as by an unexpected conflagration, or if anything of a similar nature occurs, invoke the Name of Salvation. Quickly call upon the Name of Jesus with your lips and in your heart. Have hope in the assistance of the Almighty, for He says in Psalm 90: "*he shall cry to me and I will hear him. I am with him in tribulation: I will deliver him and I will glorify him.*" And again, our Lord tells us through His prophet: "*I will protect him because he knows Mv Name.*" Finally, it says in Proverbs 18: "*the Name of the Lord is a strong tower, the just runneth to it and shall be exalted.*" which is to say that one who invokes the Name will never be harmed by the evils and calamities discussed above.

CHAPTER III

Concerning the third ray of the Name of Jesus: when burdened with the problems of illness, devotion to the Name of Jesus is productive of health.

Third, the Name of Jesus is a remedy against our infirmities, that is to say, against the evils of concupiscence. For in man, condemned to death by sin, and saved at such great cost, concupiscence persists as a morbid and sickly tendency. Therefore let us turn to the Name of Jesus, of which Peter Ravennas says: this is the Name that gives sight to the blind, hearing to the deaf, the ability to walk and even to run to those who are lame, speech to the mute, life to the dead, and even allows us to fly from and escape from the power that the devil has over the prison of the body. Hence, should you have any illness, or should any disease threaten your health, do not despair, but recall to mind the invocation of the Name of Jesus. This is true even though it often happens that one cannot apply a natural remedy for a given illness, either because we lack it, or because we are ignorant of the nature of the disease, or because there is no natural way to cure the illness in question. We are assured of this by God himself in the last chapter of the Gospel of St. Mark where He says: "and this sign shall follow them that believe: *in My Name they shall cast out devils: they shall speak with new tongues, they shall take up serpents and if they shall drink any deadly thing, it shall not hurt them: shall lay their hands upon the sick and they shall recover.*"

Do not confuse the invocation of the Name with those inane and insane and entirely erroneous incantations used by some who claim to be invoking the Name of God but who are in fact invoking the devil and using his incantations. In such formulas are interpolated unknown words and in them are always to be found mendacious things. Even though the *Pater Noster* or *Ave Maria* is added to disguise them, and even though by similar means they may appear as something noble, nevertheless—it is permitted by the justice of God you must remember that the devil can with his craftiness, make a man or a child sick, and then through erroneous and impious incantations make him well in body. The devil, however, in doing this, fastens onto the soul and heart of such a person the mortal sin of blasphemy and heresy. Such a situation is clearly demonstrated to us in the legend of B. Bartholonieus. Also David told us of this possibility in Psalm 39 saying: "*blessed is the man whose trust is in the Name of the Lord: and who has not had regard to vanities and lying follies.*" How very often I have heard from trustworthy sources that, even in our own times, when the Word of God is mentioned with the imposition of hands upon the sick, they are cured when the Holy Name of Jesus Christ is invoked. Hence it is that the prophet says in Psalm 105: *"He saved them because of his Name, that His power might be known,"* and what is even more remarkable, even sinners and pagans, when they invoke this Name, are able to perform miracles and are manifestly able to bring about the healing of the sick. Blessed Dionysius the Aeropagite gives us an example of this. It is narrated that when he was traveling with St. Paul, they came across a certain blind man, and that Dionysius said to the Apostle, "if you say to this blind man, 'in the Name of God you are cured,' and he sees, then I shall believe at once. But you must not use magic words, for I shall prescribe the form of the prayer that you shall use—namely 'In the Name of Jesus Christ, born of the Virgin, crucified and died, who was resurrected and ascended into heaven, receive your sight.'" In order that he might remove all mistrust on Dionysius' part, Paul answered him saying that he wished for Dionysius to say the words. So Dionysius spoke these words to the blind man that he might see, and at once his eyes were opened. Immediately Dionysius confessed his belief in Our Lord, Jesus Christ. Thus we see that even when this man was a sinner and an unbeliever, he was able to cure the blind man. Both then and in our own times, many have experienced similar things, for it is allowed to sinners to verify personally what is written in Psalm 102: *"He shall save thee because of his Name, that His power might be manifest."*

It is however to be noted that four things are required if a person is to obtain what he requests through the power of the Holy Name. First that he ask for himself; second, that whatever he asks be necessary for salvation; third, that he ask in a pious manner; and fourth, that he ask with perseverance—and all these things concurrently. If he asks in this manner, he will always be granted his request.

First, and I repeat it, a person must ask for himself, for only then is he assured of being heard. No one is able to merit eternal life through the worthiness of another, for it follows reason that things pertaining to the eternal life cannot be merited through the efforts of others. Hence, when a man asks for someone else, he is not always heard. As St. Jerome says in his commentary of Jeremiah: in vain does a person ask for someone else what that other person should ask for himself. St. Augustine also tells us in his commentary on John that all the faithful are heard when they ask for themselves, but not when they ask for all their friends and their enemies. When God says in John 16: *"if you ask the father in My Name, He will give it."* He does not say give it to anyone, but He says *"dabit vobis,"* which is to say, *"he will give it to you";* and even further, with regard to this, God says in Jeremiah 7: *"do not thou pray for this people, nor take to thee praise and supplication for them, and do not oppose me, for I will not hear thee."* A gloss on this passage explains that those who prayed were not heard by God for two reasons: first, their absolute and persistent heresy, and second, their complete impenitence of heart.

Second, when God says, as quoted above, *"that which you ask the Father in My Name, He will give it to you,"* it is implied that that which is asked should be necessary for salvation. Thus Rabanus in his commentary on Matthew says: no matter how often you ask the Father, He will not hear you if what you ask for is something that hinders your salvation. Or again, He may not seem to hear you because the answer to your petition is delayed to some future time, either so that you might develop greater yearning, or so that the joy which he withholds might be the more completely apprehended.

Third, it is necessary to ask with piety. This phrase implies all the attitudes which are necessary on the part of one that prays—insofar as he prays at all. Namely, he should pray with faith, with humility, and with fervor. First, he must pray with faith and confidence, for, as B. Jacobus says: ask with faith and without hesitance. Second, he must pray with humility, for it says in Psalm 101: *"he has regard to the prayer of the humble and he has not despised their petitions."* Third, he should pray fervently, for as St. Augustine says: greater worth follows prayer when it is preceded with a fervent disposition.

As we said four paragraphs above, four things were required if a person is to obtain what he requests through the power of the Holy Name. The last and fourth is that he should pray with perseverance. This is taught us by God in the parable in Luke 11. for He says: *"which of you shall have a friend and shall go to him in the middle of the night and say to him: 'friend, lend me three loaves, for a friend of mine has just come to me from a journey and I have nothing to set before him.' And He from within should answer and say, 'do not disturb me; the door is now shut, and my children and I are in bed; I cannot get up and give to thee.' I say to you, although he will not get up and give to him because he is his friend, yet because of his persistence he will get up and give him all he needs. And I say to you, ask, and it shall be given to you, seek, and you shall find; knock and it shall be opened to you, for everyone who asks receives; and he who seeks, finds, and to him who knocks it shall be opened."*

CHAPTER IV

Concerning the fourth Ray of the Name of Jesus: how he who with devotion applies himself to the repetition of this Name is filled with a wonderful joy and happiness.

Fourth, the Name of Jesus is truly a consolation to the afflicted and a protection against the evils of suffering and concupiscence. No matter what, God will not allow his servants to succumb to temptation, for in no way will He allow them to be conquered by their afflictions. There is no despair or forgetfulness in the sweet Name of Jesus if only we call upon it with the greatest possible intensity. This is why God says in Matthew 5 as a consolation to the patient: *"blessed are you when men reproach you and persecute you, and, speaking falsely, say all manner of evil against you for my sake. Rejoice and exult, for your reward is great in heaven."*

Yes indeed, for those souls inflamed with love, the Name of Jesus is a happiness beyond measure, for the Name of Jesus alone can reveal the intoxicating nature of His love and express the passionate longing of His heart. One should seek no other reward. Is not a man often happy to expose himself to danger for a friend, even though he knows him to be subject to the impermanence of his mortal nature? How much more so should we do this for God, our Jesus, who is immortal and who, as everyone knows, was so glad to suffer for us. It was because of this fact that Paul said in Acts 21: "*I am ready, not only to be bound, but even to die at Jerusalem for the Name of Christ Jesus,*" and it was because of this that the Apostles in Acts 5 "*went rejoicing before the council because they were worthy of being persecuted for the Name of Jesus.*" St. Augustine says that the Name of God, when it is written in the hearts of the just, bestows on them such great courage that they endure patiently being unconquered, she said: if you do to me the things that you threaten, only let the Name of Jesus be heard, and the tortures will be mild; and if you attack me with fire, the angels will administer to me with the saving dew of heaven. Because of the power of this Name, the holy martyrs triumphed over all their torments, whence the prophet says in Psalm 43: "*through Thy Name we will despise them that rise up against us,*" and again in Psalm 123: "*our help is in the Name of God who made heaven and earth,*" which is to say that this Name is so powerful that in our torments it consoles and assists us. Nor is it to be wondered at that the martyrs sustained so much suffering with so much joy when it was this Name that supported them. Thus it is that the Apostle says in his letter to the Philippians 2: "*it is God who of his good pleasure works in you both the will and the performance,*" and that God Himself tells the patient soul in Apocalypse 2: "*thou hast patience and hast endured for My Name, and hast not grown weary.*"

Yes, he who sings out loudly and with passion the Name of Jesus perseveres on account of this Name. He can patiently sustain all persecution because of this holy tradition of our most excellent Christian religion, for as it says in 1 Peter 4: "*let none of you suffer as a murderer, or a thief or slanderer, or as in coveting what belongs to others, but, if he suffers as a Christian, let him not be ashamed, but let him glorify God under this Name."* And lest he not merit the advantage of the virtue of patience, or even not be able to speak of it unless he perseveres to the very end, John adds: *"do not grow weary."* Let no one become discouraged, either on account of the difficulty of the effort, or because of some hidden passion of the soul, or because he is persecuted on account of his love of justice by the enemy. Let him return again to his initial undertaking, for it says in Leviticus 3 that an animal with a tail should be grasped and offered up, in which statement it is mystically implied that a work is not able to be pleasing to God unless it is carried through to the very end.

SECTION II

THE NEXT FOUR RAYS:
HOW THE NAME OF JESUS IS
OF GREAT ASSISTANCE
TO THOSE WHO WOULD BE HOLY

In this second section we shall show how the Name of Jesus is of great assistance to those who would sanctify their lives, for if it is as valuable in fighting evil as has been shown above, it must be equally powerful in producing good. Indeed, it should produce this effect in four principal ways. First, in the heart; second, in the mouth; third in actions; and fourth in all other things combined. And this is so because the Name of Jesus is the highest distinction of the believer; second, it is the most splendid of all things praised; third, it is the reward of our labors; and fourth, it is the help of those in need.

CHAPTER I

The fifth Ray: concerning the wonderful glory and honor that follows all true believers in His Name— that is the Name of Jesus

First, with respect to the heart, the Name of Jesus is the highest honor of the believer, for through their most loving faith in the Son of God, the Name of Jesus is planted in the hearts of believers. And John testifies to this when he says: *"He gave them the power to be the sons of God—to those that believe in His Name."* Great indeed is the honor of being a son of God, for as Paul says in Romans 8: *"if we are sons, we are heirs also. heirs indeed of God and joint heirs with Christ."* A very great foundation then, is the Name of Jesus, making us the sons of God, for it is on this very basis that the entire building (of the Church) is upheld, and the pillars, having been erected, mount up to heaven lasting till the end of time; for the members of the mystical body of Christ are the foundations on which this building is erected. Hence it is that Paul says in 1 Corinthians 3: *"for other foundation no one can lay but that which has been laid, which is Jesus Christ."* For the faith of the Catholic religion consists in the knowledge of Christ Jesus, and in His light, which is the light of the soul, for He is the door of life and the foundation of eternal salvation. If a person does not have this faith, or should he forsake it, he is like one going through the darkness of night without a light, like a blind and lame person walking precipitously along a dangerous path. No matter how eminent a person's intellectual achievements, he should avoid following a blind leader, a leader whose intellect, cut off from heaven, follows its own path. Such a person is like a man who builds a beautiful and resplendent house, but who ignores the foundation; he is like one who, bypassing the door, enters a house by the roof. The foundation, that is Jesus, who is also the light and the door. It is He who is a guide to those who are lost, and He who demonstrates the light of the faith to all men. This is why men who seek the unknown God come to believe in Him and believe in His coming. The Church is indeed built on the Name of Jesus which is its very foundation, and hence it is the greatest honor to cleave through faith to the Name of Jesus and to become a son of God.

The angel that John speaks of in Apocalypse 9 understood this in refusing to let himself be worshiped, for as John says: *"I threw myself before the feet of the angel to worship him, and he said to me, thou must not do that. I am a fellow servant of thine and of thy brethren who give the testimony of Jesus. Worship God."* John says: *I fell down before his feet to worship him,"* not inasmuch as he was a creature, but rather as an eager servant, with humble submission, honors God his Creator. As we know, the angels in the Old Testament allowed man to worship them in a manner now forbidden—for it is clear that he forbade this when he says *"thou must not do that."* He goes on further to explain: *"I am a fellow servant,"* that is, with you and like you I am a servant of the same God, Our Lord Jesus Christ. Do not think that the angel says this only with regard to St. John because of John's singular holiness and excellence, or even on account of his great eminence. He says this for all men who are servants of Christ, and therefore he adds: *"and of thy brethren who give testimony of Jesus"*—that is to say, those who with a pure heart confess and testify that Jesus is God and Lord of all the universes and the Redeemer and Savior of man.

Now there are three reasons why the angel forbade John to worship him. First, on account of his worthiness; second, on account of the truth; and third, because of humility. First, I say on account of his worthiness, for the angel knew how John received Christ in joy and exultation, and wished to show this to all mankind. It is as if the angel said that he could see above Him, in the seat of divine majesty, and if it can be said openly, I also see and adore the man-Christ—and hence the angel could not permit a man who believed in Christ to worship him. Second, it is so stated on account of truth: that is to say that when the angels in the Old Testament permitted man to worship them, they were not permitting that which is called worship (latria), for this was only capable of being given to God, but rather veneration. And lest the devils should desire to be worshiped—and indeed they greatly desire this—the angel adds *"adore God."* The third reason is because of humility with which the angels are thoroughly imbued. This is an attitude that those in the Church who have the highest dignity should adopt, for those that one can say serve with the greatest honor should nevertheless not ascribe to themselves that which belongs to God, or if they do, only to that degree that allows them to better serve and minister to their flocks. Hence it is that St. Luke says in Chapter 23: *"the kings of the gentiles lord it over them, and they who exercise authority over them are called benefactors. But not so with you. On the contrary, let him who is greatest among you become as the youngest, and him who is chief as the servant. For which is the greater, he who reclines at table, or he who serves? It is not he who reclines? But I am in your midst as he who serves."* And this is why Peter, the prince of the Apostles and the head of the Church, does not permit Cornelius in Acts 10 to fall on his knees and to honor him as a servant, but rather says to Cornelius: *"get up, I am myself also a man,"* and he said this that we might know that such humility is to be shown.

CHAPTER II

Concerning the sixth Ray of the Name of Jesus: that those who extol and proclaim the singular Name of Jesus who is the Savior, come to fruition in the Word of God.

Second, the repetition of the Name of Jesus is the most wonderful thing that can be advocated, because, by this, as St. Bernard says, His Word is heard and proclaimed in all its luminous splendor. In what other way can you find the light of God so greatly, so unexpectedly, and so fervently manifested, unless it be in the repetition of the Name of Jesus. With all the brilliance and sweetness of this

Name, God has called us to enter into His wonderful glory—that we might be illuminated and in this light be able to apprehend His glory. As the Apostle says in his letter to the Ephesians 5: *"for you were once in darkness, but now you are light in the Lord: walk then as children of light."* So also, in like manner, this Name should be extolled and proclaimed, that it might shine forth. It should not be hidden, nor exposed in speech that reflects an evil heart, or a polluted tongue, but rather brought forth from a person who is like a vessel of election. Hence God says in Acts 9: *"this man is a chosen vessel to me to carry My Name among the nations and kings and children of Israel."* *"A chosen vessel,"* He says—and is this not a container where the sweetest liquor is kept, a liquor that can be poured forth and imbibed while at the same time it continues to shimmer and glow in the vessel? *"To carry,"* He says, *"My Name"*—this is like the fire lit in the autumn to burn the dry and useless stubble left after harvesting; it is like the risen sun dispelling the darkness of night that covers the acts of thieves that wander about and rifle houses. Thus it was that Paul spoke to the people, like thunder pealing forth; like an overpowering fire; like the burning sun—consuming all perfidy, dispersing error and clarifying the truth, much as a strong fire burns up wax. Truly, the Name of Jesus was spread abroad by voice, by letter, by miracles and by examples, for Paul praised this Name of Jesus continuously. He extolled it in all things, and above all, he extolled it before kings, before the nations, and to the sons of Israel. The Apostle carried this Name as if it were a torch with which he illuminated his fatherland. He proclaimed it, saying in Romans 13: *"the night is far advanced, and the day is at hand. Let us therefore put aside the works of darkness and put on the armor of light. Let us walk becomingly as in the day."* He showed to all this shining lamp, like the light over the candelabrum—announcing in every place Jesus and His crucifixion. And how greatly did that light shine forth in Paul, blinding the eyes of those who listened as if with wonder and astonishment. Peter describes this in Acts 3: *"like lightning flashing, curing and making strong the crippled limbs of their bodies and illuminating the spiritual blindness of many."* Did he not dispense fire when he said: *"In the Name of Jesus Christ arise and walk"?* St. Bernard tells us, both in the source quoted above, and also in his treatise on the Apostle Mark, that "the perfect have extolled it always"—that is to say, the Name of Jesus, "and, God cooperating, the Word having been as it were confirmed, signs follow"—which signs were truly shown in the Name of Jesus. And how are these signs shown? They are shown by miracles, by the persecution that tyrants imposed upon the faithful, and by those shining lights, who by explaining the scriptures have destroyed the false teachings of heretics—and what is more, it is daily demonstrated in our own sweet meditations and in the frequent illuminations of the elect. Thus it is that the Church, the Bride of Christ, in support of this testimony, rejoices in singing from Psalm 95: *"Lord Thou hast taught me from my youth, and even now I shall pronounce Thy miraculous Name"*—that is to say, invoking it continuously. And the prophet further exhorts us to this, saying: *"sing to the Lord and bless If is Name: announce His Salvation from day to clay"*—which is to say, constantly invoke the Name of Jesus, our Savior.

CHAPTER III

The Seventh Ray of the Name of Jesus: how by the power of this Name, merit is gained in good works.

Third, with respect to our actions, the Name of Jesus is a labor of merit, for by the virtue of this Name, grace and merit are accumulated as is testified to by the Apostle in his first letter to the Corinthians 12: *"no one can say 'Jesus is Lord' except in the Holy Spirit."* Now, Alex of Ales understands in this passage a triple definition: namely, no one can say Jesus is God in his heart, with his mouth or in his actions unless he does it through the strength of the Holy Spirit. He says 'no one' because if anyone is able to bear this most Holy Name worthily, it will inevitably be efficacious in producing in him a worthy life and eternal glory. This is so because all acts that are elicited of the Holy Spirit are worthy of eternal glory. Great indeed then is the richness and treasure with which this most Holy Name of Jesus overflows. Indeed, when the Name of Jesus is continuously praised and glorified, with humble devotion and with sweetness, this hidden treasure is shared and spread abroad in the manner that is recommended in Ecclesiastes 51: *"I will praise Thy Name continuously and will extol it in all things."* St. Chrysostom in commenting on this passage says that it refers to a person who deeply loves and invokes the Name of God repeatedly, and who is, by this invoking, exulted in the Most High Lord—that is to say, by the accumulation of merit and the acquisition of graces.

CHAPTER IV

The eighth Ray of the Name of Jesus: how the luke-warm and spiritually weak, though the Name of Jesus, are brought back again to fervid charity.

Fourth, to continue our discussion regarding the Name of Jesus, know that it is the help of the infirm, whence St. Bernard, as quoted above, says: "are not all consoled as often as they recollect the Name of Jesus, which Name impinges upon the mind, and when repeatedly invoked, heals the wounded senses, strengthens the virtues, stirs up good and honest manners, and keeps the affections pure. If you are afflicted with a sluggish mind or an indolent faith, Jesus heals you by exciting fervor, and the Name of Jesus will be always in your heart, and always on your fingertips, because all your emotions and all your actions will be directed towards Jesus." And Jesus Himself invites us to this, saying in the Song of Songs 8: *"put me as a seal upon thy heart, and as a seal upon thy arm,"* for through this Name your tepid heart will be mended and you will have an arm that is both strong and dextrous. I assure you that through the invocation of the Name of Jesus, your actions, should they be depraved will be corrected, and if they are less than perfect, they will be improved; also your senses, which should be your servants, are not only protected from damage and destruction, but should they be injured (by sin) are repaired and healed. Rightly then, my brothers, as St. Bernard says, is this Name to be invoked by us, because it is a quick protection against lassitude and against the languor that follows grief; it removes aridity, the fear of isolation, disgust with spiritual reading, agitation of the soul or feelings of tepidity or scrupulosity in our affections. No matter how prolonged the prayers seem; no matter how deep the lassitude of soul, what sweetness this Name brings! When neither the desire for the kingdom of heaven, nor the fear of eternal damnation can free us from or disperse our apathy of soul, if we but retire to a quiet place and invoke the Name of Jesus with love in the depths of our heart, we will quickly be suffused with joy, and an eagerness so great will return, that tongue cannot express it, nor words in sermons portray it, for it transcends the acuteness of human understanding and the ability of all the senses taken together. The mind is, as it were, flooded with a certain kind of radiating light. One becomes inebriated with that special liquor of which we have previously spoken. So full of joy is the mind—as if in a split second—if it is still in time at all—that it can prefer nothing else. It fills the soul with such sweetness, with so many benefits, and with such a heavenly flavor, that no one can describe it. Now I hold that this is because Jesus, when one invokes His Name with a deep and humble love, recalling it secretly and silently (in one's heart), causes the apathy and sadness to disappear and to be replaced with joy. This is illustrated by the story of Lazarus. When Jesus did not come at his death, the house was filled with sadness—but behold, when Jesus arrived, the sisters were consoled by his presence—and shortly afterwards Lazarus was resuscitated.

Mary—in the time of Christ's Passion, after suffering many painful and bitter things, went to the sepulcher and asked *"where was"* as Matthew 6 says, *"Jesus of Nazareth, Crucified."* Now Jesus means Savior. Nazareth is interpreted as flower, and the word Crucified is added. It is as if you had in sequence, Savior, Flower and Crucifixion, and in all three of them you have consolation. Jesus gives one the promise of salvation; the flower gives joy in one's affections; and the cross reconciles in action. This is why the sign of the cross is made with a perpendicular motion followed by two horizontal motions. The flower, delighting the eye, makes us hope in the coming of the fruit. Jesus is Himself the blessing (of the cross) and the most blessed fruit of the Virgin's womb—the fruit, I say, the most blessed and beautiful fruit that can be imagined—most pleasant to smell and most pleasant to taste. It is also the most precious fruit to possess for which reason the bride describes her joy in the Song of Songs saying, *"His throat is most sweet and he is all lovely."* Understand in this statement that Jesus is the fullness of beauty and completely satisfies all the desires of the soul. And what is even more wonderful, and more to be wished for, just as the deeper and more firmly the root of a tree is fixed in the ground, so much the more abundantly it produces fruit; so also with the Name of Jesus—if it is fixed deep in the heart and solidly rooted, it will produce the most luxuriant crop of fruit—a crop of most sweet smelling and pleasant graces.

SECTION III

THE LAST FOUR RAYS:
HOW THE POWER OF THE NAME OF
JESUS RELATES TO THE LIVES OF THE SAINTS

Under the heading of this third Section, we delineate the characteristics of the last four rays. We do this, first, that we might complete the picture, and second, because these characteristics blend together in the contemplative and perfect soul. We discuss this first with regard to meditation which has its seat in the memory; second, with regard to the use of the Name in prayer; third, with regard to its tasting and experiencing, and fourth, the Name as our reward when we are to be transplanted out of this life. And all this is true because the Name of Jesus is the initial inspiration of meditation; second, it is the support of prayer; third, it is the savoring of contemplation, and fourth, it is the glory of the triumphant finish.

CHAPTER I

The ninth Ray of the Name of Jesus—of that great sweetness that fills one when he devoutly meditates upon the Name of Jesus.

The Name of Jesus is, as it were, the very essence of meditation and recollection. Hence it says in the Song of Songs: *"Thy Name is as oil poured forth, therefore young maidens have loved thee."* Origen explains this saying: "it is well known that when oil is poured out (as in food), it nourishes the recipient. Now in what way is the oil of His Name poured forth? Surely it is poured into the heart of the person who frequently and with devotion invokes the Name of Jesus. And what is meant by the young maidens? Surely they are the fresh souls, laboring in asceticism, who with great zeal and joy follow after that delight of love that He inspires—that is, rejoice in its great sweetness." As St. Bernard says in recalling the sweetness of Jesus: "He is to be preferred with a joyful heart above all sweetness and honey. Nothing sings more sweetly, sounds more joyful, nor is more delightful than to meditate on the Name of Jesus, the Son of God." Hence it is that Isaiah says in Chapter 25: *"O Lord, Thy Name and remembrance is the desire of my Soul."* Hence it is that Bernard says in his commentary on the Song of Songs that the Name of Jesus is not so much a light as it is a nourishment or food, and is not the person who constantly invokes this Name completely filled? The Name of Jesus is an oil: and all that nourishes the soul is dry unless flavored with this oil. Oh how much sweetness is seen to be drawn forth from the lips of innocent children when they learn the *Pater Noster* and *Ave Maria* from their devoted mothers, and while still unable to repeat the entire prayer, they nevertheless repeat with reverence the Name of Jesus! The Name of Jesus is honey to the mouth and sweet music to the ear.

It says in Apocalypse 2 that: *"to him who overcomes I will give the hidden manna, and I will give him a white pebble (or light) and upon the pebble a new name written which no one knows except him who receives it."* The hidden manna indicates the taste of divine wisdom, hidden from the unworthy, for just as the manna came from above, having in it all the delicacy of taste, so also, the knowledge of the mysteries of Jesus Christ fills all minds with sweetness. This is why John adds: *"I will give him a white pebble,"* or light. This light is the burning coal, literally a light bearing stone, or a burning pebble— that all might perceive in some mystical way the greatness of the humanity of Christ—for the humanity of Christ is manifested under the sign of a stone. For the manna signifies truth, the pebble sweetness and mercy, and the burning whiteness, justice—which particular qualities are those of the Christ-man. Hence it says in Psalm 44: *"on account of mercy and justice."* And because the human-ity of Christ is joined to it, and since we obtain an awareness of this essential wisdom through the Name of Jesus Christ, he adds, *"and upon the pebble a new name is written."*

Now truly, the new name written is the one taken by the God-Man who alone is able to save. He it is, who with His well known excess of love, abundantly renews with sweetness and transforms with stupendous grace, all those who through the truth of the Name of Jesus Christ, come to Him. And who is able to measure the bril-liance of this light? Who is able to describe the taste of this good-ness? Surely only the person who himself experiences it. This is why it says: *"which no one knows except he who receives it"* from Christ. This is because the sweet knowledge of God must be received, and because it is communicated by the mind of Christ through grace to the one who is to receive and experience this sweetness. Christ, then, is the dispenser of this treasure and is shown in Isaiah 45 where God the Father says to the prophet: *"I will give the hidden treasure and the concealed riches,"* which is to say that you O Lord dispense all good things to the members of your body, and to your elect. And in what manner do you give O Lord? The prophet tells us in Psalm 132: *"like the precious ointment"* which is to say, so plentifully that *"it runs down upon the beard,"* which beard signifies the perfect and manly soul. And because this is. something clearly experienced, the psalmist adds: *"the beard of Aaron,"* for Aaron means a strong mountain. The beard of Aaron then signifies those great and manly souls such as the Apostles, the prophets, and the leaders of God's elect in whom the graces and gifts of God are most abundantly diffused. But almost immediately the psalmist adds: *"running down to the skirt of his garment,"* which is to say that almost immediately the lesser saints and the least of God's elect were included in the diffusion of these gifts and graces. Now this pouring forth of spiritual oil is of such tremendous value to the soul and to the body, and in this both the soul and body so delight, that *"dew"* is added as an analogy—*"as the dew of Hermon which descendeth upon mount Sion."* Now Hermon means condemned by the walls, and signifies the body contaminated by original sin. Sion originally meant a watch-tower, and signifies the soul which is the image of the Holy Trinity. And the analogy is most apt, for the soul is washed clean of original sin and bedewed with an excess of grace.

CHAPTER II

The Tenth Ray of the Name of Jesus—that whatsoever is asked in the Name of Jesus, observing the necessary circumstances, is invariably obtained.

Second, the glorious Name of Jesus is the support of prayer and all entreaty. What greater force is to be heard in prayer than this Name. Listen to what our Lord says in John 16: *"if you ask the Father for anything in My Name, I will give it to you."* Now indeed, He does say "anything" because that which is evil is not just anything. Remember, He says "in My Name," which is Jesus and which means

Salvation. Therefore it follows that you must ask for that which per-
tains to salvation and then "it will be given to you." Hence St.
Augustine says in his commentary on this passage: "we ask in the
Name of the Savior when we ask for the sake of salvation." Now the
power of the Name in which we seek salvation is never denied, and
so Augustine, in the same commentary adds: "we are unable, in the
Name of the Savior, to ask for that which is against the needs of salvation." This is why Holy Mother Church, who always desires that
which is necessary for salvation, is in the habit of placing at the end
of her petitions—prayers always heard with favor such as the Divine
Office—the phrase "*through Jesus Christ our Lord.*" St. Ambrose says
in his commentary on this passage (Art. I, Chap. 3) that no one can
call himself poor in or with God, if he prays to the Father in the
Name of the Son and receives God's gifts. Rather, such a person,
who extols with devotion the glorious Name, is truly rich in God,
for whatever such a person needs of what he asks, is given to him in
the most appropriate way possible. For if there are many needy who
only place their trust in temporal goods, there are also, in contrast,
the just, who place their trust in the invocation of our Lord, Jesus
Christ. Thus it is that the prophet says in Psalm 19: "*some trust in
chariots and some in horses, but we trust in the Name of the Lord, our
God.*" Now the psalmist does not use the word "some" as a demon-
strative, but rather as a partitive, much as Matthew (25) does when,
speaking the mind of God. He says: "*and some will go into everlasting punishment, but the just into everlasting life.*" Those that trust in
"chariots" are those that place their confidence in the perpetual rev-
olutions and changeability of time, those that trust in themselves,
which is pride. Those placing their confidence in horses represent
those that put their faith in status or position or in worldly power.
Such, clearly have confidence in what is worthless. We however who
meditate upon these words, "we will call upon the Name of the
Lord," asking the Father, in the Name of his Son, for all that we
have need of.

CHAPTER III

*The eleventh Ray of the Name of Jesus—of the
immense sweetness with which those who contemplate
with delight the Name of Jesus are inebriated.*

Third, the Name of Jesus is the most sweet tasting nourishment of
contemplation, for it feeds and revives those souls that are famished
and spiritually hungry. The world that we live in is a poor and
famine-ridden land. Therefore with, we hope, a patient disposition—we await the Savior, our Lord Jesus Christ who will remake
our miserable bodies in the form of His shining image. And during
our sojourning with hope of being saved, rending as it were, our gar-
ments interiorly, we have the foretaste of the tenuous fruits of paradise, which during this earthly pilgrimage are ripened and fed
upon in contemplation. For verily, this is that most delicious manna
that satiated every soul—descending from heaven and nourishing
Israel in the desert. And this most edible fruit is the Name of Jesus
which contains every flavor and all possible sweetness. This is the
fruit whose foretaste we hope to grasp and relish during our way-
faring in this world, in contemplation. But whenever hope seems to
be in vain, let us grasp and take pleasure in this most perfect thing,
the Name. According to the prophet, when our heart rejoices total-
ly in Jesus, because we hope in His Holy Name, then we can say in
accordance with Psalm 32: *"let Thy mercy be on us, O Lord, because
we have placed our hope in Thee."* For the sweet taste of the Name of
Jesus instructs us, just as much as it did David—so that with him
we say: *"we have trust in Thy Name because it is good."* St. Augustine
comments on this passage, saying that the Name of God is good
because it is good for us if we delight in it, place all our love in it,
and praise that which gives us so much joy. And again, St. Bernard
says that through the Name of Jesus Christ we come to the thing
named and arrive at the delight and fruition of His Name. Most
meritoriously then, does Proverbs 18 state with that lofty wisdom:

"the Name of God is a strong fortress; the just runneth to it and shall be exalted." St. Jerome expounds on this passage saying: not without cause is the Name of Jesus likened unto a strong fortress, for it is the most powerful weapon, not only in attacking the enemy and protecting of oneself against the vicissitudes of life, but also in the elevated contemplation of the multitude of eternal joys. This is why St. Chrysostom says that he who profoundly loves the Name of God and calls upon it frequently, will be exalted in the high God. The Blessed Giles, the companion of St. Francis, also knew this from his personal experience, for, ever since our Lord Jesus appeared to him near his hermitage on Mount Ceton, tarrying with him for long periods of time every day from the Feast of the Nativity to that of Epiphany, ever since that time he was so full of sweetness that whenever he heard the Name of Jesus pronounced, he at once was overwhelmed with joy and fell into ecstasy, and was often even raised up above the ground. The Holy Father, wishing to see this for himself, had Brother Giles brought quietly to his privy chambers, and when he casually mentioned the Name of Jesus in his conversation, Brother Giles was elevated above the ground in ecstasy immediately. Oh, if only I might participate in such a superabundant grace! Oh, that I might be transported in such lofty contemplation! Oh, that I might share in this exquisite glory of paradisaical delight— that I might be given a spark—that a single drop might descend upon my arid soul so that I might know, taste and love Jesus with my whole heart. You are inaccessible, O Lord, to us standing as it were, outside, and wrapped up with bodily things. To many of us living in the world, the sweet graces which you have reserved for your beloved children, are like an oasis in the desert, encouraging us to run after the odor of your scent. And over and above this most sweet delight, it is because of your odor, O Lord, that the desire seems eternal. This is why the prophet says in Psalm 35: *"In the light of Thy countenance we shall see the light."* And again, Isaias 60: *"the people shall walk in Thy light and they shall praise Thy Name the whole day long,"* And finally, I would be numbered among those saying with Habakkuk (3): *"I rejoice in the Lord and exult in my God, Jesus."*

CHAPTER IV

*The Twelfth Ray of the Name of Jesus: how the saints
in heaven eternally glory in the Name of Jesus.*

Fourth, the Name of Jesus is the glory of the triumphant saints, for
it is in their perfected images that the Name finds its consummation. For where the blessed are living eternally, there is no darkness;
no error creeps in to spoil the enjoyment of truth; no impulse of
greed to corrupt divine charity—in heaven, the Name of Jesus will
be most clearly seen in all its most super-splendorous truth by the
intellect of the saints through the merit of faith. It will be kept in
the memory, in all its stupendous majesty, as a permanent possession, through the merit of hope. It will be held in the will, like the
sweet fruit of goodness, through the merit of loving. As the prophet
says in Psalm 5: "*all they that love Thy Name, shall glory in Thee.*"
And, if on account of the Name of Jesus every soul lives, is enriched
and will come to beatitude, being formed after the Triune God in
unity, enlightenment and sobriety, it is because the perfect live eternally in all good things gathered together. Thus it is that the prophet
says in Psalm 142 to God: "*Thy good spirit shall lead me into the right
land for Thy Name's sake.*" Concerning this most happy statement,
God says further in John 16: "*Hitherto, you have not asked anything
in My Name,*" which is to say, because the power of My Name was
unknown to you. But now that its power is known, "Ask," He says,
"and receive"—that is, through the power of My Name. As St.
Chrysostom says, in order that the power of this Name might be
demonstrated, this Name, not visualized, not appended to a
request—just the Name alone, worked miracles with the fathers.
And He adds: "that your joy might be complete," which is to say, it
will be complete in eternal glory.

Now eternal glory is called a joy for three reasons. First, every
desire of the soul is filled to excess, for as the psalmist says (15):
"*Thou shalt fill me with the joy of Thy countenance,*" which passage

has been adequately discussed in a preceding chapter. Second, it consists in the vision, fruition and possession, in its entirety, of the consummation of goodness, which is the Triune God, as is taught, and concerning which God Himself says in Exodus 33: "*I will show thee all good.*" Third, this joy is so great, and of such a nature, that it cannot be lost, whence John 16 says to his disciples: "*and no one will take away your joy from you.*"

In these ways, therefore, the Name will be the glory of the saints, whence John says in Apocalypse 14: "*and I saw, and behold the Lamb was standing upon Mount Sion and with Him one hundred and forty-four thousand having His Name and the Name of His Farher written on their foreheads.*" Now Mount Sion indicates the highest power in heaven, of which Sion is an image. And on this mountain stands the Lamb, Jesus Christ, the Son of God, who is above all, resplendent in the vision of His glory, and in which glory all the saints share. Hence it follows: "and with Him, one hundred and forty-four thousand"—that is to say, lambs, with the Name written over them, and they are subject to the principal Lamb. Now the number given, as explained elsewhere, represents all those in glory. By four we understand virtue; by forty, the exercise of virtue; by one hundred, those who delight in virtue and by practicing it, acquire virtue, and, by a thousand, wisdom, for wisdom is the perfection of virtue, for through wisdom God gives eternal glory. And it is added, "having His Name" that through this Name they might be well known and recognized, because, in God's eyes they cannot be known, unless it is through love—such is it to be in such a state of holiness. Putting this another way, the Name of Jesus is itself God through which God the Father and the Holy Spirit communicate in the Divine Unity. (*Seu aliter dici potest quod Nomen Jesu, id est, res Nominis Jesu est ipse Deus, in qua communicat Deo Patri, & Spiritui Sancto in divinitatis unitate*), a statement to which John testifies in the first chapter of his Gospel, saying: "*and God was the Word*" which Word is indeed distinct from the Father but to which God imparted one nature with the Father. Accordingly, while distinct in person, they deserve to be subjoined together in the unity of the Godhead. *"And the Name of His Father written on their foreheads"*— now the Father undoubtedly gives to all those in glory, the knowledge of the Son whose Father He is. Therefore, if they have the Name of the Father written on their foreheads, that is, if they have it in their mind, then they are not able to be ignorant of the Name of the Son. For the Son says in Luke 19: *"He who receives me,"* that is to say, in grace and in glory, *"receives the One that sent me."*

Moreover, Scripture tells us that the Name of the Father and the Son, written on the foreheads and minds of the saints, is written there by the finger of the Living God, which, as explained in Exodus 32, is the Holy Spirit. Thus, through the testimony of these first two, we come, in glory, to one Name in three persons, which constitutes the glory of the saints. It follows then, as St. Bernard says in his eighth sermon on the Song of Songs: those who follow the Lamb are said to have His Name and the Name of His Father written on their foreheads, which is to be glorified by this twofold knowledge.

O glorious Name! O Name so full of grace! O most powerful and loving Name! By you sin is forgiven, enemies are vanquished and the sick healed. Through you the patient are given strength and the afflicted consoled. You are the pride of the believer, a teaching theologian, the strength of the laborer, the sustainer of the weak, the fire of fervor and the heat of ardent love. You are the desire of those that pray, the inebriating liquor of the contemplative soul, and the glory of those who are triumphant in heaven, with whom, O sweet Jesus, allow us also to co-reign through Your most Holy Name, that with the Father and the Holy Spirit, together with all the Holy Saints in glory, we might glory and triumph and reign for ever and ever, Amen.

*This passage is taken from the translation of Kilian Walsh OCSO,
Cistercian Publications, Spencer, Mass. 1971*

St. John Eudes

St. John Eudes was born in 1601, at a time when France was being torn apart by conflicts between Protestants and Catholics. Educated by the Jesuits, he took a vow of chastity at the age of fourteen, and after the completion of his studies, at the age of twenty-two, joined the Oratory where spiritual formation was under the direction of Fathers de Berulle and de Condren. He was ordained priest two years later and greatly distinguished himself in caring for those stricken by the plague. After this he began to give the missions—six week courses of sermons—throughout France for which he became famous.

Many of the priests at that time were poorly educated and ineffective in the ongoing struggles with the Protestants. Aware of this, in 1643 he obtained permission to leave the Oratory and established a new order—The Society of Jesus and Mary for the education of priests and for missionary work. At the same time he established, preceding St. Margaret Mary, devotion to the Sacred Hearts of Jesus and Mary. He used to say that through the Sacred Heart the angels praise God, the Dominations adore Him, the Powers honor Him, the saints bless Him and all men atone to His divine Majesty for their deficiencies. Further, he had the honor of composing the office to the Holy Heart of Mary which was for the first time celebrated in 1648 as well as that of the Sacred Heart of Jesus which was introduced in 1672. Thus it was that in his canonization he was called "Author of the Liturgical Worship of the Sacred Heart of Jesus and Holy Heart of Mary." He is also the author of many books which are famous for their combination of both simplicity and profundity.

He was greatly devoted to the invocation of the names of *Jesus* and *Mary*. To quote him directly: "If I were to follow my own convictions, I should never speak or write any word but one, Jesus, for it seems to me that the tongue which has once pronounced, and the pen that has once written this adorable name and this divine word, *Jesus,* should never again be used to speak or write anything else. Besides, to say *Jesus* is to say everything, and after having said *Jesus,* there is nothing more to add, inasmuch as *Jesus* is an abridged word which in itself contains everything great that can be said or thought. *Jesus* is the name admirable above all names which, through its immense grandeur, fills heaven and earth, time and eternity, the minds and hearts of all the angels and saints; it even fills and possesses, from all eternity, the infinite capacity of the Heart of God, of the Father, Son, and Holy Ghost. Even if I could write nothing, therefore, save the one word *Jesus,* and could go everywhere in the world crying out unceasingly and pronouncing no other name except this one *Jesus, Jesus, Jesus,* I believe that I should be saying and writing enough to fill to capacity the minds and hearts of all the inhabitants of the earth."

In what follows, St. John Eudes provides us with his mediation on the Holy Name of Mary.

THE MYSTERY OF
THE HOLY NAME OF MARY[1]

"It is an infallible maxim," says Albert the Great, "that all the favors wherewith God honored His Saints have been accorded to the Queen of Saints, and that all that can contribute to her glory, has

---

1. St. John Eudes lists only the most common interpretations—he refers the reader to the work of Bardenhewer, *Der Namen Maria,* published in 1895 where sixty-seven are listed. The text, slightly modified, is taken from St. John Eudes *The Wondrous Childhood of the Most Holy Mother of God,* first published by the House of the Good Shepard, Peekskill, New York, 1915, and more recently republished by Preserving Christian Publ., P.O. Box 6129, Albany, N.Y., 12206. The presentation is somewhat modified from the original.

been bestowed upon her with so great excellence, that Mary surpasses all the other inhabitants of heaven in dignity and sanctity."[2]

Now, if the name of the patriarch Isaac was revealed by an Angel to his father Abraham, if the name of John the Baptist was announced by a heavenly messenger to Zechariah and Elizabeth; it is not to be doubted that the sacred name of Mary was brought from heaven by the Archangel Gabriel, who was always employed in commissions relative to the adorable mystery of the Incarnation. By an express order of the most holy Trinity, this glorious Archangel was deputed to declare to St. Joachim and St. Ann, that the Divine Majesty willed to give them a daughter who should be called Mary, which name was subsequently given her by the same St. Joachim.

Therefore we must infer that this holy name of Mary has come from heaven by order of the Sovereign Monarch of heaven and earth, and from the heart of the adorable Trinity, and the treasures of the Divinity: *"De thesauro Divinitatis,"* says St.Peter Damian, *"Mariae Nomen evolvitur."*[3]

Man had lost himself miserably and the Father of Mercies, seeking means to save him, beheld the name of Mary among the treasures of heavenly wisdom, and having placed it before the eyes of His Divine Bounty, this God of all consolation issued a decree, in His divine counsels, that the great work of man's redemption and the world's reparation, should be performed by Mary, in Mary, of Mary and with Mary; so that, as nothing had been made without the Incarnate Word, nothing should be repaired without the Mother of the Incarnate Word. This is the substance of the words of the holy Cardinal teaching us that the sacred Name of Mary has been taken from the storehouse of Divine Charity where it was hidden from all eternity.

After this, we need not be astonished that the precious Name of Mary contains in itself all the prodigies of which we shall speak below.

2.　In *Bibl. B. Mar.* ad cap. 1 Cant.

3.　*De Annunt*

SEVENTEEN INTERPRETATIONS OF THE HOLY NAME OF MARY, GIVEN BY THE HOLY FATHERS AND BY SOME CELEBRATED DOCTORS, IN HEBREW, SYRIAC, GREEK, AND LATIN.

The first interpretation of the holy name of Mary is that given by St. Ambrose, who says,[4] that Mary signifies *"Deus ex genero meo*—God born of my race,"* which gives us to understand that God having willed to be born of the noble race of Mary, daughter of Joachim and Ann, it followed that there must necessarily be a Mother of God in that royal race. This Mother could be none other than the blessed Mary, since the Mother of God was to be a Virgin: *"Ecce Virgo concipiet et pariet. Behold, a virgin will conceive and bring forth."*[5] This divine Mary is a Virgin and Queen of Virgins and the first to make the vow of virginity, for which may God be praised and glorified eternally.

The second interpretation is that of St. Jerome,[6] St Athanasius,[7] St. Anselm[8] and several others who teach that Mary means *"Domina maris*—Lady of the Sea." This signifies the great power of the Blessed Virgin. "The Son and the Mother have the same power," says Richard of St. Laurence. "The Son being all powerful renders the Mother all powerful. *Eadem potestas Matris et Fulii, quae ab omnipotente Filio omnipotens est effecta."*[9]

O Mary, be Mary to us truly, that is to say, our sovereign and absolute Lady: *"Dominare in medio inimicorum tuorum."*[10] Establish

---

4. *Lib. De Inst. Virg.*, cap, 5

5. *Is.* 7: 14

6. *Lib. De Nom. Hebr.*

7. *In Ev. De Deip.*

8. *De Exc. Virg.*, cap. 9

9. *De Laud. B. V.*, lib 4 "The Son and the Mother share the same power because from the all powerful Son, all power is actualized."

10. Ps. 109:2 "Reign in the midst of thy enemies," usually translated as "sit at my right hand until I make thy enemies thy footstool."

thy reign and dominion in the midst of our souls, notwithstanding all thy enemies, our own will, self-love, obstinacy and all our bad passions. Be Queen of our hearts, rule and govern them in all things, according to the will of thy Son.

The third interpretation is St. Ephrem's,[11] who teaches that the name of Mary signifies *"illuminata, illuminatrix, illuminans*—illuminated, illuminator, illuminating."

O Mary, be a Mary to us. Be our sun; enlighten our darkness. Do not permit us to slumber in the death of sin, but that we may know it only to flee in horror from it; that we may know God to love and fear Him; that we may know the world to despise it, that we may know ourselves in order to humble ourselves.

The fourth interpretation is from this same Saint and the others I have quoted, who say Mary means "Light of God."

O Mary, light of God! light, which is an excellent participation in the Light essential; light, Mother of the Eternal Light, be the light of our minds and have pity on so many miserably blind souls, who precipitate themselves into the horrible darkness of sin and hell.

The fifth interpretation is that of the saintly Abbot of St. Evron, in the diocese of Lisieux, in Normandy, who through humility styled himself the "Idiot," but whose real name was Raymond Jourdain. He says that Mary signifies "Doctor, Mistress of the Sea, of the people," because God has placed her in the world to teach men, to be Mistress of the "people," designated by the waters of the sea. St. Augustine[12] calls her *"Magistra gentium,"* for she brings to men the knowledge of salvation and of heavenly doctrine, teaching them not only by example, but by word. And this she did even for the Apostles, after her Son's Ascension. She is thus called by the Angel addressing himself to St. Bridget, "Mistress of the Apostles"[13] and by St. Augustin and St. John Chrysostom, "Mistress of piety

---

11. *Orat. De Laud. Virg.*
12. *Sermo* 6, de Temp.
13. *In Sermo. Angel.* Cap. 19

and truth." She is styled by the devout Abbot Rupert, "the Mistress of religion and faith,"[14] and "the Mistress of Masters,"[15] and by the pious Abbot Blosius "Mistress of the Evangelists"[16]; and by Gregory the Great "Mistress of all Doctors"[17] and by Richard of St. Laurence "Mouth of the Church—*Os Ecclesiae*"; and by the entire Church, "Queen of Apostles and Evangelists."

O divine Mistress, blessed are those who study in thy school. Oh, that I may be among the number of thy disciples, and learn at thy feet the philosophy of the children of God, and the theology of Paradise!

The sixth interpretation is that of an excellent author, Angelus Caninius, who assures us that the name of Mary signifies *"exaltata, eminens, sublimis, excelsa*—exalted, eminent, sublime, elevated," and expresses the amazing height of her dignity, sanctity, power, and glory, which are so great that there is nothing above her save God alone, to Whom she is most near: *"Deo proxima*—next to God, "says St. Thomas. All that is, not God is infinitely below Mary.

Infinite and eternal thanks be given to Him Who has made her so great and so admirable!

The seventh interpretation is that of Rev. Pere Adrian Lyere, S. J., who wrote an excellent book on the Name of Mary, *"Trisagion Marianum,"*[18] in which he teaches that Maria, according to the Hebrew etymology of the word, signifies not only *"sublimis, excelsa*—sublime and elevated," which shows the greatness of the Mother of God, but it signifies also *"stilla, vel gutta maris*—a drop of water of the sea," symbolizing her profound humility. O Queen of Heaven, which has elevated thee to the supreme dignity of Mother of God. Thou art regarded and treated as the last of all creatures, and God, Who exalts those who humble themselves, has given thee

---

14. *In Cant.* Lib. 5
15. Ibid., lib. 4
16. *In 1 Prec.*
17. *Homil. In Ev.*
18. *Trisagion Marianum seu trium mundi ordinum cultus:* Amvers. 1648

the first place in His empire. Thou hast abased thyself below all things, and He has elevated thee far above all pure creatures.

O most humble Virgin, make us share in thy humility; make us detest all pride and vanity, and love humiliation in all places, at all times, and in all things, according to the divine precept: *"Humilia te in omnibus—*humility in all things,"[19] not indeed that we may be afterwards exalted and glorified, but that God may be glorified and exalted in us; for he who exalts himself abases God, and he who abases himself, exalts God.

The eighth interpretation is that of Rutilius Benzonius, Bishop of Loretto, and several others, who declare that Maria signifies *"Dei imitatrix*—the imitator of God by excellence," for never was there, nor will there be seen, one who imitated God so perfectly in all His adorable perfections. This is why St. John Chrysostom says that she is an abyss of the immense perfections of God: *"Abyssus immensarum Dei perfectionum"*[20]; and St. Andrew of Crete, that she is an abridgment of the incomprehensible perfections of the Divinity— *"Compendium incomprehensibilium perfectionum Dei."*[21]

O my divine Mother, I desire with all my heart to bear within me the image of all thy rare virtues, by careful imitation, as thou bearest the image of the perfections of thy heavenly Father. Obtain this grace for me, I conjure thee; and annihilate in me all that may be an obstacle thereto.

The ninth interpretation is that of Canisius, S. J.,[22] and of other authors, who assure us that Mary signifies *"pluvia temporanea maris* —rain of the sea, falling at convenient time and season," which makes us see that this sacred Virgin is our consolation in the afflictions of our exile, amid the perils of the tempestuous sea of this world. For she is as a gentle rain, tempering the ardor of the fire of

---

19. Ecclus. 3: 20 "The greater thou art, the more humble thyself in all things, and thou shalt find grace before God."

20. *In Hor. Ani.*

21. Orat. *De assumpt.*

22. Lib. 1, cap. 1

tribulation, and sweetening in the time and fashion most agreeable the bitterness of the miseries of this vale of tears; watering the earth of our hearts and making them fertile and abundant in flowers of good desires, and fruits of holy deeds.

O holy and sacred rain, sink deep into our souls and hearts; extinguish therein all other fire except that which Our Savior came to enkindle upon earth; submerge us in the sacred torrents of thy divine waters.

The tenth interpretation of the Name of Mary is given by St. Peter Chrysologus. He teaches that Maria signifies *"mare, vel maria*—the sea, or the seas."[23] By this we may understand that as God having assembled the waters in one place, called them the seas, so, having gathered together all graces in the Blessed Virgin, He named her Maria to let us know that she is "an ocean and an abyss of graces." *"Abysus gratiae,"* says St. John Damascene[24]; "an immense sea of mercies," says St. Chrysostom, *"mare spatiosum misericordiarum"* [25]; a sea in which the true Pharaoh has been engulfed and drowned, as is sung in the Greek hymn.[26]

O great sea! would that thy waters might again cover the land as with a second deluge to destroy the many Pharaos that today inhabit it. Who will give me to plunge into this abyss, not indeed as Pharaoh, but as a little drop of water to be lost with thee in the sea of divine love forever, never again to find myself!

The eleventh interpretation is that of St. John Damascene,[27] and Albert the Great,[28] who teach that Maria signifies *"amarum mare—* a bitter sea."* Why is it that the most gracious Virgin, who is an ocean of sweetness and benignity, is called a bitter sea? It is to show us that,

---

23. Sermo 146
24. Orat. 2 *de Ass.*
25. *In Her. Ani.*
26. *Hymn, Graec. Apud Bution,* p. 122
27. Lib. 4, cap 1.
28. In cap I, *Luc.*

firstly, she was plunged into a sea of gall and bitterness at the time of her Son's Passion: *"Magna est velut mare contritio tua."*[29] Secondly, that being full of mercy towards men, she is filled with rigor and bitterness towards the demons. "As the Red Sea," says St. Bonaventure, "was very bitter and formidable to the Egyptians who were engulfed in it, so Mary is full of bitterness and terror for the demons."[30] For the pious and humble invocation of the Name of Mary discovers their ambushes and snares, dissipates their temptations, overthrows their designs, demolishes their work, breaks the chains of the souls whom they hold captive. In a word, the mere invocation of Mary's name causes all hell to tremble and puts to flight all the infernal powers: *"Terribilis ut castrorum acies ordinata."*[31]

Oh, how foolish and culpable we are to allow ourselves to be vanquished by these cruel enemies of our souls, seeing that, on the one side, they are very feeble, and, on the other side, God has given us such powerful arms with which to combat them. Have always the sacred Name of Mary in your heart, and often upon your lips, and you will be more terrifying to all hell than an army, well ranged, well equipped and well conducted, is to a small troop of feeble enemies.

The twelfth interpretation of the Name of Mary is given by St. Jerome[32] and St. Epiphanius,[33] who announce that Maria means *"myrrha maris*—myrrh of the sea." Several celebrated authors say that there is a certain precious stone found in the sea, called myrrh, from the fact that it has an odor like myrrh. It is said that it is made into saucers and drinking cups and sells at a higher price than gold.

Now our admirable Mary is the most precious cup of the great King, in which is presented to Him a nectar very delicious, being composed of the wine of her love and charity, and the honey of the sweetness of her humility. This wine so inebriates Him that He for-

---

29. Lam. 2:13. "Her suffering is great like unto the oceans."
30. *In Spec. B. V.,* lect. 3.
31. "Terrible as an army arrayed for battle."
32. Lib *De Nom. Hebr.*
33. Orat. *De Laud. Virg.*

gets the grandeurs of His Divinity, and plunges into the baseness and miseries of our humanity, that He may draw us thence and raise us even to the throne of the Divine Majesty.

O Mary, what hast thou done? What obligations towards thee has the whole human race! What praise shall we offer thee? What thanksgivings can we render for such benefits?

May I dare supplicate thee, my divine Mother, to give me a little of that precious wine which has inebriated my Redeemer, that being intoxicated therewith, I may forget myself entirely for love of Him, as He has forgotten Himself for love of me, and that I may no longer think except of Jesus, no longer love any one except Jesus, no longer live except to serve and honor my adorable Jesus and my all amiable Mary.

The thirteenth interpretation is that of Rev. Fathers Canisius and Salazar[34] of the Society of Jesus, who assure us that Maria interprets itself as *"jaculatnix maris*—the archer of the sea." This is an appropriate title for the Mother of God, for she is a generous warrior, and general of the armies of the Most High God, who combats incessantly upon the sea of this world, being armed with darts and arrows which she discharges continually against sin, against heresy, against the demons, and all God's enemies.

O most powerful Archer, discharge the arrows of thy indignation against the enemies of our souls, against that innumerable army of infernal dragons with which the earth is covered. They devour so many souls ransomed by the precious blood of thy Son. Shoot thy darts deep into our bosoms to kill there the love of the world and the disordered love of ourselves. O divine Archer I hear the King of heaven complain lovingly to thee "Thou hast wounded my Heart, my Sister, my Spouse, thou hast wounded my Heart."[35] Or, as another version has it, "Thou hast shot thine arrows into my heart—*Sagittasti con meum.*" Ah! since thou hast

---

34. Lib. 1., *de Virg.*; In Cant.
35. Cant. 4:9

not spared the heart of the Father, spare not that of the child. Turn thy arrows towards my heart, transpierce it with the inflamed darts of divine love, so that, dying to all created things and living only for God in the languors of His holy love, I may incessantly cry out to all the inhabitants of the heavenly Jerusalem: "Go, say boldly to my well beloved Jesus, and to my most dear Mary, that I languish with love for them."[36]

The fourteenth interpretation is from St. Epiphanius,[37] who declares that Maria signifies *"spes maris*— the hope of those who voyage on the stormy sea of this world."* This is conformable to the words the Holy Ghost causes her to speak, saying: "I am the Mother of holy hope: in me is all hope of life and virtue."[38] And St. Augustin fears not to say that she is the unique hope of sinners, that is, after God: *"Tu es spes unica peccatorum."*[39] And St. Ephrem says she is the only hope of the despairing and the most powerful succor of all those who implore her aid: *"Beatissima Virgo, unica spes despe-natorum et ad illam recurrentium auxilium potentissimum."*[40] "My little children," cries out St. Bernard, "behold here the ladder on which sinners may mount to heaven; here is my great confidence, the subject of all my hope—*Filioli mei, haec peccatorum scala, haec tota ratio spei meae.*"[41]

O most benign Virgin, blessed are those who, being diffident of themselves, have placed all their hope in thee; for, being very powerful, very wise and very good, thou canst, thou knowest how and thou wilt protect and favor them so truly and efficaciously, that those who address themselves to thee with filial confidence will never be deceived nor confounded.

---

36. Cant. 5:8
37. *Tract. De Laud. Virg.*
38. Ecclus. 24:24-5
39. Sermo, 18 *de SS.*
40. *Orat. Ad Virg.*
41. *Sermo de Nat. Virg.* "My children, this is a ladder for sinners, and this is the entire reason for my hope."

The fifteenth interpretation is that of St. Jerome, St. Bernard,[42] and several others who say that Maria signifies *"stella maris*—star of the sea."* For God has given us this star to enlighten us amid the dark mists of the sea of this world and to conduct us, through the innumerable perils we shall encounter there, to the desirable port of eternal salvation. "She is a star so resplendent," says St. Peter Damien,[43] "that, as the sun when it appears causes all the other lights of the heavens to fade from sight, so the marvelous splendor of Mary's sanctity and glory is such that it altogether eclipses all that is most brilliant among the Angels and the Saints, who in presence of Mary's glory and brilliancy, appear as though they were not."

She is a star, Daughter and Mother of the Eternal Sun. She is a star born of a Sun, and herself bringing forth a Sun. Alas! what should we do without this beautiful star amid so many dangerous tempests and whirlpools, surrounded by so many pirates and monsters, in the darkness which covers the sea whereon we must voyage? "Take away the sun out of the heavens," cries St. Bonaventure,[44] "what will become of the world?" Take away Mary, who is the torch of the obscure night of this miserable life, and what will happen? Where shall we find ourselves, if not in the shadow of death and the thick darkness of despair? "And consequently," says St. Bernard, "you who waver in the midst of the tempestuous sea of these our times, keep your eyes always fixed upon this star. If the winds of temptation beat against you, if you encounter the storm of tribulation, look up to your star, call upon Mary to succor you. If you are agitated by the waves of pride or ambition, envy, or detraction, look up to your star, invoke Mary. If anger or avarice or the passions of the flesh menace you with shipwreck, cast your eyes upon Mary. If horror of your crimes, a disordered conscience or the terrors of God's judgments cast you into the abyss of sadness or despair, turn

---

42. In Ps. 118; *Sermo. De Nat. B. Virg.*
43. *In Sermo. De Ass.*
44. St Bonaventure quoting St. Bernard: *In spec. B.V.* Lect. 3

your thoughts to Mary. In all perils, in all trials, think of Mary, call upon Mary. May Mary be always in your heart and upon your lips; and, that you may obtain the favor of her prayers, do not forget the example of her holy conversation."[45]

The sixteenth interpretation is from Lyere, who, as has been said above, is author of the seventh interpretation. He teaches that Maria, in the Greek etymology, signifies *"aquaeductus,* a water conduit." And the Holy Ghost uses these words to His divine spouse: *"Ego sicut aquaeductus exivi de paradiso*—I am like an aqueduct coming out of paradise,"[46] words attributed to the Mother of grace in this manner. Jesus is in the Church as the first fountain of grace; the Blessed Virgin is there as the channel through which graces are given to the faithful. The Saints are the streams which contain each one its portion of this same grace. All graces are in the fountain as in their prime source. They are found also in the streams, where they are proportioned according to the capacity of each stream, but they are all together unreservedly in the channel which receives them from the fountain to communicate them diversely to the streams, in such sort that it loses nothing at all, preserving them entirely in itself, like the torch, which while giving part of its light, loses nothing of its brightness.

"Nihil nos Deus habere voluit, quod per Mariae manus non transiret." "There is a decree in the eternal counsels of the Divine Majesty," says St. Bernard,[47] "that never will a grace be dispensed to any one without having first passed through the hands of Mary." Wherefore hast Thou willed this, my God? Why hast Thou sent forth such a decree? It is because of Thy love for this most amiable Virgin and Thy charity for us: Thy love for her obliging all men to recognize and honor her as the source of their salvation, after Thee: Thy charity towards us, giving us easy access through her to the

---

45. *Hom. 2, Super Missus est* and referred to in the Office of the Sacred Name of Mary which was composed by St. John Eudes.

46. Ecclus. 24:41

47. Sermo 3, *in Virg. Nat. Dom.*

primitive fountain of our eternal happiness; for which mayst Thou be blessed, praised and glorified eternally.

The seventeenth and last interpretation is from Theodore, surnamed the "New Confessor," who salutes the Blessed Virgin thus: "I salute thee, O Mary, who (according to the Greek word closely resembling thy Name) containeth within thyself innumerable wonders and prodigies." *"Innumera enim de te si quis dicat, numquam te digne collaudavenit.* For though one should say of thee and never cease to repeat all imaginable praises, one would never be able to praise thee worthily."

Behold what grand and admirable things are contained in the marvelous Name of Mary. I have endeavored to speak of them, because they relate to her divine Infancy, when this name was bestowed upon her by the order of that God Who knows infinitely better than the first man knew, how to give a proper and suitable name to each of His creatures. Add to this that the Church in several places, as we shall see, keeps the feast of the Name of Mary during that period of the year consecrated to her blessed Infancy, of which this Name is one of the principal mysteries. Thus it was thought well to open here this inestimable treasure and expose it to the eyes of the children of this glorious Virgin, to excite them to solemnize this feast with greater fervor.

I style the Sacred Name of Mary an inestimable treasure, and it will be seen in the following chapter that it is altogether right and proper so to do.

THE HOLY NAME OF MARY THE TREASURE OF THE ETERNAL FATHER'S LOVE

We have seen before these beautiful words of the blessed martyr St. Methodius, who thus salutes our amiable Mary: *"Salve, amoris Dei*

Patris thesaure—I salute thee, O Mary, the treasure of the Eternal Father's love."[48] They are so sweet and charming, however, for those who pronounce them and so advantageous to this divine Mary, that I would wish thus to salute her forever. And in order to excite every one thus to salute her, I would wish to go about through all the earth, preaching that Mary, daughter of Joachim and Ann, is the treasure of the Eternal Father's love.

In the first place, Mary is a treasure which contains in itself, according to the common language of the holy Doctors, all that there is most rich, most beautiful, most precious and most desirable in heaven or upon earth; in time and in eternity, in nature, in grace, in glory and in all pure creatures.

This treasure was hidden from all eternity in the love and in the Heart of the heavenly Father. In the fullness of time a little of this treasure was discovered to us, but it is now and will be eternally hidden in this same Heart, and hidden much more closely than we can understand.

For Mary signifies Mother of God, according to the first interpretation, given by St. Ambrose. There is so much that is rich and marvelous in this immense treasure of the divine Maternity, that all that the Angelic or human spirits comprehend of this mystery is but little in comparison with that which they do not know of it.

St. Augustin cries out that there is no heart capable of conceiving, nor tongue capable of expressing its grandeur: *"Nec cor concipere, nec lingua valet exprimere."*[49] And St. Andrew of Crete says it is only God who can worthily praise the miracles He has wrought in her: *"Deus solus pro dignitate potest laudare miracula quae fecit in illa."*[50]

Listen to St. Bernadine of Siena, who announces that, "as the perfections of the Divinity are incomprehensible to all understandings, so the excellence and graces which accompany the divine Maternity are so eminent, that there is no mind except the mind of

---

48. *De Orat. De Hypap.*
49. Serm. *De Ass. Virg.*
50. Orat. !, *De Dorm. Virg.*

God, the Man-God, and the Mother of God, able to comprehend them; and in order to dispose Mary for this high dignity, it was necessary to elevate her to a certain equality, if we may dare so speak, with God, by a certain infinity of graces and perfections." *"Oportuit, ut sic dicam ipsum elevari ad quamdam quasi aequalitatem divinam, per quamdam infinitatem perfectionum et gratiarum."*[51]

St. Andrew of Crete has already given us to understand that "this admirable Virgin is a declaration, that is to say, an expression and an image, of the hidden mysteries of the Divine Incomprehensibility—*Declaratio occultorum et profundorum divinae incomprehensibilitatis."*[52] And the Angelic Doctor says the same when he declares to us that Mary "is an infinite image of Divine Goodness," that is to say, an image representing infinitely well, and with infinite perfection, the immense grandeur of the Divine Goodness— *"Divinae bonitatis infinita imago."* [53]

St. Peter Chrysologus would repeat the same thing in saying: "The greatness of Mary is, in some sort, the measure of the grandeur and immensity of God, and whosoever knows not the one well, cannot know the other—*Tanta est Virgo, ut quantus sit Deus satis ignoret, qui hujus Virginis mentem non stupet, animam non miratur."*[54] And truly it can be said that the divine Maternity is the just measure of divine Omnipotence, since it is very true that God, Who can easily make a world grander than this, a heaven more extensive, a sun more brilliant, cannot make a more worthy or more noble mother than the Mother of a God.

We understand then how our divine Mary is a hidden treasure in the mind and heart of the Eternal Father, since there is none other Who knows her price and value.

---

51. Sermo. 61 *de B. Virg.*
52. Orat 2 *de Assumpt.*
53. Opusc. De Char.
54. Sermo 104

In order better to understand the second manner in which Mary is a treasure altogether hidden, it is to be remarked that there are three loves in the adorable Heart of the Divine Father, which are, however, but one: the first is the infinite love which He bears to His Son, Jesus; the second is His immense love for the Holy Ghost; the third is the very ardent love He has for the Angels, the Saints, and all His other creatures—*"Diligis omniaquac sunt, et nihil odisti eorurn quae fecisti."* [55]

Now, the most amiable Mary contains these three loves in herself. For, firstly, the Eternal Father regards her as the Mother of His Son, and in a certain measure even as He regards His Son, since they have together the same flesh, the same blood, the same nature, spirit, heart, and will. He therefore loves her with the same love He has for His Son. Thus this same Son speaking to His Father of all his members, that is, of all faithful souls, says: *"Dilexisti eos sicut et me dilexisti* [56]—Thou hast loved them as Thou hast loved me."* If the Divine Father so loves the servants of His Son, how much more must He not love the Mother of His Son?

Secondly, regarding Mary as the Spouse of the Holy Ghost, consequently, in a certain manner as one with Him, the heavenly Father loves her with the same love He bears His Holy Spirit, Who is His heart and His love.

Thirdly, not only does He love her as He loves all His Angels, His Saints, and all His other creatures, but, as Mary's love for Him is far greater than the love of all the Angels and Saints together, the Eternal Father loves her in return incomparably above all else which He has made. And thus she contains in herself all the loves of the Adorable Heart of the Divine Father.

Now the third manner in which this all amiable Virgin is the treasure of the Divine Father's love, is that He regards her in that quality which the Holy Spirit accords her by the mouth of the

---

55. Sap. 11:25 "For Thou lovest all things that are, and hatest none of the things which thou hast made."

56. John 17:23

Church and the holy Fathers.[57] He calls her "a vessel of honor and glory, a vessel fashioned by the hand of Wisdom, a vessel chosen by God, a vessel of grace and devotion, a vessel most pure and precious, a vessel of life and salvation and sanctification, in a word, an admirable vessel." In this vessel, the Eternal Father placed His most precious treasure, His well beloved Son, the first object of His love. He placed His treasure in her virginal bosom and her maternal heart. This treasure, infinitely precious to the Father, was hidden during nine months in the sacred womb of Mary, while it has always been and ever will be enclosed in her maternal heart. So it must be avowed that Mary is the treasure of the Eternal Father's love.

The fourth manner in which this most holy Mary is the treasure of the Eternal Father's love, is that the Father of mercies has amassed and combined in her all the effects of the bounty and love, which emanate or shall ever emanate from His Paternal heart, that is, He has replenished and overwhelmed her alone, with all the gifts, graces, favors, powers, privileges, perfections, glories, felicities, that He has divided among all the Angels and Saints. For which reason, St. Peter Damien calls her "the treasure of all God's graces—*Thesaurus gratiarum Dei*"[58]; and St. Andrew of Crete, "the most holy treasure of all sanctity—*Thesaurus sanctissimus omnis sanctitatis.*"[59]

Once more not only does Mary possess all the gifts and graces of God for herself, but she holds the possession and disposition of all the treasures and riches of the most Holy Trinity, to distribute to those who, addressing themselves to her, beg some alms or favor, and the blessed Raymond Jourdain styles her "the treasurer of God's graces;" and St. Bonaventure says: "She is a Mother most rich—*Mater ditissirna*—having the keys of all the treasures of the most Holy Trinity—*quae clavem thesaurarum sanctissimae Trinitatis tenet.*"[60]

---

57. Sts, Adam of St. Victor, Ephrem, Epiphanius, Anselm, Ildephonsus.
58. Sermo de Nat. B.V.
59. Orat 2, de Ass.
60. John 16:27

Behold the four ways in which our most amiable Virgin is the treasure of the Eternal Father's love.

This being so, if you wish to find this treasure of treasures, you must seek it in the infinitely amiable Heart of the Father of love. For has He not said: "Where thy treasure is, there is thy heart also?"[61]

Seek, then, this Paternal Heart in Mary, and you will find it there, since Mary is its treasure. Love, serve, and honor Mary with all your heart, and you will gain and possess entirely the heart of the Heavenly Father. He will love you and bless you abundantly, and she will repeat, after her Divine Son: "For the Father Himself loveth you, because you have loved me—*Ipse Pater amat vos, quia vos me amastis.*"[62]

THE HOLY NAME OF MARY
THE TREASURE
THE HEART OF THE CHURCH

There are two other qualities which holy Doctors attribute to the Sacred Name of Mary, which are very consoling to us.

In the first place, St. Epiphanius tells us that "Mary is the prodigious and admirable treasure of the Church—*Thesaurus Ecclesiae stupendus.*" "She is an inexhaustible treasure of grace and benediction," says Richard of St. Laurence, "for all the children of men who will use this treasure—*Thesaurus inexhaustus hominibus.*"[64] Is a treasure of joy and jubilation for the Church triumphant; a treasure of goodness and holiness for the Church militant," says St. Bonaventure. "She is a treasure of incomparable mercy for the Church suffering—*Thesaurus rnisericordiae incomparabilis,*" says St. Cyril of Jerusalem.[65]

---

61. Luke 12:27
62. John 16:27
63. *Orat. De Laud. Deiparae*
64. Lib. 4, *de Laud. Virg.*
65. *Super Salve; Sermo. De B, Virg.*

But let us listen to the other holy Fathers upon this subject.

"The name of Mary is jubilee to the heart, honey to the mouth and music to the ear," says St. Anthony of Padua: "*Nomen Mariae jubilus in corde, mel in ore, melos in aure.*"[66]

"Happy he who loves thy Name, O Mary," it is St. Bonaventure who speaks, "for this holy Name is as a refreshing fountain to the weary soul, bringing with it the fruits of justice."[67]

"O Mother of God," continues he, "how glorious and admirable is thy Name! Whoever carries it in his heart will be freed from the terrors of death. We need but to pronounce that Name to make all hell tremble and the demons flee away. Whosoever would possess peace and joy of heart, let him honor thy Name."[68]

"The Name of Mary," says St. Peter Chrysologus, "is a name of salvation for those who are regenerated; it is the insignia of virtue, the honor of chastity, the sacrifice agreeable to God, the virtue of hospitality, the school of sanctity, a name altogether maternal."[69]

"O Mary," cries out St. Germain of Constantinople, "thy greatness has no bounds, and thy meditation is all sweetness—*Quae magnitudinis non est finis; te cogitandi nalla satietas.*"[70]

"O great, O gentle, O most lovable Mary," cries out St. Bernard, "thy Holy Name cannot be spoken without inflaming the heart. To

---

66. *Dom. In Quad*

67. "*Beatus vir qui diligit Nomen tuum, Maria Virgo, gratia tua animam ejus comfortabit. Tamquam aquarum fontibus irrigatum uber in eo fructum justitiae propagabis.*—Happy is the man who loves your Name, O Virgin Mary; your grace will be a comfort to him. Her breasts, as an overflowing fountain will generate in him the fruit of justice." *In Psal. Virg.*

68. "Glorious and admirable is your Name, O Mary, he who has it in mind will not fear when faced with the moment of death. . . . This Name is so remarkable that he who has it in his heart, cannot be harmed by any evil whatsoever." Ibid.

69. Serm. 142 and 146.

70. Serm. 2 *de Dormit B.V.*

those who love thee, it is unspeakable consolation and joy even to think of thee; thou art a sweet memory to those who honor thee."[71]

"How wonderful!" says St. Anselm, "it sometimes happens that salvation is obtained by the invocation of the Name of Mary, rather than by that of Jesus. But how can that be? Is Mary greater and more powerful than Jesus? No, for Jesus has not received His greatness and power from Mary, but rather, Mary has received hers from Jesus. But the Son of God, being Lord and Sovereign Judge, must necessarily treat each one according to his merits, and according to the order of justice, which demands that the prayers of a criminal shall not be heard; but if he invoke the Name of the Mother of Mercy, although his sins render him unworthy of all grace, he is, nevertheless, heard through the intervention of Mary."[72]

"O Mary," says the holy Raymond Jourdain, "the Most Holy Trinity has given thee a name, which, after that of thy divine Son, is above all names; a name at sound of which all creatures in heaven, earth and hell, bow the knee; its grace, glory and virtue all tongues confess and honor. Thy Name, after that of thy Son, is most powerful to assist us in obtaining eternal salvation. Thy Name, above the names of all the Saints, has virtue to comfort the weak, to cure the sick, to give sight to the blind, to soften hearts, to encourage the weary, to fortify those who combat and to overthrow the tyranny of the demons."[73]

The Blessed Alain de La Roche, O. P., who had an extraordinary devotion to the Mother of God, was so highly favored by this Queen, all heart and love towards those who love her ardently, that she chose him as her spouse, and herself placed a ring upon his finger to mark the holy alliance that she had contracted with him; a grace worthy of the inconceivable charity of the Mother of fair love. She would imitate the infinite bounty of her divine Son, Who has willed to be the Spouse of miserable and sinful souls. This same

---

71. *In deprec, ad B. Virg., et in laude quae seq. Post Serm. In Signum magnum.*

72. *Lib. De Excell. Virg.*, cap. 6

73. *Lib. Contempl.*, part 4, cont. 1

grace was accorded by our heavenly Queen to St. Robert, Abbot of Citeaux, St. Edmund, Archbishop of Cantebury, Blessed Herman of Premontre and several others. This blessed spouse of the Queen of Angels, relating thirty-three praises of the Holy Names of Jesus and Mary, which he attests were revealed to him by the most holy Virgin, expresses the seventeenth in these terms: "These holy Names, Jesus and Mary, are two furnaces of ardent love and charity, which torture and trouble the demons, mortify the passions of sensuality, purify pious souls, and light up the fire of sincere devotion in the hearts of the faithful."[74]

The Holy Virgin thus speaks to St. Bridget: "My Son has so honored my Name that the Angels, hearing it, rejoice and thank God for the great things He has done in me and by me. The souls in Purgatory receive much consolation from it, as an invalid on his bed is comforted by the kind words of his friend. The Guardian Angels, hearing this Name, approach nearer to the souls whom they guard and redouble their care and vigilance towards them. All the demons are vanquished when they hear this Name; they tremble and are constrained to flee away from the soul who was already their prey; but if this soul amend not they will soon return. Finally, there is no sinner, howsoever cold his love for God, if he be not already lost, that the devil will not abandon, if he but call upon my Name, with resolution to quit his sins."[75]

Mary is not only the treasure, but the very heart of the Church and the holy priest Hesychius explains this in connection with these words of the forty-fourth Psalm, *"Eructavit cor meum*—my heart bellows forth,"* saying that the divine Mary is the heart of the Church—*"Cor Ecclesiae."* This is most true, for is not the heart the principle of life? And does not St. John Damascene say that Mary is the fountain whence life has come? *"Fons ex quo vita orta est."* [76]

---

74. In *Ps. Seu Ros.*, p.2, cap. 7
75. *Revel.*, lib. 1, cap. 9
76. Orat. 2, *de Assumpt.*

Holy Church herself states that by Mary life is given to us: *"Vitam datam per Virginem."* She is our life, our consolation, and our hope: *"Vita, dulcedo et spes nostra."* In her we find all hope of life: *"In me omnis spes vitae*—in me is all hope of life."[77]

But let us hear St. Germain of Constantinople: "As respiration is not only the sign of life but the cause of life, so, when we see Christians devout to the Name of Mary, it is a sign that they are living the true life, and a singular affection for this sacred Name gives life even to the dead, preserves the living, and fills them with joy and benediction."[78]

Mary, Mother of Jesus, is "the joy and glory of all priests," says St. Ephrem—*"Laetitia omnium sacerdotum,"*[79] "sun and light of religious," says St. Andrew of Crete—*"Lumen monachorum"*[80]; "the magnificence of the Christian people," says St. Germain the Patriarch—*"Magnificentia populi christiani,"*[81] and he adds that she is the spirit and life of the Christian—*"Spiritus et vita christianorum."*[82]

"In a word, whoever says 'Mary,' names the most precious treasure of the Holy Trinity," as says Origen: *"Thesaurus Trinitatis."* Whoever names Mary, names the most brilliant ornament of the house of God. Whoever names Mary, names the glory, love, and delights of heaven and earth. Finally, whoever names Mary, names the treasure, heart, mind, soul, life, love, and the heavenly delights and all the hope, after Jesus, of the last of all men, most unworthy and unfaithful of all the servants of this great Princess—the one who writes these lines and would wish to sign with the last drop of his blood all that he has written to the praise of this admirable Mary.

---

77. Ecclus. 24:25

78. Orat. De Seipar: "Just as the continuity of breathing is a sign of life, and indeed, its very cause: so also the Name of Mary when assiduously repeated in the mouths of God's servants, gives proof both that said servant lives and also that his life is preserved and effective, and always fills him with joy."

79. Orat. 1 *de Laud. B.V.*

80. *In depos. Zonae S. Mar.*

81. *Orat. De Dorm. Virg.*

82. In encomia zonae Vir.

He would wish to write and imprint these things upon the hearts of all who are or ever will be upon earth, yielding up a hundred million lives, if he had them, to excite the whole world to love and serve this amiable Mary, and to bless and praise incessantly Him Who has made her Name so amiable and so admirable.

Oh, who will give me to engrave upon all hearts these beautiful and holy words of Venerable Thomas a Kempis? "All hell trembles at the august Name of the Queen of Heaven. It is the terror of all the malignant spirits, who fear and flee from it as from a raging fire. They dare not appear in those places which are illumined by this beautiful Name, for it is a sun chasing away all infernal darkness. If you would rout all the diabolical troops, you have but to pronounce with devotion the terrible Name of Mary. It is like a frightful peal of thunder, terrifying them and precipitating them, in one moment, into the awful abyss. It frustrates their wicked machinations, brings to naught their cruel snares and dissipates all their deceits: *Tanquam ad tonitruum de caelo, factum, sic prosternuntur ad sanctae Mariae vocabulum.* The more you pronounce and lovingly invoke this amiable Name, the more promptly you will chase away and keep far from you those cruel enemies of your salvation."[83]

The glorious Name of Mary should be held in singular veneration by all the faithful. It should be, after God, the first and continual object of their love and devotion. Religious should ardently love this Name and cherish it tenderly, and should recommend seculars to do the same. It should sound without ceasing in the ears of the afflicted and be invoked amid the numerous perils wherewith this miserable life is fraught: *"Mariae Nomen omnibus fidelibus venerandum, devotis semper amandum, religiosis amplectendum, saecularibus com-mendandum, peccatoribus predicandum, tribulatis insonandum, in periculis omnibus invocandum."*[84]

---

83. Serm. 4 ad *Nov.* "like a frightful peal of thunder from heaven, the sounding of the holy Name of Mary precipitates them."

84. Lib. S, Oracul. *Cf. Vega. Theol. Mar.,* n. 1364.

SEVERAL OTHER PREROGATIVES OF THE HOLY NAME OF MARY, AND EIGHT MEANS OF HONORING IT.

While the Divine Majesty had, from all eternity, borne in His adorable Heart this holy Name, it was not manifested to men until the time should arrive for it to be given to our holy Infant. However, several centuries beforehand and even from the beginning of the world, this name was not unknown.

By the oracles of the Sibyls, the Holy Ghost foretold many things concerning the Savior of the world and His most holy Mother, and this, to dispose the Gentiles to believe in them. These oracles, and especially those of the Sibyl Erythraea, proclaimed the birth of a new light upon the earth, and that this new luminary should be born of a Virgin called Mary.

Besides this, in the Ecclesiastical Annals of Cardinal Baronius, there is related a remarkable circumstance attested by Latin and Greek historians. In the year 780, a certain man engaged in excavating some walls in Thrace, came upon a tombstone bearing the following inscription: "Christ will be born of the Virgin Mary. O Sun, thou shalt see me again under the Emperor Constantine and the Empress Irene." It is not known whom this tombstone covered. Some have believed it to be Mercurius Trismegistus or Plato; but, be this as it may, it is quite certain that the man who lay buried there had lived a long time before the birth of the Son of God or of His holy Mother.

John of Leyden, Carmelite, in his chronicle of the Counts of Holland,[85] states a remarkable fact, the truth of which is attested by a Doctor in Theology, named John de domo Villarii, an eyewitness of the affair. Writing to another Doctor in Flanders, he declares that in the year 1374, there was found in the valley of Josaphat a subterranean tomb, wherein lay the body of a remarkably large man, with

---

85. Lib. 31, cap. 25

beard and hair very long. The body was intact. In front of the tomb there was a tablet on which was inscribed in Hebrew the following: "I am Seth, third son of Adam. I believe in Jesus Christ, Son of God, and in the Virgin Mary, His Mother, who shall be born of my race."[86]

Another proof of how precious and honorable before God is the sacred Name of Mary is that there are enclosed within this name, according to several holy Doctors, the names of the five most illustrious women of the Old Testament, of which the first four are very excellent figures of this incomparable Mary, the fifth being her mother. The first letters of the names of these holy women compose the name of Mary: Mary, sister of Moses; Ann, mother of the Prophet Samuel; Rebecca, wife of the holy patriarch Isaac, and mother of Jacob; Judith; and Ann, wife of St. Joachim and mother of the blessed Mary.

Several celebrated Doctors remark that the Divine Majesty has confined within the five letters of the glorious name of Mary, the rarest of ornaments. The first letter *M* signifies that Mary is Mother of God, Mother of all Christians, Mother of the truly poor, of orphans, Mother of love and grace and mercy, and Mediatrix between God and man.

The second letter *A* marks her as Advocate of sinners, Asylum of the afflicted, Aid of those who invoke her, Anchor of our hope, Ark of holiness, and Aurora preceding the Sun of Justice.

The third letter *R* designates Mary as *(Reine or Regina)* Queen of men and Angels, of heaven and earth, Ray of the Divinity, as S. Bernard says: *"Radius Deitatis,"* the Repose of the most Holy Trinity, according to St. Bonaventure: *"Requies sanctissimae Trinitatis,"* Rose without thorns, Refuge of the miserable, Repairer of the Ages.

The fourth letter *I* gives us to understand that she is the infinite Image of divine Bounty, according to St. Thomas, the Illuminator of the blind; the Ideal of all virtue, the *(Imperatrice)* Empress of the universe.

---

86. *Cfr, Vega. Theol. Mar.,* n. 1364

The fifth letter *A* shows Mary as an Abyss of wonders, Admirable in all things, Amiable above all created objects, and the *(Amour)* Love of those who love her Son, Jesus.

After all the eminent perfections of the adorable Name of Mary, and all the favors we have received through it, what ought not we to do, to honor and thank this most holy Mary?

There are eight means that will serve this purpose:

First, we should celebrate devoutly the feast of this most august Name. The discalced Carmelites, friars and nuns, keep the feast on September 17, and the Mathurin Fathers on the same day. Besides this feast, these latter religious recite the office of the feast under semi-double rite every Saturday which is not occupied by an office having three nocturns. In the Congregation of the Seminaries of Jesus and Mary, we solemnize the feast on September 25, with proper office and hymns, and sequence in the Mass,[87] containing many beautiful eulogies of this sacred Name.

Second, recite every day, or at least sometimes, according to your devotion, the *"Magnificat"* and the following Psalms, the first letters of which compose the name, Mary: *"Ad Dominurn cum tribularer clamavi; Retribue servo tuo,"* as far as: *"Adhaesit pavemento anima mea;" "In convertendo;" "Ad te levavi animarn rneam."*[88]

Several authors attest that Pope Gregory XIII, in 1580, accorded one hundred days' indulgence each time to those who should practice this devotion in honor of the holy Name of Mary. And

---

87. This office will be found in the *Liturgical Works* of Blessed John Eudes. The feast of the Holy Name of Mary arose in Spain, in the diocese of Cuenca, about 1513. Later on it was extended throughout the country and was kept on September 22, fourteen days after the Nativity, because among the Jews it was the custom for girls to receive their names fourteen days after their birth. On November 26, 1683, Pope Innocent XI extended the feast to the universal Church in thanksgiving for the victory gained by John Sobieski over the Turks who menaced Venice. It is now celebrated on the Sunday in the Octave of the Nativity. *Cf* Benedict XIV, *De Festis B. Mariae.*

88. Ps. 119, 117 verse 17 (usually separated as a separate psalm in the office), 125, 24.

some very famous authors, among them John Molan, recount signal miracles wrought upon those who had practiced this devotion, for, after their decease, there were seen to fall from their mouth, eyes and ears, five beautiful roses, upon each of which was written a letter of the name, Mary, with the first verse of the Psalm beginning with the same letter, thus manifesting how agreeable to the only Son of Mary is the praise bestowed upon His most worthy Mother.[89] In place of the five Psalms, may be recited the *"Magnificat," "Alma Redemptoris," "Regina Caeli," "Inviolata," "Ave Regina Caelorum."*

Third, accustom yourself to repeat as your first words upon awaking, and your last words before sleep, the names of Jesus and Mary, so that God will give you grace to die with these holy Names on your lips and in your heart. Pope Pius V has granted an Indulgence of seven days to those who belong to the Confraternity of the Holy Rosary,[90] every time they pronounce the Names of Jesus and Mary.

Fourth, when you pronounce these adorable Names, or hear them pronounced, make a reverence, or an inclination of the head. This is what Holy Church prescribes to her children in reciting the Divine Office.

Fifth, in time of, temptation, invoke the Holy Names of Jesus and Mary, saying: "O Jesus, be to me a Jesus! O Mary, be to me a Mary!" or "Jesus, Mary!" We learn from ecclesiastical history that Chosroes, King of Persia, who was Christian at heart, gained a signal victory over the Jews through the merits of the most sacred Virgin, whose blessed Name he had adopted as his war cry. Let this powerful Name be our war cry against the infernal demons who molest us, and we shall assuredly vanquish them and put them to flight.

---

89. *In Nat. ss. Belgii ad diem 30 Nov.*

90. There is an indulgence of 25 days, each time, for pronouncing devoutly the Holy Name of Jesus, independently of belonging to any confraternity, and the same regarding the Holy Name of Mary. Moreover, there is a plenary indulgence at the hour of death for all those who have had the pious habit of invoking the Holy Names of Jesus.

Sixth, bear upon your hearts the most amiable Names of Jesus and Mary, written or printed upon paper, or a medal, or some other emblem, as testimony of your desire that these sacred Names be engraved deep in your heart, and as protestation of love, submission, fidelity and praise to Jesus and Mary.

Seventh, if you have the care of very young infants not yet able to speak, say and repeat so often to them the words, "Jesus, Mary," that these two holy words may become engraved in their hearts, and may be the first words they will utter. This will draw down a blessing upon them.

Eighth, have devotion to the words I am about to quote, wherein, after having blessed the most loving heart and the sweet Names of Jesus and Mary, we ask their blessing, a favor certain to be accorded us, since the Eternal Father has promised to His Son, that He will bless those who bless Him (the Son)— *"Benedicam benedicentibus tibi."*[91]

Pope Clement IV, at the instance of St. Louis, King of France, granted an indulgence of three years in the year 1299 each time that the faithful should devoutly invoke the Holy Names of Jesus and Mary, as is reported in the Ecclesiastical Annals, and according to the testimony of Wernerus Rolerinck, of Chartres.[92] Another thing which I counsel you to do morning and evening, at the commencement of your most important actions and at the end of your prayers, is to bless the Sacred Heart and the holy Names of Jesus and Mary and to ask them to bless you in all your works by the following: *"Benedicturn sit Cor amantissimum, et dulcissimum Nomen Domini nostri Jesu Christi, et gloriosissimae Virgin is Mariae Matris ejus, in aeternum et ultra. Nos cum prole pia benedicat Virgo Maria. Amen."* A shorter form is as follows: *"Benedictum sit Cor amantissimum et dulcissimum Nomen Jesu et Mariae, in aeternum et ultra. Nos curn prole,"* etc.[93]

---

91. Gen. 12:3

92. Pope Pius X has accorded an indulgence of three hundred days, once a day, and a Plenary indulgence once a month, to those who daily recite this prayer. (Nov. 30, 1905)

93. "Blessed is the loving heart and the most sweet Name of Our Lord Jesus Christ and the Glorious Virgin Maria, His Mother in all eternity and even beyond. We with her holy child bless the Virgin Maria. Amen."

I find in the life of Blessed Henry Suso, O. P., written by himself, that, one day he saw the evil spirit with a frightful countenance and flaming eyes holding in his hands a bow, from which he was seen to hurl fiery arrows at a religious who fell to the earth as one dead.

Satan attempting to vanquish the Saint after the same fashion, the Blessed Henry raised his eyes towards heaven and said the words: *"Nos cum prole pia benedicat Maria,"* and the demon at once fled away.

Some persons have written or printed the words: *"Ben edictum sit Cor amantissimum,"* etc., which they suspend over the heart, after protesting to God, and renewing from time to time their intention of offering every pulsation of their hearts as so many voices to bless incessantly the most amiable Heart and venerable Names of Jesus and Mary, and beg, in return, their holy blessing, of which we have an extreme and perpetual need.

I exhort you, my dear reader, not to neglect these industries of piety suggested by the loving Hearts of Jesus and Mary, to those hearts which love them ardently, for they are very agreeable to the Son and the Mother, and most advantageous to those who practice them through love. There is nothing so small but that it becomes great when done for love and through love of the most adorable Jesus, Son of Mary, and the most amiable Mary, Mother of Jesus, who recompense even the good will that we bring to their service.

For the rest, I shall add in concluding this chapter what is related in the life of St. Peter Thomas, Carmelite, Patriarch of Constantinople, and Martyr. This holy man had a wonderful devotion to the Mother of God, and, after his death, the Holy Name of Mary was found written upon his heart. This fact was attested by several persons who had seen the prodigy.

The Blessed Alain de La Roche relates that the name of Mary was found written in gold in the heart of the Blessed John, of the Order of Citeaux, whose body was opened after death by St. Bernard's command.[94]

---

94. Cap. 57

O my all good and all love worthy Mother, who will give me that thy holy Name may be written in letters of gold upon my heart? and that it may be engraven in the hearts of all men who are, or are yet to be? May all creatures, in heaven, in earth and in hell, bend the knee to adore and glorify forever the most august name of Jesus, and to revere and praise eternally the most worthy name of Mary.

Oh, how cordially I offer and give myself to the Son and to the Mother, to do and suffer for this end whatsoever it may please them, and for as long a time as shall please them, without reserve or limitation.

St. Patrick and the Golden Legend

Modern scholars are quick to condemn the Golden Legend as implausible and superstitious, and to treat as fools those who love to hear or tell of feigned miracles. However, despite this the Golden Legend has remained a favorite of the faithful from the thirteenth century, when it was written, down to the present time. It was one of the two books that Saint Ignatius Loyola read on his sick bed and which subsequently resulted in his conversion and entering the life of religion. What the modern scholar fails to understand is that it is not the facts that are important, but the content of truth which the facts convey. One may debate about the truth of the miracles that are reported, but no one can fault the theology they convey. The text may be dismissed as fable, but the content cannot be condemned as heretical.

In presenting the legend of Saint Patrick, one has a clear demonstration of the use of the Jesus Prayer in the western Church under the patronage of one of her greatest saints. What is of especial interest is that the form of the prayer is precisely that used by the Hesychast monks of Mount Athos down to the present day—"Jesus Christ, son of the living god, have mercy on us." Amen.

The translation is that of Granger Ryan and Helmut Rippergar, published by Longmans, Green and Co., and is reprinted with their permission.

Saint Patrick

March 17

Saint Patrick lived about the year of the Lord 280. One day, while he was preaching the Passion of Christ to the king of Scotland, he pierced the king's foot by accident, with the point of the staff on which he was leaning. And the king said nothing, and suffered without protest, thinking that the holy bishop had knowingly inflicted the wound, and that in order to be admitted to the faith of Christ, he had first to suffer as Christ had suffered. And when the saint became aware of the king's pious error, he was filled with wonderment. He healed him by prayers, and in addition obtained that no venomous beast could do hurt to anyone throughout the kingdom. It is said moreover, that in Scotland, thanks to Saint Patrick, the bark of trees is efficacious against poisons.

A certain man had stolen a sheep from his neighbor and had eaten it. Saint Patrick several times called upon the thief to confess his theft and to do penance; but when no one came forward, he commanded in the name of Christ, in the midst of the whole congregation, that the stolen sheep should disclose his whereabouts by bleating in the thief's stomach. And at once the sheep began to bleat in the belly of the thief, who confessed his sin and did penance. And thenceforth the other inhabitants refrained from stealing.

Whenever Saint Patrick came upon a cross, he used to bend the knee before it. But one day he passed by a large and beautiful cross without seeing it. His companions asked him why he had not seen and venerated it. But at that moment a voice came out of the earth and said to him: "Thou hast not seen this cross because the man who is buried underneath is a pagan, and is unworthy of the sacred sign!" And Saint Patrick had the cross taken away and placed elsewhere.

He then went to preach in Ireland, but his preaching bore little fruit. Therefore Saint Patrick implored God to reveal Himself to the Irish by some sign which would strike terror into their hearts, and lead them to repentance. Then, at God's command, he traced a wide circle with his staff, and a very deep pit opened within it. And it was revealed to Patrick that the pit was the opening to a purgatory, and that those who chose to go down into it could expiate their sins therein, and would be spared their purgatory after death; but also that most of those who entered the pit would never come out again, and that those who would come out would have remained in the purgatory from one morning to the next. And a few persons went down into the pit, and, in very deed, never came out again.

But long after Saint Patrick's death a nobleman named Nicholas who had been guilty of many sins, bethought himself to do penance by going down into the saint's purgatory. For a fortnight he made ready by fasting and prayer, as was the custom. Then he entered the pit and found himself in a chapel where monks vested in albs were singing the divine office; and these told him to put on the armor of constancy, that he might be able to withstand the deceits of the Devil, with which he was about to be assailed. He asked them what he must do to resist the demons. The monks replied: "When thou art aware that they wish to torture thee, call out at once, 'Jesus, Son of the living God, have mercy on me, a miserable sinner.'" Then the monks disappeared, and Nicholas was surrounded by demons, who at first sought to win his obedience by flattering promises. But when he spurned them, he heard a sound like to a roaring of wild beasts, and it was as if the whole world was tumbling into chaos. Then, trembling with fright, he cried out: "Lord Jesus Christ, Son of the living God, have mercy on me, a miserable sinner." And at once the tumult subsided. Next Nicholas was led into another place, where a horde of demons surrounded him and said: "Thinkest thou that thou canst escape us? Escape thou shalt not: for thy torture is only beginning!" Thereupon a huge fire sprang up before him and the demons said: "Yield, or we shall throw thee into the fire!" And indeed, they seized him and cast him into the flames. But the instant he felt the heat of the fire, he called upon Jesus Christ and at once the flames died out. Then he was taken to another place, where he saw some men being burned alive, others being crushed down upon hot iron spikes, others lying prone on the ground and gnawing the earth, crying out for pity, while the demons rained blows upon them. Serpents were devouring the members of some; monsters were tearing out the vitals of others with red-hot iron hooks. And when Nicholas still refused to obey the demons, they made ready to work these divers torments upon him. But again he invoked the name of Jesus, and was delivered from these pains. Next he was carried to another place where he saw men being thrust into huge frying-pans, and where there was a gigantic wheel, with men bound to each of its spokes; and the wheel spun round so swiftly that it seemed to form a circle of fire. He also saw a large house in which were trenches filled with molten metal; and some men had one foot in the metal, some two feet, some their bodies up to the knees, some up to the waist, some up to the chest, some to the neck, and some to the eyes; but Nicholas passed through all these places by calling upon Christ. Farther on he saw an enormous hole out of which poured a vile, stinking smoke; and men were struggling to escape from the hole, but the demons pushed them back. And the demons said to Nicholas: "The place which thou seest before thee is the circle of Hell wherein dwells our master Beelzebub. And if thou dost not now obey us, we shall cast thee into this hole, and never again shalt thou emerge from it." But Nicholas still refused and the demons pitched him headlong into the hole. The pain which then seized him was so fierce that he well-nigh forgot to invoke the name of the Lord; but after a time he cried out in his heart (for he was no longer able to speak): "Jesus Christ, son of the living god, have mercy on me." And instantly he emerged from the hole, and the horde of demons fell back before him.

Next he was led to a place where he had to cross a very narrow bridge, which was as slippery as ice, and beneath which flowed a great river of fire and sulphur. He almost abandoned hope of crossing the bridge, when he remembered the prayer which had already saved him so many times; and setting his foot in all confidence upon the bridge, he cried out once more: "Jesus Christ, son of the living God, have mercy on me:" Then there arose a shouting so fearful that Nicholas barely kept himself from falling; but again he called upon the name of Jesus, repeating his prayer at each step, and thus made his way across to the other side. And when he had traversed the bridge, he came into a verdant meadow, in which bloomed a thousand varieties of sweet-smelling flowers. And two fair youths came to meet him, and led him to the gate of a city which shone with gold and precious stones; and from the gate came forth a perfume so delightful that Nicholas, breathing it, forgot all the terrors and sufferings through which he had passed. And the two young men told him that this city was Paradise. But when Nicholas started forward to enter it, his two companions said that he must first return to his own folk on earth, going back over the same way by which he had come; but that this time the demons would not molest him, but would flee in consternation at the sight of him. And the youths added that within thirty days Nicholas would go to his rest in the Lord, and become forever a citizen of the heavenly city. Then Nicholas made his way back to earth, to the very spot whence he had departed. He gave account of all that had befallen him; and thirty days later, he fell asleep happily in the Lord.

Richard Rolle, Hermit

Little is known about Richard Rolle's life apart from the information to be found in the office prepared to be used in the event of his canonization, the process for which was halted because of the English Reformation. Despite this, to quote Hope Emily Allen, "Probably at the time of the Reformation 'Richard Hermit's' influence was as great as, or greater than that of any other mediaeval writer of devotional works. The 'cult of the Holy Name of Jesus,' in which his, though far from being the only, had probably been the decisive influence, had permeated general popular devotion. A 'Feast of the Holy Name of Jesus' with an office in nine lessons had been established in the calendars of Sarum, York, etc., with such a pressure of popular devotion behind it that it was able to survive the great change, and to pass over into the calendar of the Church of England where it still remains."[1] The same author says elsewhere that this devotion was so strong that the Reformers felt freer to move against the Mass than to attack this form of prayer. And indeed, one can even today see on many of the Altars which were converted into Anglican tables the carved symbolic forms of the Name.

We learn from his Office that he was born in the village of Thornton, in the Diocese of York. His youth was apparently ordinary, and he was sent up to Oxford for his studies which were paid for by Master Thomas de Neville, archdeacon of Durham. There is some evidence that he spent as much as seven years at the Sorbonne, but this was probably later in life. In any event, at the age of nineteen, "he fled to solitude" leaving his sister to think he had gone mad. He

---

1. *Writings attributed to Richard Rolle* Modern Language Association of America, 1927.

adopted the garb of a hermit and was supported on the estate of John de Dalton, a friend of his father's. He later moved his habitation on several occasions and according to the English Martyrology, "led a solitary life in a wood near to the Monastery of Hampole." During his life he gave public sermons and wrote several works. His literary output was first gathered together by William Stopes, his disciple, and copies of manuscripts attributed to Rolle are to found throughout Europe, especially in the houses of the Carthusians.

The selections given here are taken from G.E. Hogson's *Some Minor Works of Richard Rolle,* published by Watkins in 1923. (The early English and Latin has been retained.)

IN PRAISE OF THE NAME OF JESUS

Oleum effusian nomen tuum. That is, in English, "Oil outpoured is Thy Name." The Name of Jesus comes into the world, and as such it smells as oil out-poured. Oil! that is taken for the everlasting salvation which is hoped for. Truly "Jesus" is as much as to mean, savior or healthful. Therefore, what means "Oil outpoured is Thy Name,"[2] save "Jesus is Thy Name?" This Name is oil out-poured, because Jesus, the Word of God, has taken man's nature. Jesus! Thou fulfillest indeed what Thou art called in name; soothly one says— Thou, Whom we call Savior. Therefore, Jesus is Thy Name.

Ah! that wonderful Name! Ah! that delectable Name! This is the Name that is above all names, Name altogether highest, without which no man hopes for health. This Name is sweet and joyful, giving truthful comfort into man's heart. Soothly, the Name of Jesus is, in my mind, a joyous song, in mine ear a heavenly sound, in my mouth honey-full sweetness. Therefore, it is no wonder if I love that Name, which gives me comfort in every anguish. I cannot pray, I cannot meditate but in sounding the Name of Jesus. I savor no joy

---

2.　Cant. 1:33.

that is Un-mingled with Jesus. Wheresoever I be, wheresoever I sit, whatsoever I do, the remembrance of the Name of Jesus departs not from my mind. I have set it as a token upon my heart, as a token upon mine arm; for "love is as strong as death." As death slays all, so love overcomes all. Everlasting love has overcome me, not to slay but to quicken me. But it has wounded me in order to heal me; it has struck through my heart that it may be the more healthfully healed; and now, overcame, I yield. Unless I live for joy, very soon I must die, for I, in this feeble flesh, cannot suffice to bear so flowing a sweetness, and ever it falls into inebriation; the flesh cannot fail in its virtue awhile the soul in such joy is ravished to joy. But wherefore cometh such joy to me but for Jesus? The Name of Jesus has taught me to sing, and has lightened my mind with the heat of uncreated light.

Therefore I sigh and cry; who shall shew to the beloved Jesus that I languish for love? My flesh has failed, and my heart has melted into love, in yearning after Jesus. The whole heart fixed in yearning after Jesus is turned into Fire of Love, and with the sweetness of the Godhead is it fully filled. Therefore, O good Jesus, have mercy on this wretch, shew Thyself to this languishing one, be leech to this wounded one. If Thou comest, I am whole: I do not feel sick, only languishing for Thy love. Seeking Jesus Whom it loves, with Whose love it is seized, Whom alone it covets, let my soul seize on Thee.

Soothly the mind touched with sovereign sweetness, sighs to wax hot in the Maker's love, while it strives to hold busily within it the sweetest Name of Jesus.

Truly, there rises thence a great love, and whatever thing it truly touches it ravishes it utterly to it. It inflames affection, and binds thought; and draws all men to its service.

Soothly Jesus, desirable is Thy Name, lovable and comfortable. None other so sweet song may be heard, none other so sweet joy be conceived; none other so delectable solace may be had in mind.

Therefore, whosoever thou beest that makest thyself ready for the love of God, if thou wilt neither be deceived nor deceive, if thou wilt be wise and not unwise, if thou wilt stand and not fall, remember busily to hold the Name of Jesus in thy mind. Thine enemy shall fall, and thou shalt stand: thine enemy shall be made weak and thou shalt be made strong; and if thou wilt loyally do this, thou shalt be, far from fear, a glorious and lovable overcomer. Therefore, seek the Name of Jesus, hold it, and forget it not. Soothly no other thing so quenches hell flames, destroys all ill thoughts, puts out venemous affections, does away with curious and vain affections from us.

Also this Name Jesus, loyally held in mind, drags up vices by the roots, plants virtues, sows charity, pours in the savor of heavenly things, drains away discord, reforms peace, gives everlasting rest, utterly does away the grievousness of fleshly desires, turns all earthly things worthless, and fills His lovers with ghostly joy. So that it may well be said: *Et gloriabuntur omnes qui diligunt nomen tuum, quoniam tu benedices justo;* that is "All that love Thy Name shall rejoice; for the righteous Thou shalt bless."

For the righteous has deserved to be blessed if he have truly loved the Name of Jesus. Therefore, what can be wanting to him who incessantly desires to love the Name of Jesus? Soothly, he loves and he yearns to love; for we have known that the love of God so is that in so far as we love more, the more we long to love; wherefore it is said : *Qui me edunt adhuc esuriunt, et qui me bibunt adhuc siciunt;* that is "they that eat Me hunger still, and they that drink Me still thirst." Therefore the Name of Jesus and the love of it, is in itself delectable and to be coveted.

Therefore joy shall not be wanting to him who busily desires to love Him "Whom the Angels yearn to behold." The Angels ever see, and ever yearn to see, and they are so filled that their filling does not quench desire: and they so desire, that their desire does not do away with their filling.

This is full Joy, this is unending Joy, this is glorious Joy, wherewith we being filled, use lastingly without pain, and if we use it we shall be filled for ever without any loss. Therefore, Jesus, all shall rejoice that love Thy Name. Soothly now shall they rejoice for the inpouring of grace, and in time to come for the sight of Joy; and, therefore, shall they rejoice because they love Thy Name. Soothly were they not loved, they could not rejoice. And they that love more shall rejoice more; for why, Joy comes of love. Therefore, he who loves not shall be evermore without Joy. Therefore, many wretches of the world expecting to rejoice with Christ, shall sorrow endlessly because they loved not the Name of Jesus. "Whatsoever ye do, if ye give all that ye have unto the needy, except ye love the Name of Jesus, ye travail in vain." Alonely they may rejoice in Jesus, who love Him in this life: and they who fill themselves with vices and venomous delights, no fear but they are put out of Joy. So, let all men know that the Name of Jesus is healthful, fruitful and glorious. Therefore, who shall have health who loves it not? Who shall bear fruit before Christ who has not the flower? and he shall not see Joy, who, rejoicing, loved not the Name of Jesus. The wicked shall be done away so that he sees not the joy of God. Truly, the righteous seek joy and life and they find it in Jesus, whom they loved.

I went about by covetousness of riches, and I found not Jesus. I ran by the wantonness of the flesh, and I found not Jesus. I sat in companies of worldly mirth and I found not Jesus. In all of them I sought Jesus, but I found Him not; for He let me know by His grace that He is not found in the land of softly living. Therefore, I turned by another way, and I ran about by poverty and I found Jesus, poorly born into the world. laid in a crib, lapped in cloths. I went by suffering of sharpness; and I found Jesus weary in the way, tormented with hunger, thirst and cold, filled with reproofs and blame. I sat by my lone, fleeing the vanity of the world, and I found Jesus, in the desert, fasting, in the Mount, praying alone. I ran by pain and penance, and I found Jesus, bound, scourged, given gall to drink, nailed to the cross (hanging on the Cross) and dying on the Cross. Therefore, Jesus is not found in riches but in poverty, not in delights but in penance, not in wanton joying but in bitter weeping, not among many but in loneliness.

Soothly, an evil man finds not Jesus, for where He is he seeks Him not. He forces himself to seek Jesus in the joy of the world, where never shall He be found. Soothly therefore, the Name of Jesus is helpful, and needs must be loved by all who covet salvation. He well covets his own salvation who busily keeps within him the Name of Jesus. Soothly, I have no wonder that he, who puts not the Name of Jesus lastingly in his mind, falls when tempted. Certainly, only he may choose to live who has chosen the Name of Jesus for his special own; for no wicked spirit can trouble when Jesus is much in mind and named by the mouth.

Therefore, the Name of Jesus is to be held busily in mind.

When I had taken my singular purpose, and left the secular habit, and I began to serve God more than man, it fell on a night, as I lay in my rest, in the beginning of my conversion, there appeared to me a full fair young woman, the which I had seen before, and she loved me not a little in good love. And when I had beholden her, and I wondered why she came so, in the night, in the wilderness, suddenly, without more speech she laid herself beside me. And when I felt her there, I feared lest she should draw me to evil, and said, I would rise up and bless us in the Name of The Holy Trinity. And she constrained me so stalwartly that I had no mouth to speak, nor no hand to stir; and when I saw that, I perceived well that there was no woman, but the devil in the shape of a woman. Therefore, I turned me to God, and with my mind I said; "My Jesus, how precious is Thy Blood," making the Cross with my finger upon my breast; and at once she waxed weak, and suddenly, all was away; and I thanked God, who delivered me. And soothly, from that time forth, I forced myself to love Jesus; and ever the more I increased in the love of Jesus, the sweeter I found it; and from that day it never went from my mind.

Therefore, blessed be the Name of Jesus in the world of worlds. Amen.

Richard Rolle

ANOTHER PASSAGE ON THE NAME OF JESUS

If thou wilt be well with God, and have grace to rule thy life right and come to the joy of love; fasten this Name of Jesus so fast in thine heart that it can never come out of thy thought. And when thou speakest to Him, saying, through habit, Jesus! it shall be in thine ear joy, in thy mouth honey, in thy heart melody; for all shall think joy to hear that Name named, sweetness to speak it, mirth and song to think it. If thou thinkest on Jesus continually and holdest Him stably, it purges thy sin, and kindles thy heart; it clarifies thy soul, removes anger, and does away with slowness. It wounds in love, it fills full with charity; it chases the devil and quenches fear, it opens heaven and makes a contemplative man. Have Jesus in memory, for that puts all vices and phantoms far from the lover. If thou wilt not deceive nor be deceived: if thou wilt be wise and not unwise, think on this Name, Jesus, continually. It destroys all vices and vanities. It sows charity and virtues in the soul, and pours in the savor of heaven, and the fullness of God's grace into earth. Whosoever loves this Name, Jesus, without forgetting, dies in wonderful melody, and is is taken by angels and brought before Him Whom he loved. This Name Jesus is above all names, to which all knees kneel, of heaven and earth and hell.

Eat and drink, sleep and wake, speak and hold silence, pray and think, work, and all that thou dost do it in the Name of Jesus, bids St. Paul.

God bless you, and keep you and give you good perseverance, through the virtue of this joyful Name, Jesus, Amen.

AN EPISTLE ON SALVATION
BY LOVE OF THE
NAME OF JESUS

Wit thou well, dear friend, that though thou hadst never done sin with thy body, deadly nor venial, but only that which is called Original, because it was the *first* sin, which is the losing of thy righteousness in which thou wast made, thou shouldst never have been safe if our Lord Jesus Christ by His passion had not delivered thee and restored thee again.

And thou shalt wit that thou, be thou never so great a wretch, though thou hast done never so much sin; forsake thyself and all thy works good and ill, cry mercy, and only ask salvation, by the virtue of His precious Passion, meekly and sorrowfully. and without doubt thou shalt have it; and from this original, and from all other sin, thou shalt be safe. Yea, and thou shalt be as safe as an anchorite enclosed: and not only thou but all Christian men and women who believe in His Passion, and meek themselves, knowing their wretchedness, asking mercy and forgiveness and the fruit of His precious Passion, only yielding themselves to the Sacraments of Holy Church; though it be that they have been cumbered in and with sin all their lifetime and never had any feeling of ghostly savor, or sweetness, or ghostly knowledge of God, they shall, in this faith and in their goodwill be saved by the virtue of the precious Passion of our Lord Jesus Christ, and come to heaven's bliss.

See here the endless mercy of our Lord, how low He falls to thee and to me, and to all sinful caitiffs. Ask mercy and have it; thus said the prophet in the person of our Lord. "*Omnis enym quicunque inuoeauerit nomen domini saluus erit* —Everyman, whatever he be, that calls on God's name"—that is to say asks salvation by Jesus and by His passion, "he shall be safe."

But this courtesy of our Lord, some men take and are thereby saved: and some, in trust of His mercy and His courtesy, live still in their sins, and ween that they can have it when they list; and then they may nor, for they are taken or ever they know, and so they damn themselves.

But now thou sayest thou wonderest greatly if this be true, "on account of what I find written in some men's sayings. Some say, as I understand, that he who cannot love this blessed Name, Jesus, nor find nor feel in it ghostly joy and delectability with wonderful sweetness, here in this life, he shall be alien from the sovereign joy, and ghostly sweetness in the bliss of heaven, and never shall he come thereunto. Soothly, these words when I hear them or read them, astonish me and make me greatly afraid; for I hope, as thou sayest, that many by the mercy of God shall be safe by keeping of His commandments, and by very repentance of their aforetime evil life, though they never felt ghostly sweetness nor inward savor in the Name of Jesus nor in the love of Jesus. And, therefore, I marvel the more that these say contrary hereto as it seems."

As for this, I may say as I think, that their saying, if it be well understood is true, nor is it contrary to what I have said. For this Name, Jesus, is nought else but to say in English Healer, or Health. Now, every man who lives in this wretched life is ghostly sick, for there is no man who lives wirhout sin, which is ghostly sickness; as St. John says of himself and other perfect men thus: "*Si dixerimus quia peccatum non habemus ipsi nos seducimus,* etc.—If we say that we have no sin, we beguile oursclves, and soothfastness is not in us;" and therefore, he may never feel nor come to the Joys of heaven until he first be made whole of his ghostly sickness. But this ghostly health may no man, with the use of reason, have, unless he desire it, and love it, and have delight therein in as much as he hopes to get it. Now, the Name of Jesus is nought else but this ghostly health. Wherefore it is truth that they say that there may be no man safe unless he love and like in the Name of Jesus, for there may be no man whole but if he love and desire ghostly health. For just as, if a man were bodily sick, there were no earthly thing so dear nor so needful to him nor so much to be desired by him as bodily health—

for though thou wouldest give him all the riches and honors of this world and nor make him whole though thou couldest, thou shouldst please him nor—just so is it to a man who is ghostly sick, and feels the pain of ghostly sickness: nothing is so dear, so needful, so much to be desired by him as his ghostly health; and that is Jesus, without Whom all the joys of heaven cannot pleasure him. And this is the reason, as I hope, that our Lord when He took human nature for our salvation, He would not be called by any name betokening His endless being, or His, might, or His wisdom, or His righteousness, but only by that which was the cause of His coming and that was the salvation of man's soul, which salvation was most dear and most needful to man, and this Name, Jesus, betokens this salvation. Then by this it seems that there may no man be safe except he love Jesus, for there may no man be saved unless he love salvation, which love he may have who lives and dies in the lowest degree of charity. On another wise also, I may say that he who cannot love this blessed Name Jesus with ghostly mirth, nor enjoy it with heavenly melody here, in the bliss of heaven he shall never have nor feel that fulness of sovereign joy, which he, who in this life could by abundance of charity enjoy in Jesus, shall have and feel; and so may their saying be understood. Nevertheless, he shall be safe and have full praise in God's right if, in this life, he be in the lowest degree of charity by keeping God's commandments.

For Christ says in the Gospel: *In dorno patris mei mansiones multe sunt* " In My Father's house are many separate dwellings." Some are for perfect souls, who, in this life were filled full of the Holy Ghost's grace, and sang praises to God, contemplating Him with wonderful sweetness and heavenly savor. These souls, because they had most charity, shall have highest reward in the bliss of heaven, for these are called God's darlings. Other souls who, in this life, are imperfect and are not disposed to the contemplation of God, nor had that fulness of charity as, in the beginning of Holy Church, apostles and martyrs had; these shall have the lower reward in the bliss of heaven; for these are called God's friends. Thus our Lord has chosen souls in Holy Writ, saying thus: *Comedite amici; et inebri-amini carissirni:* "My friends eat ye, and my darlings be ye drunken," As if our Lord said on this wise: "Ye that are My friends because ye kept My commandments, and set My love before love of the world, and loved Me more than any other earthly thing, ye shall be fed with ghostly food of the Bread of Life. But ye, who are My darlings, and not only kept my commandments, but also of your own free will fulfilled my counsels, and beyond that loved Me only, entirely with all the powers of your soul, and burned in My love with ghostly delight as did, first of all, the Apostles and Martyrs and all others who should come, by the gift of Grace, to perfection, ye shall be made drunken with the freest wine in My cellar, that is the sovereign joy of love in the bliss of heaven."

To the which bliss may He bring us, Who bought us with His precious Passion, Jesus Christ, God's Son of Heaven. Amen.

St. Bonaventure

Cardinal, Seraphic Doctor and Saint "It would require both the illumination and the brilliance of the Seraphs to properly speak of this incomparable man" (Bollandist's Life). He was called by Pope Leo XIII the "Prince of Mystics." He was on intimate terms with St. Thomas Aquinas and an advisor to the holy king St. Louis.

Little is actually known about his life, and no contemporary biography exists. He was born in 1221 at Bagnorea near Vitorbo in Tuscany, and in either 1238 or 1243 was clothed in the order of Friars Minor. In 1257 he received his Doctorate in Theology at the University of Paris and nine months later he was chosen as minister general of his order. He was raised to the Cardinalate in 1273 and took a prominent part in the Council of Lyons, which council led to the founding of the Holy Name Society. He died in 1274 at the age of fifty-three.

His writings are little known today, but in mediaeval times he was one of the most widely read and copied of theologians. The passage which follows is taken from his *De quinoue festivitatibus*—On the Five Feasts of the Child Jesus. It was translated by Jose de Vinck and published in the Works of Bonaventure; it is reprinted with the kind permission of St. Anthony Guild Press, Patterson, New Jersey.

THE SECOND FEAST

How the Son is spiritually born in the Devout Soul

Now, let us behold and consider how this blessed Son of God, spiritually conceived, is spiritually born in the soul. He is born when, after proper thought, sufficient pondering, and holy and divine patronage, the resolve is brought into effect: that is, when the soul sets out to do in fact what it had long entertained in mind, but had been reluctant to undertake for fear of eventual failure. The angels rejoice in this most blessed birth; they glorify God and promise peace: when the concept, long in mind, is led to the perfection of good work, peace is restored to the inner man. In that kingdom— the human soul—God's peace is not well preserved if the flesh wars against the spirit, and the spirit against the flesh; if the spirit loves solitude, and the flesh seeks the world; if the spirit pursues the repose of contemplation in God and the flesh craves the honor of high temporal positions. On the contrary, if the flesh obeys the spirit, and if good work, long obstructed by the flesh, now finally comes to fruit, internal peace and joy are restored. Happy the birth that brings such gladness to angels and to men! "How sweet and delightful it would be to act in harmony with nature! Alas, our own folly rules it out. Allay that folly, and nature is reconciled with men."(quoted from St. Bernard) Experience confirms the truth of the Gospel text: "*Take my yoke upon you etc. . . .*" And what follows: "*You will find rest for your souls. For My yoke is easy and My burden light.*"

At this point, O devout soul, if you rejoice in happy birth, remember that first you must be Mary. For the name Mary means "bitter sea," "giver of light", and "masterful."

Be therefore a BITTER SEA through your tearful repentance, regretting bitterly your past sins, bemoaning profoundly the good you failed to do deploring without cease days you wasted and lost. Be also a GIVER OF LIGHT, through honest living, virtuous deeds and zealous efforts to teach others the ways of good. Finally, be MASTER of your senses, of your fleshly desires, and of all your works, conforming your acts to right reason, ever seeking and desiring salvation for yourself, edification for your neighbor, and praise and glory for God.

This indeed, is being like Mary, the fruitful one, who pines and weeps over the sins of the world, who shines and sparkles with virtue, who dominates the passions of the flesh. From such a Mary, Jesus Christ does not disdain to be spiritually born in joy without pain or labor. After such a happy birth, this Mary knows and tastes how good the Lord Jesus is. For He is truly sweet as we feed Him with holy meditation, bathe Him in a flow of warm and devout tears, swaddle Him in the cloth of chaste desire, carry Him in the arms of holy love, kiss Him over and over again with heartfelt devotion, and keep Him warm in the folds of our inner mind. That is how the Child is spiritually born.

THIRD FEAST

How the infant Jesus is spiritually Named
by the devout soul.

Thirdly, we should consider what name to give to this blessed Infant now spiritually born. There is no better name for Him than Jesus, for it is written: *His name was called Jesus.* This is the sacred Name foretold by the prophets, announced by the angel, proclaimed by the Apostles, desired by all the saints.

O Name so full of power, grace and joy; full of delight and glory! Full of POWER, for it overcomes the enemy, restores strength, and refreshes the mind. Full of GRACE, for in it faith is founded, hope confirmed, love increased, and justice brought to perfection. Full of JOY, for as St. Bernard writes, "it is exultation to the heart, music to the ears, honey to the tongue," and splendor to the mind. Full of DELIGHT, for according to the same Bernard, "it nourishes when remembered, soothes when uttered, anoints when called upon." Full of GLORY, for it gives sight to the blind, agility to the lame, hearing to the deaf, speech to the dumb, and life to the dead. Blessed is the Name that brings forth such powerful effects!

O soul, whether you write, read, teach, or do anything else, may nothing have any taste for you, may nothing please you besides Jesus. Give, therefore, to the Infant spiritually born in you the Name Jesus, that is, Savior in the wretched state of this present life. May He save you from the world's vanity that threatens you, from the devil's deceit that assails you, from the fleshy weakness that tortures you.

O soul, amidst the scourges of this life, call out: "Jesus, Savior of the world, save us, having redeemed us through Your Cross and Blood. Come to our assistance, O Lord our God Most sweet Jesus Savior, we beg of You, save us! Strengthen the weak, console the despondent, assist the frail, sustain those who waver!"

After this blessed Name had been given, how often did a feeling of sweetness come upon the Virgin Mary, fruitful Mother by nature, true Mother in spirit, when she saw, in this very Name, the demons cast out, miracles multiplied, the blind made to see, the sick returned to health, and the dead made to rise from the tomb.

You, therefore, O soul, you a spiritual mother should certainly and with good reason rejoice and exalt as you see, within yourself and others, Jesus casting out demons through the remission of sins, enlightening the blind by infusing true knowledge into them, raising the dead through the gift of grace, curing the sick, healing the lame, straightening the palsied and the twisted through spiritual consolations, so that those who had been weak and diseased in their sin might become strong and manful through grace. Oh, how fruitful and blessed is the Name endowed with so great a power and efficiency!

St. Thomas Aquinas

Saint, philosopher, theologian, and Angelic Doctor, Thomas Aquinas is still considered the "official theologian" of the Roman Church. While he wrote no specific piece concerned with the Name of Jesus, references to this devotion are to be found scattered throughout his writings. The selections made are such as confirm many of the statements made in the Introduction.

The first selection is taken from *Sermon Matter from St. Thomas Aquinas* edited by C. J. Callen, O. P. and published by B. Herder Book Co., St. Louis, Mo. It is printed here with their permission. The second selection is taken from his Commentary on the Lord's Prayer, Opuscule VIII, Chapter V and translated by the editor. It is entitled *On the First Petition*.

HIS NAME WAS CALLED JESUS

"His Name was called Jesus." Names are supposed to correspond to the nature or qualities of the things they designate; and in the case of human individuals they are conferred on account of some personal attribute or circumstance. Thus, some persons are named from the time of their birth (e.g., from the saint on whose feast they are born); some from their relatives, as when the neighbors objected to the name of John for the Baptist and wished him to be called after his father Zacharias (Luke 1:61); others from some event or circumstance, as when Joseph called his first born Manasses (i.e., one who causes to forget), because this birth made him forget his labors (Gen. 41:51); still others from their appearance, as Esau (i.e., hairy) was named from his hairy appearance at birth (Gen. 25:25).

When, however, names are imposed by God they always indicate some free gift from Him. So it was with the patriarch of the Jews, when God named Abraham (i.e., father of the great multitude), because he had been divinely chosen as the parent and ancestor of many peoples (Gen. 17:5). Thus also the first pope received from Christ the name of Peter (i.e., rock), because Christ made him the cornerstone or foundation of His Church (Matt. 16:18).

Hence we see why our Lord, who was sent to bring salvation to the world, was called Jesus (i.e., Savior) by the angel before He was conceived in the womb and received that Name at His circumcision. And to this Name can be reduced all the other names foretold of Him, since they all refer to salvation. For example, He is called Emmanuel (i.e., God with us), because it is the union of the divine and the human in Him that caused our salvation (Isa. 7:14); He is called Admirable, because of God's wonderful design that sent Him for our salvation (Isa. 9:6); He is called orient or sunrise, because as Savior He brought light to those who were in darkness (Zac. 6:12 and Ps. 111:4). Others before our Lord's time bore the name of Jesus, but only in a limited and temporal sense. He alone deserved it in its full meaning, because He alone is the Savior of mankind, and in the highest manner, as being our delivery from soul bondage.

Abraham received his name at the time the law of circumcision was made known to him; and this explains how it became the custom among the Jews to name their children on the day they were circumcised. The giving of the name also indicated that a new being was received in the rite, just as children are named today at their baptism, which is a second or spiritual birth. In the case of Our Lord, there was a further, special fitness in the conferring of the name Jesus at the moment of His Circumcision, because He was to save the world by the pouring out of His blood, and this first shedding of His blood coincided with the giving of the name Jesus, or Savior.

ON THE FIRST PETITION

"Hallowed by Thy Name." This is the first petition that we address to God, in which we ask Him to manifest and make known His Name among us. Now the name of the Lord is most admirable because it works wonders in all living things; for as it says in the last chapter of the Gospel of St. Matthew, "they cast out demons in my Name." Secondly, it is most lovable. As it says in the fourth chapter of Acts: "there is no other Name under the sun by which we can be saved." Now everyone should love salvation. An example of this is furnished by St. Ignatius of Antioch who so greatly loved the Name of Jesus Christ that when Trojan demanded of him that he deny this Name, he replied that it was not possible for this name to be taken from his lips. When they threatened to cut off his head to prevent him from repeating it, he cried out that though they might stop his lips by cutting off his head, they could never efface the Name from his heart, for it was written there, and that was why he could not stop invoking it. Trojan listened to what he said, and wishing to verify it in detail, cut off his head and afterwards removed the heart of this servant of God and he found written on it in letters of gold, the Name of Jesus Christ, for this Name was as it were placed as a seal on his heart.

Thirdly, this name is most worthy of veneration. The Apostle says in his Letter to the Philippians, "in the Name of Jesus every knee shall bend, of those that are in heaven, on earth, and under the earth." In heaven by the angels and the saints; on earth by those people in the world who do it for love of the glory that they bring to themselves, and on account of the fear of chastisement that they wish to avoid; and in hell by the damned on account of the fear it inspires in them.

Fourth, this Name is inexplicable, for no tongue is capable of explaining it. This is moreover why on certain occasions one has recourse to natural things to explain it. One can for instance give

Him the name of "rock" in order to express the quality of stability. It is written in Matthew 16: "on this rock I will build my Church, and the gates of hell shall not prevail. . . ." He is also named "fire" on account of fire's quality of purifying, for the Name is a means of purifying the hearts of sinners just as it purifies metal. This is why it says in the fourth chapter of Deuteronomy that "the Lord you God is a consuming fire." He is also given the name of "light" because he is the source of illumination, for just s the torch disperses shadows, so also does He illuminate the shadows of the soul. It is thus written in Psalm 17: "O Lord, scatter the shadows that envelope me." Now these things are asked that this Name might be manifest, known, and considered Holy.

Now Holiness has three qualities. First, it signifies the quality of stability, whish is why the blessed in heaven are called saints, for they are firmly established in eternal happiness. The saints cannot live for ever on this earth, for this world is always in motion. Thus St. Augustine says: "I am estranged from you O Lord, I have greatly erred and I have wandered from your stability."

Secondly, Holy means other-worldly such as is the quality of the saints in heaven who have no earthly attachment. The Apostle says on this subject in the Epistle to the Philippians 3: "I have considered all things as dung . . . etc." Now the world signifies sin which is appropriate first of all because of its nature. The earth in effect, if not cultivated, produces only thorns and thistles—so also the soul of the sinner, if not cultivated, produces only the thorns of tribulations and the barbs of sin—as it says in Genesis 3: "she produces thorns and thistles." The earth also signifies sin because it symbolizes the clouding of the spirit, for the earth is dark and full of shadows which is also characteristic of the sinner—as it says in Genesis 1: "and darkness was on the face of the earth." Thirdly, it does so because of its material nature, for the earth is in effect a dry material that does not give forth its fruits unless it receives moisture from the waters; for God has established the earth upon the waters—as it says in Psalm 91: "who has established the earth upon the waters." The dryness and aridity of the earth is circumscribed by the waters just as the soul of the sinner is dry and arid as we understand from the words of Psalm 142: "my soul is for you like the earth without water."

Finally, Holy implies "covered with blood," which is why the saints are so described, for it says in the Apocalypse [Revelation] 7: they are covered with blood—"those they are who have undergone the great tribulations and have their robes washed in the blood of the Lamb," and again, as it says elsewhere, "He has washed our sins in His blood."

The Blessed Thomas à Kempis

BORN ABOUT THE year 1380 at Kempen in Holland—whence his name, Thomas à Kempis spent his boyhood days at the school of the Brethren of the Common Life at Deventer, and in 1399 entered the order of the Canons of St. Augustine at Mount St. Agnes near Zwolle. In 1412 he was ordained priest and in 1425 he was appointed Superior and later Master of Novices. He died at Mount St. Agnes "at the age of one hundred years less eight."

There has been considerable debate as to the authorship of the works attributed to his pen. He is best known for the spiritual classic, *The Imitation of Christ* of which thousands of editions have been published. It is not my intention to enter into a discussion as to whether he was the author or only the copier of the various works ascribed to him. The medieval reader, being traditional in his outlook, was unconcerned with authorship as such as is illustrated by the fact that so few of the medieval works of art have any name ascribed to them. What is important is that by ascribing the name of Thomas à Kempis to these works, the faithful saw in them a guarantee of orthodoxy—that is of the truth.

The present selections are translated from the Latin by the editor. The Latin original is taken from the *Opera Omnia of Thomas à Kempis* collected and edited by the Jesuit Henri Sommali and published in 1680. I am indebted to the Corrigan Memorial Library of Dunwoodie Seminary in New York for the loan of the original.

SELECTIONS FROM THOMAS À KEMPIS

O sweet Name of Jesus, holy above all names in heaven and on earth, and to which every knee, both of men and of angels in heaven, on earth and in hell bends. You are the way of the just, the glory of the saints, the hope of those in need, the balm oif the sick, the love of the devout and the consolation of those that suffer. O Jesus, be to me a help and a protector so that your Name may be blessed for all times. . . . (*Manualis Parvulorum* XII)

ON THE INVOCATION OF THE HOLY NAME OF JESUS AND OF THE VIRGIN MARY, HIS BLESSED MOTHER

"Direct my ways in thy sight O Lord my God." In your ways, O Lord Jesus Christ, in your beautiful ways, pure and secure, that I might walk in them with justice and in perfection. For all your paths are peaceful and holy, leading the faithful and those of humble heart into you heavenly kingdom.

Whenever you go, wherever you walk of stand or rest, invoke Jesus and invoke Mary, his sweet mother, and consider as you go this short verse with a willing spirit: "Direct my ways in thy sight O Lord" adding to it in a like manner, "perfect, O sweet Jesus, my goings in thy paths that my footsteps may not be moved to the vision of empty things, or the speaking of vain words that may be harmful to my soul." And as you travel on this earthly pilgrimage, take for yourself as a provision (*viaticum*), much as a shepard's staff held firmly in the hand, this short prayer, "JESU-MARIA". Say it often and with great devotion. JESU-MARIA be with me always on the way, in every place and at all times. Be my strong guide lest I wander in error from the true path or be frightened by inner or outer imaginings. The holy prayer "JESU-MARIA" is brief of speech, light to carry, easy to hold and sweet to contemplate. It is a strong shield, faithful as a guardian, friendly as a companion, delightful as a refreshment, sweet as a consolation and powerful as a help. The prayer JESU-MARIA is a most powerful method for all of us poor pilgrims on the way to the eternal life, a way to be traveled with justice and with contempt of the world. This holy prayer of "JESU-MARIA" makes better allies and more powerful soldiers than all the kings and princes of this world. It makes better and loftier saints than all the saints in heaven and on earth. This holy prayer attracts to him who says it, the whole heavenly court, for this court follows with all reverence its Lord Jesus Christ and his holy mother Mary, for she is worthy of all dignity and is honored by all. Do not forsake that Jesus that—along with Mary—with whom you wish for all eternity to live and rejoice. He who carries Jesus and Mary in his heart, repeats JESUS and MARY with his lips, blesses JESUS and MARY with his mouth, clapping with his hands and dancing with his feet; he belches out JESUS and MARY with his voice, with his heart rejoicing, his eyes beseeching, his face expressing his longing, embracing JESUS and MARY with his arms, kissing them with his lips and adoring them on his knees. Such a person travels on this earthly pilgrimage in a beneficial and secure manner.

Truly he is blessed who sedulously invokes Jesus and Mary, salutes them with devotion, remembers them with love, honors them to the extreme, praises them with joy, loves them with the greatest ardor, and glorifies them to the highest. He speaks forth their Names with the greatest sweetness, singing and enjoying the very sound of their Names with the greatest joy. O how sweet is the Name of JESUS and MARY, his most blessed mother. O how happy is the pilgrim who everywhere in this time of exile remembers his heavenly homeland where Jesus together with Mary enjoy with all the saints and the angels the greatest joy and eternal glory. Blessed are the poor and the beggers who daily solicit the bread of heaven, and until they receive a crumb do not cease to humbly suplicate before the table of the Lord. Blessed is he who is called to the supper of the Lamb, and until he comes to the heavenly supper is satisfied with the sacrament of it here.

Just as when the devout communicate, or when the priest celebrates Mass with devotion and reverence, so also when a person blesses JESUS and his mother by calling on their Names, do they partake of the sacred bread and wine. Those who invoke the divine Names are the disciples of Christ and the chaplains of the Blessed Virgin MARY. They are the companions of the angels, fellow citizens with the Apostles, dwellers in the house of God, relatives of the saints and friends of heaven. Such a person flees the crowds, hates gossip, meditates on the words of Jesus, and guards his heart and his senses with care lest JESUS, MARY and all the saints be offended.

As soon as one cries out "JESUS", he receives blessings and mercy from Our Lord, for no matter where he is, nor in what danger he finds himself, as soon as he cries out JESUS, our Lord hears him from heaven. Is this not what happened to the disciples in the sea of Galilee? When they were about to be drowned, they invoked JESUS, and at once He appeared and said, "Why are you afraid? Have faith, I am here, do not be afraid." the very sound of the word JESUS is a sweet consolation, a strong protection, a joy and a happiness; it is a blessing and an indulgence, a grace and a most powerful support leading us to the eternal life (*Vallis Lilliorum* XIII).

"I shall be remembered by all generations." Mary loved to live, from the time of the birth of Jesus until He died on the cross, in poor circumstances, in humility and in all perfection. . . . If anyone flies to her and cleaves to her with humility, and if he invokes her glorious and sweet Name, he will never retire from her presence with his hands empty. Whole choirs of angels are subservient to her commands, and she can send them to assist those who call upon her. She also commands the demons, lest any of them should dare to bother or molest anyone who submits to her care and authority. Our Queen defeated and ejected the malignant spirit from heaven, and as son as her holy Name was heard, they fell straight into the fires of hell. The devil hates and fears the holy Name of MARY which Christians everywhere so greatly love and repeat. Nor do the demons dare to appear and to exercise their evil mockeries in a place where they know the holy Name of Mary shines forth. Before the Name of MARY, they prostrate themselves, as if it were thunder hurled at them from heaven itself. On the other hand, the holy angels and saints rejoice and delight together with all the devout faithful when they remember MARY (which they do frequently and with a good will), whose most honorable Name is extolled within all the boundaries of the Church—a Church dedicated in a special manner to that Name. Indeed, it is most honorable and right that all the holy saints should honor the Name of the mother of His earthly birth which all the angels of the universe venerate and praise in the highest. Indeed, all the faithful venerate, all the devout adore, all the religious embrace, all the laity commend, all sinners extol, all those in trouble are familiar with, and all those in danger invoke this very Name. It is the closest to God and the most loved of His only Son, Our Lord Jesus.

Choose the Blessed Mother of Jesus ahead of your own parents and friends as a special mother and advocate before death. Greet her frequently with the Angelic Salutation, for she listens to this most willingly. If the malignant one attacks you and hinders your prayer, pay him no heed, increase your praying and praising, but even more, invoke with greater intensity the Name of MARY. Salute MARY, think MARY, honor MARY, lean on MARY, commend yourself to MARY and repeat the Name of MARY. Be with MARY in your cell, be silent with MARY, pray with MARY, rejoice with MARY, be sad with MARY, work with MARY, walk and sit with MARY and be recollected with MARY,

Seek the things of the spirit with MARIA-JESU, bear MARIA-JESU in your arms, live with MARY and JESUS in Jerusalem even to the cross, weep with MARY and JESUS, be buried with JESUS and MARY, rise again with JESUS and MARY, ascend into heaven with JESUS and MARY and desire to die with them. Brothers, if you know and practice this method, the devil will fly away from you and you will become proficient in the spiritual life. MARY will willingly intercede for you in her mercy and JESUS willingly listens to MARY out of His respect for her. It is little enough that we do, but if we approach the Father with a humble and contrite heart through JESUS and MARY, we shall be recipients of His mercy and grace now and of His glory in the future for ever and ever. . . . It is indeed good to often repeat the Ave Maria and to invoke the Name of the Mother of JESUS frequently (*Sermons to Novices*).

Blessed Henry Suso

HENRY SUSO HAS long been well known as an exponent of the "Name," and indeed he went so far as to cut the Name of Jesus over his own heart with a knife. In doing so he prayed: "O most unique love of my soul, O my Jesus, see with what great ardor my love for you burns. I have written your Name upon my flesh, but I am not satisfied with this. I would actually have written it on my heart. This I cannot do, but if You will accede in your tenderness to my prayer, you can make up for what I lack in ability, and do this. Engrave your Holy Name in the very center of my heart, and do it with the letters of eternity so that nothing can ever efface or destroy them in me." He was a disciple of Meister Eckhart whom I have quoted extensively in the Introduction, and once had a vision of his master "in exceeding glory, into which his soul was quite transformed, and made Godlike in God."

He was born near Constance in Germany in 1300 of parents who were themselves of noble descent. His mother was a person of eminent sanctity and he called himself by her maiden name. When he died, among his papers was found a note to the effect that God had changed his name to Amandus, or Beloved. At the age of thirteen he entered the Dominican Order and underwent a course of studies aimed at obtaining a degree of Doctor of Theology. Shortly before he was finished, he was instructed by God not to take this degree, but to enter a life of preaching. He died in 1365 and was buried in the Dominican convent in Ulm. Two hundred and forty-eight years later, when the city was Protestant, the body was exhumed by workmen building the foundations of a new building and was found incorrupt and emitting a sweet odor.

The passages below are taken from his *Life* (written under obedience) and translated by Thomas F. Knox, (Methuen, London): and from his letters as translated by Sister M. A. Edward, O. P. and published under the title of *The Exemplar* by Priory Press, Dubuque, Iowa. The latter is published with the kind permission of the publisher.

A POEM ON THE LOVABLE NAME OF JESUS

Jesus is the soul's abyss
    Is sweeter far than earthly bliss:
A tower strong is that Name mild
    Ne'er disturbed by tempest wild.
Far lovelier than a diamond bright,
    That Name of Jesus sweetly rings
    Like rarest zither's silver strings.
Ah, Jesus, for your Name's blest sake,
    Forgive my sins, exceeding great.
Grant, dear Lord, that your fair Name,
    May wound my heart with holy pain.
Jesus, choicest Lover mine,
    May my heart's love be ever thine.
Bless me Jesus, God of power,
    Now and in death's departing hour.

A LETTER ON
HOW A PERSON SHOULD
PRACTICE DEVOTION TO
THE SACRED NAME OF JESUS

The eternal God asks a favor of the pure soul: "Hold me close to thy heart."

A true friend of God should always keep some good images or thoughts in his soul's mouth and chew on them in order to inflame his heart with love or God. The most perfect thing we can do in this life is to think frequently of God's love, to languish for his love; to speak often about him, to meditate on his words, to do all our actions for him, and to think of him alone. The eye should look at him; the ear should listen to his desires; the heart, soul, and emotions should embrace him tenderly. If we have offended him, we should supplicate him; if he exercises us, we should bear with him; if he hides himself, we should seek our Beloved and not desist until we have found him. And when we have found him, we should embrace him tenderly and reverently.

Whether we walk or stand still, eat or drink, we should at all times wear the golden locket IHS upon our hearts.

If we are unable to do anything else, we should press it upon our souls with our eyes and revolve this gracious Name in our mouths. We should think of it so often during the day so that we will dream of it during the night.

Say with the prophet Jeremiah (Lam. 3:25): "Good is the Lord to one who waits for him, to the soul that seeks him."

Behold this is the best practice you can acquire. The crown of all spiritual exercises is fervent prayer, and everything else must be subordinated to it as to the final goal.

What else do they do in heaven except contemplate and love the gracious Beloved, love and praise him? Therefore, the more tenderly we press the divine love to our hearts, and the oftener we gaze upon it and embrace it with the arms of our heart, the more will we be embraced by him here and in eternal bliss.

Take, for example, the great lover of God, St. Paul. He lovingly inscribed the sweet Name of Jesus in the deepest depths of his heart. At his martyrdom, when his head had been severed from his holy body, the head spoke three times: "Jesus, Jesus, Jesus!." During his excruciating martyrdom, St. Ignatius repeated the Name of Jesus with intense fervor. When he was asked the reason for this, he replied that the Name of Jesus was engraved in his heart. After his death, the astonished executioners opened his heart and found written there in golden letters: "Jesus, Jesus, Jesus."

AN ACCOUNT OF THE DEVOTION TO THE MOST HOLY NAME OF JESUS

The Servitor sent this last letter to his spiritual daughter. This ardent lover of God had often noticed the intense devotion and firm faith which her spiritual father had in the lovable Name of Jesus. She had also heard from his own lips the manner in which he had engraved this same Name into his heart. She cultivated in her own heart a burning desire and love for this holy Name, and in order to increase her devotion she embroidered the Name with red silk on a small piece of white cloth in this fashion: IHS. She carried this namesake always with her, and embroidered countless others in the same way.

When the Servitor of Wisdom came to visit her, she devoutly begged him to touch all these names to his heart and then to return them to her. And he did so.

Then she took the one she had made for herself and sewed it to her underclothing, so that no one could see it. Her purpose herein was to augment her love of God and to obtain his perpetual blessing. The other names which she had prepared she sent to his numerous spiritual children, asking them to wear them for the same intention, and they did so. She wore this Name secretly the rest of her life; it was buried with her.

It happened shortly before her death that the Servitor came to visit her for the last time. She addressed him thus: "Dear father, may God be praised for all the blessings I have received from him through you. Now, my dear spiritual father, I ask one more favor from your virtuous heart. Please do not refuse me. And I confide to you that I have often been admonished by God in prayer to ask this of you. It is his wish that you grant it."

He spoke: "Dear daughter, whatever you desire in God shall be done."

She answered: "Father, whoever knows your loving heart as God and I do, and hears or reads your enthusiastic words, will observe the fiery and profound devotion you have towards this sacred Name and the immense benefit all persons should derive from this same devotion. Therefore, I, a poor suffering creature, beg you in God's stead and for the sake of this sublime Name, that before you die, you would in the this hour lay your anointed hand against the saving Name which you engraved upon your heart. Then, with the same hand make the Sign of the Cross over all of us who because of you holy instructions venerate this Name and daily repeat the morning prayer which God taught you as a means of honoring him and encouraging all people to practice this same devotion. If they are prevented from saying this prayer, they will say a Pater Noster and an Ave Maria, accompanied with a venia to honor him before whom all knees bow, in heaven and on earth. This will assure them of God's protection in all life's events, and help them to conquer all obstacles to God's praise and their eternal welfare."

Seeing in her earnestness and devotion sign of God's will in the matter, the Servitor devoutly placed his hand upon his heart, touched the Name of Jesus, and then in the almighty power of that same Name he made the Sign of the Cross and blessed all those who would devoutly repeat the aforementioned morning prayer in honor of the sacred Name. He begged God to grant them a holy death and eternal blessedness. And may God help all of us to attain this through the merits of his Holy Name! Amen.

MORNING PRAYER

This is the aforementioned praiseworthy greeting and excellent morning prayer which a person should say in order to honor God and ward off from himself all harm:

"O Thou most beautiful, most brilliant Eternal Wisdom, my soul has yearned for you during the night. Now in this early morning hour, my heart and soul have awakened to thee, my love. I beg thee, my gracious Lord, that your coveted presence will drive all evil far from my body and soul, pour precious graces into every dark nook of my being, and inflame my cold heart with the fire of divine love. Ah, Sweetest Jesus Christ, turn your gracious countenance kindly toward me, because this morning my soul turns to you with all its faculties. I tenderly greet you from the deepest depth of my heart and desire that the thousand times a thousand angels who serve you would today greet you for me, and that the ten thousand times a hundred thousand heavenly spirits who dwell with you would praise you worthily. May the fair loveliness of all creatures praise you today in union with me, and gratefully bless your sacred Name, our comforting shield, now and throughout the ageless eternity. Amen."

St. John Chrysostom

ST. JOHN CHRYSOSTOM was born at Antioch around the year 344 of a noble and wealthy family. He was well educated and for a while practiced law while living at home. In 374, after his mother died, he retired to a monastery and four years later became a hermit. He was however raised to the priesthood by Flavian and began as such to preach. Indeed his sermons were so beautiful that he was called the "golden-mouthed."

He tells us in his Eight Homily on St. Paul's Letter to the Romans that "We too, have our spiritual incantations, the name of our Lord Jesus Christ, and the power of His Cross. This spell not only drives the dragon from his lair and casts him back to the fire, it also heals our wounds. This Name is terrible to demons, and salutary to the troubled and the sick. Let us honor His Name, and rest secure in its power to defend us." He says elsewhere that "I beseech to hold the Name as a staff. If none of you would go abroad unclad or unshod, so neither go forth without this Name, but speak it as you cross the threshold. Never go forth without it. It will be to you as staff, armor and tower of defense" (*Catech. II pr. Finem*).

The Homily that follows is taken from the *Greek Patrology*, Volume 62, page 363 and is translated by Father F. M. Toal. It was initially published in *Patristic Homilies on the Gospels*, Vol I (Regnery, Chicago, 1954) and is reproduced with the kind permission of Father Toal.

HOMILY OF ST. JOHN CHRYSOSTOM

"All whatsoever you do in word or in work, do all in the Name of the Lord Jesus Christ, giving thanks to God and the Father by Him" (Col. 3:17)

If we do this, there will indeed be nothing of evil, nothing impure, in our invoking of the Sacred name. If you eat, if you drink, should you marry, if you set out on a journey, do all in the Name of Jesus, that is, calling on Him to help you. And having in all that you do invoked Him, then apply yourself to the thing at hand. Should you wish to speak concerning any business, do this beforehand. For this reason do we also place the Name of the Lord at the head of all our epistles. Wherever there is the Lord's name, everything will be well. For if the name of the consuls are affixed to documents, to insure that they are authentic, how much more the Name of Jesus.

Again, the apostle likewise means: say and do everything as is right and fitting in relation to God. But do not bring in the Angels. Offer thanks to God, both before you eat, and afterwards. Do you sleep? Give thanks to God, both before and after. Are you going out among people? Do the same; not some worldly thing. Do everything in the name of the Lord, and all that you do will bring you happiness. Wherever the Name of the Lord is set up, all things prosper. If it has power to drive away demons, if it can banish illness, much more will it aid you own actions.

And what does he mean when he says: *whatever you do in word or in deed.* Whether you pray, or whether you do anything else whatever. Recall how Abraham sent his servant in the Name of God. And David in the Name of the Lord slew Goliath; great and wonderful is His Name. Again Jacob says to his sons, saying: *and may Almighty God make him favorable to you.*[1]

---

1. Gen. 43:14.

He who does this has God for his helper: without Whom he can do nothing. And the Lord, accepting the honor of being called upon returns the honor by making possible what we strive to do. Invoke the Son, give thanks to the Father. For invoking the Son, we invoke the Father; and giving thanks to the Father, we give thanks also to the Son. Let us learn these things, but not restricting ourselves merely to the words, but fulfilling them in our deeds. Nothing is so great as this Name, that in every place is wondrous. *Thy name is oil poured out.*[2] He who speaks it is filled with its fragrance. *And no man can say the Lord Jesus Christ, but by the Holy Ghost.*[3]

So many are the wonders wrought by this Name! If you say with faith: in the Name of the Father, and of the Son, and of the Holy Ghost, you have done what is asked. See what great things you have done; for you have created within you a man, a new man, as well as the other effects that also follow from baptism. So likewise in commanding the sick this is a name of power. For this reason the devil, envying the honor given to us, has brought in the use of the name of angels. These are incantations of the demons. Even if it should be an angel, even an archangel, or even the very Cherubim, do not suffer it. For these very Powers will not hearken but turn away, when they have seen that it is but an affront to the Lord.

I have honored thee, He says, and I have said, Call upon Me; and dost thou offend Him with dishonor? If you chant this hymn with praise, you will put to flight both demons and infirmities; and if you banish not sickness, this happens, not from want of power, but because it is not expedient for you.

According to Thy Name, so also is Thy praise.[4] By this Name was the whole world changed, tyranny laid low, the devil trodden under foot, and the heavens thrown open. What do I say: the heavens? We by this Name are born again. If this has happened to us, we are

2. Song of Sol. 1:3.
3. 1 Cor. 12:4.
4. Ps. 47:11.

already glorified! This name makes both Martyrs and Confessors; let us hold fast to it, as to a great gift, that we may live in glory, and that we may be pleasing to God, and be held worthy of the good things that are promised to those who love Him in grace and generosity of heart, through Jesus Christ Our Lord, to Whom be honor and glory, now and for ever. Amen.

Elsewhere in his Homily 8 on the Fourth Chapter of Romans he states:

> We too, I repeat, have our spiritual incantations, the Name of Our Lord Jesus Christ, and the power of His Cross. This spell not only drives the dragon from his lair, and casts him back to the fire, but also heals our wounds. This Name is terrible to demons, and salutary to the troubled and the sick. Let us honor His Name, and rest secure in Its power to defend us.

St. Bernard

IT IS ALMOST an act of futility to introduce the reader to St. Bernard. For of all the saints of the Church, he is among the best known and loved. The following passages are taken from his commentary on the Song of songs as translated by a religious of C.S.M.V. (Mowbray, London, 952). It consists of a selection of passages on the Scriptural phrase (Canticle of Canticles) "*Thy Name is as oil poured forth,*" taken from his Sermons 12, 15, 18–20, and his fifteenth Sermon on Conversion.

SERMONS ON THE SONG OF SONGS

"Your Name is oil poured out." This is plainly Israel's witness of praise to the Name of the Lord, not indeed the Israel that lives by the law of the flesh, but he that lives by the law of the Sprit. For how could the carnal Israel utter such words? It is not that he has no oil, but that it is not poured out. He has it but keeps it hidden; he has it in his scriptures, but not in his heart. In the sight of men he clings to the letter of the law; he clutches in his hand a jar that is full but sealed, nor will he open it and be anointed. It is within you, deep within, that the Spirit's unction is poured out: open and be anointed and you will no longer be a rebellious house. Why store oil in jars and never apply it to your limbs? Of what use to ponder over your books on the Name of our holy Savior if you exclude his love from your lives? You have the oil: pour it out and experience its threefold power. The Jew scorns these monitions but you will listen to them. I wish now to tell you what I have so far left unmentioned: why the

Name of the Bridegroom is compared to oil. There are three reasons. But because he is called by many names, since that which is adequate to him is known to none—for it is ineffable—we must first invoke the Holy Spirit that he may be pleased to reveal to us that one Name above all others on which he wishes us to concentrate in this instance, for he has given no written indication of it. This topic however must wait for another time. For even if I now knew all I should need to know, even if you should not feel oppressed nor I wearied, the hourglass indicates the end. Hold fast to all that I have drawn to your attention, for tomorrow I shall not repeat it. The job I have undertaken, the task in hand, is to explain why the Bridegroom's Name is compared to oil, and what this Name is. And since I may not trust in my own powers for what I am to say, prayers must be offered that the Bridegroom Himself, Jesus Christ, our Lord, may reveal it to us by His Spirit. To him be all honor and glory for ever and ever, Amen.

Wisdom is a kindly spirit, and easy of access to those who call upon him. Quite often he anticipates their request and says: "Here I am." Listen now to what, because of your prayers, he has revealed to me about the subject we postponed yesterday; be ready to gather the ripe fruit of your intercession. I put before you a Name that is rightly compared to oil, now rightly I shall explain. You encounter many names for the Bridegroom scattered through the pages of Scripture, but all these I sum up for you in two. I think you will find none that does not express the gift of His love or the power of His majesty. The Holy Spirit tells us this through the mouth of one of his friends: "*Two things I have heard: it is for God to be strong, for you, Lord, to be merciful.*" With reference to His majesty we read: "*Holy and terrible is His Name*;" with reference to His love: "*Of all the names in the world given to men, this is the only one by which we can be saved.*" Further examples make it clearer still. Jeremiah says: "This is the Name by which He will be called: '*the Lord our righteous one*'"—a Name suggesting power; but when Isaiah says: "Thy Name will be called Emmanuel," he indicates his love. He himself said: "*You call me Master and Lord.*" The first title implies love, the second majesty. Love's business is to educate the mind as well as to provide the body's food. Isaiah also said, "*His Name shall be called Wonderful, Counselor, God, the Mighty One, Everlasting Father, Prince of Peace.*" The first, third and fourth signify majesty, the others, love. Which of these therefore is poured out? In some mysterious way the name of majesty and power is tranfused into that of love and mercy, an amalgam that is abundantly poured out in the person of our Savior Jesus Christ. The Name "God" liquifies and dissolves into the title "God with us," that is, into "Emmanuel." He who is "Wonderful" becomes "Counselor;" "God" and "the Mighty One" become the "Everlasting Father" and the "Prince of Peace." "The Lord our righteous one" becomes the "gracious and merciful Lord." This process is not new: in ancient times "Abram" became "Abraham" and "Sarai" became "Sara;" and we are reminded that in these events the mystery of the communication of salvation was prefigured and celebrated.

So I ask where now is that warning cry: "I am the Lord, I am the Lord," that resounded with recurring terror in the ears of the poeple of old? The prayer with which I am familiar that begins with the sweet Name of Father, gives me confidence of obtaining the petitions with which it continues. Servants are called friends in this new way, and the resurrection is proclaimed not to mere disciples, but to brothers.

Nor am I surprised if, when the time has fully come, there is an outpouring of Jesus' Name as God fulfills what he had promised through Joel, an outpouring of his Spirit on all mankind. . . .

I recognize now the Name hinted at by Isaiah when he said (65:15): "*My servants are to be given a new Name, Whoever is blessed on earth in that Name will be blessed by the Lord, Amen.*" O blessed Name, oil poured out without limit! From heaven it pours down on Judea and from there over all the earth, so that round the whole world the Church proclaims: "*Your Name is oil poured out.*" And what an outpouring! It not only bathes the heavens and the earth, it even bedews the underworld, so that all beings in the heavens, on earth and in the underworld should bend the knee in the Name of Jesus, and that every tongue should acclaim: "*Your Name is oil poured out.*"

Take the Name Christ, take the Name Jesus; both were infused into the angels, both were poured out upon men, even upon men who rotted like animals in their own dung. Thus you became a savior to both men and beasts, so countless are your mercies, O God. How precious your Name, and yet how cheap! Cheap, but the instrument of salvation. If it were not cheap, it would not have been poured out for me; if it lacked saving power it would not have won me. Make me a sharer in the Name, I share too in its inheritance. For I am a Christian, Christ's own brother. If I am what I say, I am the heir of God, co-heir with Christ. And what wonder if the Name of the Bridegroom is poured out, since he himself is poured out? For he emptied himself to assume the condition of slave. Did he not even say: "*I am poured out like water*"? The fullness of the divine life was poured out and lived on earth in bodily form, that all of us who live in this body doomed to death may receive from that fullness, and being filled with its life-giving odor say: "*Your Name is oil poured out.*" Such is what is meant by the outpouring of the Name, such its manner, such its extent.

But why the symbol of oil? I have yet to explain this. In the previous sermon I had begun to do so when another matter that seemed to demand mention suddenly presented itself, though I may have dallied with it longer than I intended. In this I resembled the valiant woman, Wisdom, who put her hand to the distaff, her fingers to the spindle. Skillfully she produced from her scanty stock of wool or flax a long spool of thread, out of which she wove the material that made warm clothes for the members of her household. The likeness between oil and the Name of the Bridegroom is beyond doubt, the Holy Spirit's comparison of the two is no arbitrary gesture. Unless you can persuade me otherwise, I hold that the likeness is to be found in the threefold property of oil: it gives light, it nourishes, it anoints. It feeds the flame, it nourishes the body, it relieves pain: it is light, food, medicine. And is not this true also of the Bridegroom's Name? When preached it gives light, when meditated it nourishes, when invoked it relieves and soothes. Let us consider each point.

How shall we explain the worldwide light of faith, swift and flaming in its progress, except by the preaching of Jesus' Name? Is it not by the light of this Name that God has called us into his wonderful light, that irradiates our darkness and empowers us to see the light? To such as we Paul says: "*You were darkness once, but now you are light in the Lord.*" This is the Name that Paul was commanded to present before kings and pagans and the people of Israel; a Name that illuminated his native land as he carried it with him like a torch, preaching on all his journeys that the night is almost over, it will be daylight soon—let us give up all the things we prefer to do under the cover of the dark; let us arm ourselves and appear in the light. Let us live decently as people do in the daytime. To every eye he was a lamp on its lamp-stand; to every place he brought the good news of Jesus and him crucified. What a splendor radiated from that light, dazzling the eyes of the crowd, when Peter uttered the Name that strengthened the feet and ankles of the cripple, and gave light to many eyes that were spiritually blind! Did not the words shoot out like a flame when he said: "*In the Name of Jesus Christ of Nazareth, arise and walk*"? But the Name of Jesus is more than a light, it is also food. Do you not feel increase of strength as often as you remember it? What other name can so enrich a man who meditates? What can equal its power to refresh the harassed senses, to buttress the virtues, to add vigor to good and upright habits, to foster chaste affections? Every food of the mind is dry if it not dipped in that oil; it is tasteless if not seasoned by that salt. Write what you will, I shall not relish it unless it tells of Jesus. Talk or argue about what you will, I shall not relish it if you exclude the Name of Jesus. Jesus is honey in the mouth, music in the ear, a song in the heart.

Again, it is a medicine. Does one of us feel sad? Let the Name of Jesus come into his heart, from there let it spring to his mouth, so that shining like the dawn it may dispel all darkness and make a cloudless sky. Does someone fall into sin? Does his despair even urge him to suicide? Let him but invoke this live-giving Name and his will to live willl be at once renewed. The hardness of heart that is our common experience, the apathy bred of indolence, bitterness of mind, repugnance for the things of the spirit—have they ever failed to yield in the presence of this saving Name? The tears dammed up by the barrier of our pride—how have they not burst forth again with sweeter abundance at the thought of Jesus' Name? And where is the man, who, terrified and trembling before impending peril, has not been suddenly filled with courage and rid of fear by calling on the strength of that Name? And where is the man who, tossed on the rolling seas of doubt, did not quickly find certitude by recourse to the clarity of Jesus' Name? Was ever a man so discouraged, so beaten down by afflictions, to whom the sound of this Name did not bring new resolve? In short, for all the ills and disorders to which flesh is heir, this Name is medicine. For proof we have no less than his own promise: "Call upon me in the day of trouble; I will deliver you, and you shall glorify me." Nothing so curbs the onset of anger, so allays the upsurge of pride. It cures the wound of envy, controls the thirst of covetousness and banishes the itch of unclean desire. For when I name Jesus, I set before me a man who is meek and humble of heart, kind, prudent, chaste, merciful, flawlessly upright and holy in the eyes of all; and this same man is the all-powerful God whose way of life heals me, whose support is my strength. All these re-echo for me at the hearing of Jesus' Name. Because he is man, I strive to imitate him; because of his divine power, I lean upon him. The examples of his human life I gather like medicinal herbs; with the aid of his power I blend them, and the result is a compound like no pharmacist can produce.

Hidden as in a vase, is the Name of Jesus. In it, you my soul, possess a salutary remedy against which no spiritual illness will be proof. Carry it always close to your heart, always in your hand, and so ensure that all your affections, all your actions, are directed to Jesus. You are even invited to do this: "*Set me a seal*," he says, "*upon your heart, as a seal upon your arm.*" Here is a theme we shall treat of again. For the moment have this ready medicine for heart and hand. The Name of Jesus furnishes the power to correct your evil actions, to supply what is wanting to imperfect ones; in this Name your affections find a guard against corruption, or if corrupted, a power that will make them whole again.

Judea also has had her Jesuses—Messiahs in whose empty name she flourished. For they give neither light nor food nor medicine. Hence the synagogue is in the darkness still, enduring the pangs of hunger and disease, and she will neither be healed nor have her fill until she discovers that my Jesus rules over Jacob to the ends of the earth, until she comes back in that evening, hungering like a dog and prowling about the city. True, they were sent on in advance, like the staff preceding the Prophet, to where the child lay dead, but they could not see a meaning in their own names because no meaning was there. The staff was laid upon the corpse but produced neither voice nor movement since it was a mere staff. Then he who sent the staff came down and quickly saved his people from their sins, proving that men spoke truly of him when they said: "*Who is this man that he even forgives sins?*" He is no other than the one who says: "*I am the salvation of my people.*" Now the Word is heard, now it is experienced, and it is clear that, unlike the others, he bears no empty Name. . . .

O Wisdom, sweetly powerful and powerfully sweet, with what skill of healing in wine and oil do you restore my soul's health. Powerfully for me and sweet to me. You deploy your strength from one end of the earth to the other, ordering all things sweetly, driving off all hostile powers and cherishing the weak. Heal me, Lord, and I shall really be healed, I shall sing praise to your Name and cry out: "Your Name is oil poured out." Not wine poured out—for I do not wish to be put on trial—but oil, for you crown me with love and tenderness. Oil by all means, for it floats above all other liqids with which it mixes.

O Name utterly dear, utterly sweet! O Name renowned, predestined, sublime and exalted above all for ever. This is truly the oil that makes a man's face shine, that anoints the head of a man who fasts, causing him to ignore the oil of sinners. This is the new Name which the mouth of the Lord has conferred, the Name given by the angel before he was conceived in the womb. Not the Jews only, but all who call on that Name shall be saved, for it has been poured out without limit. This is the Father's gift to the Son, the Church's Bridegroom, our Lord, Jesus Christ, who is blessed for ever. Amen.

I will protect him because he knows my name. In the presence of God's countenance glorification is made manifest and protection in the knowledge of his name. In the name is hope, the thing hoped for is in his presence. Who hopes for What he sees? Faith comes by hearing, and, according to the same apostle, is the assurance of things hoped for. *I will protect him because he knows my name.* No one knows this name who takes it in vain; he merely says Lord, Lord, and does nor do what he says. No one knows his name who neither honors him as Father nor fears him as Lord. No one knows his name who turns aside to vanities and false follies. *"Blessed is the man whose hope is the name of the Lord and who does look back at vanities and false follies."* Peter knew this name and he said, *"There is no other name given among men by which we may be saved."* We are too, if we know this holy name called down upon us, which we should desire always to be sanctified in us, and should pray according to the teaching of the Savior, "Our Father, you are in heaven, hallowed be your name." So listen to what follows in the psalm: *"He has called upon me and I will hear him."* Calling out in prayer is the fruit of knowing his name; and the fruit of calling out is the Savior's listening. For how can someone be heard who does not call out or invoke the name of the Lord, without knowing it? Thanks be to Him who showed men the Father's name, placing the fruit of salvation in the invocation of this name, as it is written, Whoever calls upon the name of the Lord shall be saved.

St. Anthony of Padua

ST. ANTHONY, A DOCTOR of the Church and one of the most popular Franciscan saints, was born in Lisbon on the Feast of the Assumption of Our Lady (August 15) in the year 1195. His father was Martin de Boullion, a descendant of the renowned Godfrey de Boullion, commander of the First Crusade and his mother was a descended from Froila I, the fourth king of Asturia. At the age of fifteen he joined the Canons Regular of St. Augustine and spent some eight years studying in Coimbra.

In 1220, seing the bodies of the first five Protomartyres of the Franciscan Order being transferred from Morocco, he determined to preach the Gospel to the Saracens in hopes that he might achieve martyrdom. With this in mind he joined the Franciscan Order— taking the name of Anthony—and proceeded to embark for Morocco. But God wished otherwise and he became too ill to continue. On returning home, a storm took him to the island of Sicily where at first he was taken for a simple brother. When he had completely recovered he was sent to a hermitage where he led a solitary and penitential life for two years. During this period, because of the lack of a preacher for an ordination ceremony, he was asked to give a sermon, which when delivered, astonished all who heard it. As a result he was sent out to preach throughout the Romagna and it was during this period that the miracles of his preaching to the fishes, and the adoration of the Blessed Eucharist by a beast of burden occurred.

Because of his erudition and sanctity, he was successively professor of theology at Bologna, Toulouse, and Montpellier and received the title of Pater Scientiae and Doctor Veritatis.

He continued however to preach and indeed, did so before the Popes and the Curia. So popular were his sermons that they had to be given in the open air to crowds as large as 30,000 listeners. He died in Padua after receiving Extreme Unction and singing the touching hymn to the Blessed Virgin "*O Gloriosa Domina. Excelsa super sidera.*" When his body was exhumed, it had disintegrated into dust, except for the tongue. St. Bonaventure who was present said: "O Blessed Tongue, that always praised the Lord and made others bless Him, now it is evident what great merits thou hast before God." This tongue is still miraculously preserved in the Basilica of St. Anthony in Padua in a precious reliqauary donated in 1745 by the Cardinal Rezzonico.

St. Anthony was considered as a doctor of the Church in the Franciscan Order from the time of his Canonization by Pope Gregory IX in 1232. In 1946 Pope Pius XII declared him to be a doctor of the Church Universal with the title of Doctor Evangelicus—the twenty-ninth saint to be so designated.

A SERMON FOR THE FEAST
OF THE CIRCUMCISION

As Scripture says, *Vocatum est nomen eius* Iesu. O Name of sweetness, O Name of delight, O Name of blessed hope and of strength for the sinner. This Name is jubilation in the heart, melody in the ear, and honey upon the lips. The spouse in the Canticle of Canticles exultingly exclaims "*Thy Name is as oil poured out.*" Now oil has five qualities or functions. It floats upon all other liquids—thus indicating that the Name of Jesus is above all names; it is an emollient that softens what is hard; it sweetens what is bitter; it illuminates the darkness, and it satiates the body. This Name of Jesus by far surpasses all the names of men and angels and hence it is that "*in nomine Jesu omne genus flectit genu.-*in the Name of Jesus every knee bends." Hence it is that preachers use it to soften the hardened of heart. If you invoke it, it will sweeten the bitterest of temptations; if you think it, and it will illuminate your heart; if you read it, and your mind will be filled with contentment.

But it should be noted that this Name of *Jesus* is not just called an *oil*, but in addition, an *oil poured forth*. From where and on what? From the heart of the Father in heaven, on earth and in hell. In heaven providing joy to the angels as we know from the Apocalypse where they are described as crying out with a loud voice saying: "*salvation to our Lord who sitteth on the throne, and to the Lamb*" (Apoc. [Rev.] 7:10), which is Jesus, for Jesus means Savior. On earth for the consolation of sinners in accordance with the statement of Isaiah: thy Name and Thy remembrance are the desire of my soul. My soul hath desired thee in the night" (26:8–9). And in the nether world for the liberation of those held captive, for which reason they cast themselves down on their knees and cry out, "come Thou redeemer etc., as is found in the Office for the Dead.

Let us consider the words of Pope Innocent III (1198–1216), even though they are brief: "The Name of Jesus comprises two syllables, five letters, three vowels, and two consonants. The Name has two syllables because Jesus has two natures, which is to say human and divine. Divine from the Father from which He is born without any mother; human from His mother from whom he is born without a father. Indeed, there are two syllables in this one Name because He has two natures and is one person. And it should also be noted that the two consonants make it possible for the Name to be sounded. The three vowels in the Name point to the divinity of Christ which while it is One in itself, is manifested in three persons, *For there are three who give testimony to Him in heaven, The Father, the Word, and the Holy Spirit, and these three are one* (Athanasian Creed). The two consonants signify the twofold elements of Christ's humanity, namely his body and soul. These are not pronounced in isolation but in conjunction with the other letters for these two elements are conjoined in the unity of His person. *For just as the ratio-*

nal soul and flesh are united in man, so also God and man are united in one Christ (Athanasian Creed).

Elsewhere he tells us that the Name of Christ in Hebrew is *Messias*; in Greek, *Christos* or *Soter;* in Latin, *Salvator* or the Savior. Let us then, he exorts us, pray the Father to confer upon us the privilege of His love if not on account of our merits, at least on account of those of His Son, through Whom He redeemed the world. And again, he says "in the name therefore of Christ Jesus, we ask Thee, as He commanded us, give us Thyself, for without Thee there is no life," For as St. Paul said, "in Him we live, and move, and have our being" (Acts 17:28).

O Sweet Jesus: what is there sweeter than Thee? Sweet is Thy memory, sweeter than that of honey or any other object. Thy very name is a Name of sweetness, a Name of Salvation. For what does the name of Jesus signify, if not Savior? Therefore good Jesus, for Thy own sake, be to us a Jesus; so that Thou Who gavest us the beginning of sweetness; i.e., faith, mightest give us also hope and charity, so that living in it we might die in Thee and come to Thee.

This name which is so holy and glorious "*quod invocatum est super nos – which is invoked over us,*" is none other than that of which Peter spoke when he said "there is no other name under heaven in which we can be saved."

These two paragraphs are taken and adapted from
St. Anthony of Padua
by Father Raphael Huber, O.F.M.,
Bruce: Milwaukee, 1948.
The second passage is from the
Festo Purificationis Mariae.

.

St. Peter Canisius

ST. PATER CANISIUS, a doctor of the Church, and entitled the Apostle to the Germans because of his effective preaching and efforts during the Reformation, also had a great devotion to the Names of Jesus and Mary. Herein he quotes two significant passages from Sts. Augustine and Gregory on the reasons Christ's promise that whatsoever ye shall ask in my name, I will do it, is not always fulfilled. For those who follow this way of prayer, his admonitions should be kept in mind.

ST. AUGUSTINE

The Lord, by His promise, gave those whose hopes were resting on Himself, a special ground of confidence, when He said "for I go to the Father; and whatsoever ye shall ask in my name, I will do it." His proceeding, therefore, to the Father, was not with any view of abandoning the needy, but of hearing and answering their petitions. But what is to be made of the words. "Whatsoever ye shall ask," when we behold His faithful ones so often asking and not receiving? Is it, shall we say, for no other reason but that they ask amiss? For the Apostle James made this a ground of reproach when he said *ye ask and receive not, because ye ask amiss, that ye may consume it upon your lusts*" (James 4:3). What one, therefore, wishes to receive, in order to turn to an improper use, God in His mercy rather refuses to bestow. Nay, more, if a man asks what would, if answered, only tend to his injury, there is surely greater cause to fear, lest what God could not withhold with kindness, He should give in His anger. Do we not see how the Israelites got to their own hurt what their guilty lusting craved? For while it was raining manna on them from heaven, they desired to have flesh to eat (Num. 9:32). They disdained what they had, and shamelessly sought what they had not; as if it were not better for them to have asked not to have their unbecoming desires gratified with the food that was wanting, but to have their own dislike removed, and be made themselves to receive aright the food that was provided. For when evil becomes our delight, and what is good the reverse, we ought to be entreating God rather to win us back to the love of the good, than to grant us the evil. Not that it wrong to eat flesh, for the apostle speaking of this very thing says: "every creature of God is good, and nothing is to be refused that is received with thanksgiving;" but because, as he also says, "it is evil for that man who eateth with offense" (Rom. 14:20).

How then are we to understand "whatsoever ye shall ask in my Name, I will do it," if there are some things which the faithful ask, and which God, even purposely on their behalf leaves undone? Wake up O believer, and give careful heed to what is stated here: "in my name." In these words He does not say "whatsoever ye shall ask" in any way, but "in my name." How, then, is He called, who promised so great a blessing? Jesus Christ of course: Christ means King and Jesus means Savior. Clearly, it is not any king that will save us, but only the Savior-King. And therefore, whatsoever we ask that is adverse to the interests of salvation we do not ask in the name of the Savior. And yet He is the Savior, not only when He does what we ask, but also when He refuses to do so; since by not doing what He sees to be contrary to our salvation, He manifests Himself the more fully our Savior. For the physician knows which of his patient's requests will be favorable, and which will be adverse to his health; and therefore does not give into to the patient's wishes when they are prejudicial to his recovery. Accordingly, when we wish Him to do whatsoever we ask, let it not be in any way, but in His name, that is, in the name of the Savior that we present or petition. Let us not then ask anything that is contrary to our own salvation, for if He give what is contrary to our salvation, He does it not as our Savior which is the name He bears to His faithful disciples. For He who condescends to be our Savior is also a Judge to condemn the ungodly. Whatsoever, therefore, any one that believeth on Him shall ask in that name which He bears to those who believe in Him, He will do it; for He will do it as the Savior. But if one that believeth in Him were to ask something through ignorance that is injurious to his salvation, he asketh it not in the name of SAVIOR, for He would no longer be his Savior if he did anything that would impede his salvation. In such a situation He would not be doing what He is being asked to do. His way is kept the clearer for doing what His name states that He is.

There are some things which, although asked in His name, that is to say, in harmony with His character as both Savior and Master, which He does not respond at the time that we ask, and yet He faileth not to do them. For, when we pray that the kingdom of God may come, it does not imply that He is not doing what we ask, because we do not begin at once to reign with Him in the everlasting Kingdom. For what we ask is delayed, but not denied. Nevertheless, let us not fail to pray, for in so doing we are like those who sow the seed; and in due season we shall reap. And even when we ask Him for things that appropriate, let us at the same time ask Him not to do what we ask amiss; for there is also reference to this in Our Lord's Prayer when we say "lead us not into temptation." For surely the temptation is no slight one if thine own request be hostile to thy cause. (From the 75th Tractate on John.)[1]

---

1. Translated with assistance from Eerdmans edition of *The Nicene and Post Nicene Fathers* where it is listed as Tractate 74.

ST. GREGORY

If the Father gave us everything that we asked for in the Name of the Son, how is it that the Apostle Paul asked the Father for something three times and did not merit to receive it, but rather the Father said to him: "My grace is sufficient for you, for virtue is made perfect in infirmity." How is it that so great a petitioner asking in the name of the Son is not responded to? In what way then is it true that whatever we ask the Father in the name of the Son will be given to us? How could it be that a satanic angel asking the Apostles in the name of the Son should be refused? The answer is that the name of the Son, Jesus, means and is Savior, and therefore what is asked in the name of the Savior must pertain to salvation. And hence it follows that whatsoever is not expedient for salvation cannot be asked of the Father in the Name of Jesus. And so it is that our Lord said to Paul who was still suffering from his infirmity "hitherto you have not asked anything in my name" (John 16:24). It is as if He openly said, do not ask in the name of the Savior anything which does not pertain to your eternal salvation. And so it is that Paul's petition that he might be freed from temptation was not heard, for his request was not conducive to salvation. And so we see, dear brethren, that many come together to celebrate the feast days of the martyrs, on bended knee, striking their chests, offering up their prayers, and shedding copious tears. But examine, I beg you, what it is you are asking for. Consider whether or not what you are asking for is in the name of Jesus, that is to say, whether or not it is for the joy of eternal salvation. If in the temple of eternity you are seeking temporal things, you are not seeking Jesus in the house of Jesus. Some in their prayers ask for a wife, others for a country estate; some ask for clothing, others for food. And almighty God is asked for similar things. But we should always bear in mind that in accordance with His teaching, we should always desire our redemption. Seek ye first the kingdom of God and His justice, and all these things shall be added unto you. To ask this of Jesus is no mistake, and nothing greater can be asked for. But instead, which is even more serious, some ask for the death of their enemies—those who the sword cannot get to are to be struck dead with prayers. But God told us to love our enemies, so how is it possible that we should ask God to destroy them. Anyone who prays for such things is fighting against his Creator, and as it says in the Psalms "let their prayer be turned to sin" (Ps. 108:7). Their prayer is indeed turned to sin, for they ask for what is forbidden. For it is truly said that when one stands in prayer, "you should first of all forgive, if you have aught against any man in your heart" (Mark 11:25).

Alban Butler

WHILE NOT A CANONIZED saint, Alban Butler is nevertheless a person of considerable authority in the Church. He along with Bishop Challoner, are considered to be the two most prominent Catholics that graced the English isles during the eighteenth century. Born in 1710, he was brought up as a Catholic and, after finishing his early education, was sent to Douai in Belgium where he went through the full course and was ordained priest in 1735. Because of his scholarly achievements—he was known to study even when riding a horse—he was asked to stay on, first as professor of philosophy, and then as professor of theology. He is best known for his Lives of the Saints, the product of some thirty years of research and published between 1756–59. This text even today remains a standard reference, though readers should avoid the version edited by Father Thurston who in typical modernist fashion as removed all that smacks of the miraculous. He returned to England in 1746 and acted as a mission priest in various parts of the Midland District, and later as chaplain to the Duke of Norfolk. In 1766 the presidency of the English college at St. Omer in France fell vacant and Alban Butler was appointed to this position. Among his many works are *The Moveable Feasts and Fasts* from which the following is taken.

THE FEAST OF THE HOLY NAME OF JESUS

The devout Christian soul which has learned to know her divine Redeemer, the author and finisher of her salvation, and being crucified to the world, and all sensual appetites, and having purified her affections from all infection of their poison, is capable of tasting the sweetness, and comprehending the glory and happiness of his holy love, finds him in every mystery and in every circumstance, infinitely amiable and infinitely adorable. Every feast in his honor, she embraces and celebrates with unspeakable spiritual joy and devotion. That of his holy Name seems in some measure to comprise every mystery, every mercy, every title of honor, every benefit, every grace, every effort of divine love, which we adore in the whole process of His Incarnation, Life, Death, Resurrection, Ascension, and Coming as sovereign Judge of the living and the dead. This sacred Name of Jesus presents to our mind the majesty and glory of His Divinity, the most endearing charms of his humanity under the character of the divine Savior and eternal spouse of our souls. The adorable Name of Jesus was given by the Father to his only co-eternal Son, to be the title of his supreme majesty, power and dominion, and of his glorious victory over sin and hell, and to express in Him the unexhausted source of all grace, blessings and comfort which He is to us.

The holy Name Jesus was given to our blessed Redeemer at his Circumcision. It was a devout custom among Jews to name the male children at that religious ceremony, a custom derived from their holy Patriarch Abraham; for when he was circumcised, God changed his name, i.e., High Father, into Abraham, which signifies Father of Multitudes.[1] It was indeed most fitting, that at the time when a person is enrolled among the children of God, honored with His alliance, and most precious graces, and made heir to His eternal

---

1. Gen. 7.

promises, he should then take a name, which may be a title, or badge of honor, and always put him in mind of the sublime character which he bears, from which he dates a new heavenly life. Christ would take His August Name at his Circumcision, to conform Himself in all things, not only to the ordinances, but even to the pious customs of the people of God, and of the law, to teach us to conceive the greatest love and esteem of, and the most scrupulous fidelity in all the religious practices and rites of the Church. This ceremony was also most suitable for taking this sacred name which signifies savior, because he showed Himself our Savior, by offering the first fruits of His precious blood, the price of our redemption.

We must not imagine that an angel, or St. Joseph, or the Virgin Mary herself, gave this name to the divine Infant; St. Luke assures us that the archangel Gabriel brought it from heaven before the Christ was conceived.[2] It was then revealed to Mary; it was again discovered by an angel in another vision to St. Joseph.[3] These visions and revelations serve to raise our expectation and veneration of this mystery, lest we should look upon it with indifference; they were only preparatory; the mystery was reserved to God Himself; it was necessary that God Himself should give the name to His own Son. None but the eternal Father had such a right amongst men; even it is the father's prerogative to name his children, and those names are most suitable which agree to, or express the nature and most essential excellence of the things which they signify. Adam, who knew the natural properties of all living creatures upon earth, gave to each a name expressive of its nature. Among the ancient patriarchs and our own remote ancestors, parents who knew not the characters of future dispositions or actions of their children, often borrowed their names from trifling circumstances which attended their birth, or from imaginary qualities with which they hoped they would be endowed; in which how often did the event disappoint

---

2. Luke 1:31.
3. Matt. 1:21.

their expectations? We frequently see the most illustrious names borne by the most infamous of men; Christ ought to bear the name which best expressed His most adorable character: The Father alone knew perfectly the unmeasurable excellencies of his dignity, nature and functions: He alone fully comprehended His con-substantial and co-eternal Word: the boundless perfections of His divine nature and person; the unsearchable mystery of His Incarnation, or His quality of Redeemer of the world. No angel, no creature, in heaven or earth, is capable of comprehending these His perfections and mysteries, each of which is an abyss which no finite understanding can fathom. The Father alone to whom the right belonged, and who knew Him from eternity, could give Him a name agreeable to His sacred character and dignity. Some prophets have received names from heaven, but not as Jesus, to whom God Himself assigned a title, which He bears to eternity. For this mystery God chose the most suitable time; beholding His son the object of His infinite complacency and love, clothed with the veil of a created nature, in the likeness of sinners, subjected to the humbling knife of circumcision, in order to honor Him before all creatures, declared that he was no sinner, but that he was innocence and sanctity itself who came to justify sinners. This He did by bestowing on him a name of glory; a name above all other names, at the sound whereof all creatures are bound to bend their knees and adore Him. The word Jesus signifies Savior[4]: The Jews could not be surprised to hear the divine infant called by this name which had been taken by many others. We meet with Jesus or Johosuah the son of Nun, of Jesus the son of Sirach, and Josephus mentions a certain Jew called Jesus, who foretold the impending ruin of their city and nation; but in these, the name was only an appellative, a shadow, not expressing any reality,

---

4. Jesus in Hebrew Josuah or Jehosuah, i.e., Savior. See St. Thomas Qu.47, a. 2. Suarez 2. In 3. St. Thomas. Tom. ii Disp 15, Secl. 2. *Non ad instar priorum meus iste Jesus Nomen vacuum and inane portat: est in eo magni nominis Umbra sed veritas.* St. Bern. *Serm.* I. Dominica.

or at most, it denoted only a deliverer of a particular nation from slavery or other temporal calamities: It was not so in our divine Redeemer. "This my Jesus," says St. Bernard, "He does not bear an empty name which imports nothing: it is not just the shadow of a great name, but the Truth." He is truly and actually our great, our only Savior, who has rescued us from sin and that deluge of infinite evils and endless miseries into which it had plunged us, moreover purchased for us all good, all the advantages of grace, and an immense eternal bliss and glory; lastly, has subdued and triumphed over death and evil, and delivered man from their jaws by his redemption. This wonderful salvation he has wrought at the infinite price of His incarnation, sufferings and death, from which mystery the God-head itself receives an infinite glory, superior beyond all comparison to that which accrues to him from the homages and fidelity of all mere creatures; a glory commensurate to his own immensity and worthy of him. In recompense of this victory is Christ's humanity exalted above all mere creatures; as man. He is declared by the Father in an order far above them all, and appointed by Him supreme judge of all men, the living and the dead. The most illustrious Roman conquerors often took names or titles of honor from countries which they had subdued, or from some great victory or exploit; as the African, the Asiatic, the Parthian, the Germanic, the Dacic, etc. This was foolish flattery and idle vanity: But nothing in God Himself challenges our homages of adoration and love in a stricter and more sacred manner than His goodness and mercy which is over all His works. Nor does this attribute shine forth in any of them with such a bright and overpowering blaze as in the Incarnation. It was therefore most suitable that He should take His name from this glorious work of our salvation, and his victory over the devil and sin: Nor could any name be more glorious in Him, or more amiable to us. He hath saved us, and that by humbling Himself even to the death of the cross; for which cause God has exalted Him, and hath given Him a name which is above all names; that in the name of Jesus every knee should bow, of those that are in heaven, on earth and under the earth, and that every tongue should confess that the Lord Jesus Christ is in the glory of God the Father.[5] This name presents to us the God-Man, who is the true God, proceeding from the true God, infinitely holy, wise, powerful and merciful, made man to become our savior, showing pledges and tokens of mercy and love, bearing the marks of His sufferings for us, prints of His wounds, and displaying all the charms of grace and virtue; Him in whose faith and name alone we can be saved[6]: in whose redemption Adam believing was raised from his sin; Him at the sight of whose day to come Abraham exulted with joy[7]; Him whom all the prophets foretold, and all the ancient just sighed after, and solicited heaven for with continual tears; who was the desired of all nations,[8] and the desire of the eternal hills[9]; the end of the law[10]; the omnipotent Word, who from eternity dwells in the bosom of His Father[11]; in whom are locked up all the treasures of wisdom and science[12]; who is one with His Father[13]; born of Him from eternity[14]; truly the Son of God; whom the Father loves and in whose hands he has put all things[15]; and loves all who love Him[16]; the perfect substantial image of the Father, in whom all his infinite perfections are expressed[17]; the figure of His substance, the splendor of the eternal light, the uncreated wisdom, His eternal

---

5. Phil. 2:9-11.
6. Acts 4:12.
7. John 3:10; 14:6.
8. Haggi 2:8.
9. Gen. 69:26.
10. Rom. 10:4.
11. John 1.
12. Col. 2:3.
13. John 10:20.
14. Ps. 119.
15. Matt. 17:5; John 3:35.
16. John 14:23.
17. Heb. 3; Sap. 6.

self-existing Word[18]; who doeth all that the Father does[19]; by whom all things were made[20]; in whom all things are and subsist[21]; the heir of all things[22]; to whom the Father has given us and all nations[23]; He is our only mediator[24]; brings us to the Father and reconciles us with Him[25]; takes away all our iniquities[26]; and effaces the handwriting which was against us, and all the bonds of our debts[27]; is our most merciful Redeemer[28]; delivering us from the slavery of sin and all evil with the price of His blood[29]; our eternal high priest offering himself for us[30]; in whom we are filled with all blessings[31]; our victim voluntarily offering Himself[32]; and presenting supplications for us[33]; our victim on the cross by the effusion of his blood[34]; and continued in an unbloody sacrifice on our altars[35]; our pattern and model in carrying his cross and in all sanctity and virtue.

Our father of whom we are born not only by creation but more gloriously in spirit, and by predestination to his grace and glory[36]; the king of kings and lord of lords, whose spiritual kingdom is of all

---

18. John 1, etc.
19. John 5:29.
20. John 1:3.
21. Col. 1, Sap 9:26.
22. Heb. 1; Heb. 11:1–8; Ps. 8.
23. John 16; 16; Ps. 11.
24. Tim. 2:5.
25. John 14:6; Eph. 4:19.
26. Eph. 1:16.
27. Col. 2:14.
28. Isa. 12:14; Col. 1:13; Rom. 8:2; Gal. 4:4; Heb. 9:14–15.
29. 1 Pet. 1:18; 1 Cor. 6:20; Tit. 2:14.
30. Heb. 5:5; Ps. 100:9; Ps. 44; Heb. 7:26, 10:11–12.
31. Eph. 1:4.
32. Eph. 5:2; 1 John 3; 1 Pet. 1:24; John 5.
33. Heb. 5:7; John 17:17.
34. Heb. 7:22.
35. Mal. 2; 1 Cor. 11; Heb. 10:14, 11:28.
36. Isa. 9:6; Heb. 11:13.

nations, and of all ages[37]; in particular, king of our souls by his love, by which he reigns in us by the continual display and effusion of his graces, and by the homage and obedience of our hearts and all our powers and faculties[38]; our head, in whom we are fellow members and one with him[39], by the union of charity, and the most sacred incorporation in him, with the abundant effusion of his merits and graces; our most loving and faithful spouse[40]; the way which leads us to God; the life of our souls, the eternal and unchangeable truth; our doctor and legislator; our bread and our strength, our light and comfort and joy; our peace, our judge, our happiness, and our true end. All these and other titles which the Holy Scriptures attribute to Christ, this holy name comprises, with the abstract of all the other names which are given him by the Holy Ghost, as the strong God who disarms the power of hell, the admirable, whose life and doctrine are full of incomprehensible mysteries; the father of the age to come, or of the church of saints, the prince of peace who reconciles all things in heaven and on earth; the Christ, or anointed by his Father, with the plenitude of grace, the Messiah or who was to be sent, Emmanuel, or God with us; the prophet emphatically so called, etc. For all his other qualities flow from, or make up his character of Savior. This glorious name calls to our mind the holy zeal, love, and ardent desire of our salvation, his meekness, mercifulness and goodness, with all his other divine virtues, the torments and ignominies which he suffered for us, the mysteries which he performed, and all he has done for us, and all the benefits he has conferred upon us. This glorious name expresses also in him the source of all graces.

---

37. Eph, 1; John 12; 1 John 3.

38. Apoc. [Rev.] 19:6; Zach. 9:19; Luke 3; Ps. 144:13; Luke 13; 1 Cor. 12:24–28.

39. Eph. 3:17; John 4:16.

40. Eph. 1; John 14:5; Mal. 9:5; Col. 1; Eph. 5:30; Apoc. 19:7, 21; 2 Cor. 11:2; Apoc. 22:17.

The faith, hope, charity, humility, purity, devotion, and other virtues of all the saints, all the gifts, spiritual beauty, and glory, with which they are adorned, are the rich fruits of Christ's salvation. There is no other name under heaven given to men whereby we must be saved.[41] Of his plenitude we have all received.[42] From his salvation and victory we derive also all our strength, and all the victorious graces, by which we overcome our spiritual enemies. This name must always excite our veneration and love, and give glory to God, and be most pleasing to him. This name of Jesus, pronounced or repeated in the heart in a spirit of love and prayer, is most powerful. By it the servants of God have often commanded all nature, restored the dead to life, cured all distempers, and filled the world with miracles. St. Peter healed the lame man, by saying "in the name of Jesus of Nazareth, arise and walk."[43] By it the powers of darkness have been disarmed in every part of their empire; of it we may repeat, the name of the Lord is to be praised from the rising of the sun to the setting thereof.[44] Over all nations and provinces is the sound of the name of Jesus heard. St. Bernard cries out, "O name! Worthy of all blessing and praise." Its sweet perfume was shed from heaven upon Judea and thence spread over the whole earth. The Church in all parts of the world sings, thy name is oil poured out; its perfumes have not only filled the heaven and earth, but have also reached hell, though in a very different manner. All creatures are invited or compelled to pay their homages and repeat in concert, thy name is an oil poured out.

It is a name of terror to the devils, who tremble at the sound when it is devoutly pronounced; not that the material syllables contain any virtues or charm, but they are drove away by the power of him who is pleased with the love, confidence and devotion of those

---

41. Acts, 4:12.
42. John 1:16.
43. Acts 3:6.
44. Ps. 112:3.

who in these sentiments honor and invoke his name. And the infernal spirits are dismayed and disarmed at the thunder of that holy name by which they are vanquished and which they are compelled to adore. Hence it has often chased them out of those whom they corporally possessed, and when devoutly invoked, it weakens the power of the tempter in his assaults. That Christians thus, by an ordinary rule, expelled devils out of demoniacs in the primitive ages is attested by the unanimous consent of the Fathers, and other writers of those early times. Any devil adjured by the name of Christ, is vanquished and subdued, says St. Justin,[45] the most learned and ancient primitive Father and martyr. And in his second apology before the Roman senate, within fifty years after the death of the Apostles, he says he is called Christ because he is anointed; which very name has in it a mystical signification. As also the appellation God, is not a name but a sign of something unutterable added to a human nature. But Jesus has both the name and the signification of Savior: For he was made man according to the decree of him who is God and the Father, for the salvation of men who believe in him, and to overthrow the devils; as you may understand from the things which you now see. For many over the whole world, and even in your own city (Rome) itself, possessed by devils, were cured and set free. The devils themselves have been vanquished and driven away by some of our Christians adjuring and exorcizing them in the name of Jesus, after all other exorcists and enchanters had tried their skill in vain to help them.[46] The devils are vanquished by the name of Jesus Christ.[47] St. Gregory Nazianzen says Julian the apostate passed a law, commanding Christians to be called Galileans, not from Christ, because he looked upon this latter as a name of honor, unless, perhaps he did this because like the devil, he dreaded the name of Jesus. And writing to Nemesius a heathen, he says, nor

---

45. *Dial cum Tryphone* 161.
46. St. Justin, *Apol.* ii, ad Sen. n. 5, p. 172 ed, Cantabrig. Anne. 1768.
47. 1b. No. 8, p. 178.

ought it to seem surprising that Christ had so great power, for I myself, who believe in him, most frequently have scarce pronounced his name, when the devil speedily betakes himself away with noise and indignation, proclaiming the power of the immortal God, which has also frequently happened to me when I formed the figure of his cross, not only on a board, but even in the bare air: For the figure alone is his standard erected. It is affirmed by Tertullian, the most ancient Latin Christian writer, who bids the Pagans spill on the spot the blood of that Christian whose prayer, in the name of Jesus, should fail to cast the devil out of a demoniac presented to him.[48] With such confidence did the Christians of those days challenge the heathens to the trial, that none of their oracles, and no fiends in persons possessed by them, could stand the sound of the holy name of Jesus, or the sight of the cross. This is more powerfully experienced against the spiritual assaults of the devil. St. Theresa and others show from daily experience, the like powerful succor in time of temptations from the humble and earnest invocation of Jesus through his sacred cross and precious blood.

The Name of Jesus is the strongest incentive of emulation and edification in every virtue, with the ardent love and sentiments of which it inspires us from the perfect model which he sets before us, and by the grace of him who is honored and invoked by it. When we religiously pronounce it, or call Jesus to mind, we represent to ourselves the most humble, the most tender, charitable and meek of heart, the most spotless, innocent, and holy, the most chaste and merciful of men; a divine man endowed with all sanctity, all grace, all virtues. We, at the same time, represent to ourselves that this man is also the omnipotent God, who whilst he sets before us on one side, the example of his holy life to imitate, gives us on the other, light, strength, and grace to copy after it, and to form our hearts and conversation upon this perfect model: All manner of good things present themselves to my mind, when the name of Jesus sounds in

---

48. *Apolog.* C. xxiii.

my ears, says St. Bernard. We must never repeat the holy N
without sentiments of adoration and love, and without feeling a
earnest desire and resolution of imitating him who is the Holy of
holies and the perfect pattern of sanctity. This requires great fervor
and courage, for the world and the passions raise violent storms, and
throw snares and difficulties in our way. But we must be resolved to
pursue steadily the path set before us, without regarding any dis-
grace, contradictions, and sacrifices, which it may cost us. We have
not yet resisted to blood, nor borne a cross like our Redeemer's. If
we have him before our eyes, we shall cheerfully embrace all tribulations and ignominies for his sake. Jesus will be our strength if we
carry his name always in our hearts: If we ask the apostles, martyrs,
and all other glorious saints, whence they drew their invincible
courage, by which they conquered the world and hell, they will all
point out Jesus, and proclaim the power of his Name, in which
alone they were saved. He who said to his disciples: "In my Name
they shall cast out devils,"[49] has promised to all who call upon his
Name, strength to repulse all their fiery darts, and triumph over all
tribulations. The cross on which is written the name of our great
Captain, is the standard of our spiritual warfare, in which we place
our glory and all our confidence: "We shall rejoice in thy salvation,
and in the Name of our God we shall be exalted."[50]

If the adorable name of Jesus, when invoked with devotion be
a shield of omnipotence to protect us in battle, it is a fountain of
inexpressible sweetness and joy to all true lovers of their God and
redeemer: Its very sound filled their whole hearts with love and pleasure, awaking our attention and love to our infinitely gracious and
amiable God and Savior, made man for our sake. For us he lay in a
manger, wept, was circumcised, loaded with calumnies and
reproaches, was buffeted, scourged and crucified. For our justifica-
tion he rose from the dead, ascended in glory, and sits at the right

49. Mark 16:17.
50. Ps. 19:6.

hand of the Father. The saints never could satiate their souls, burning with his love, in repeating this sacred Name with adoration and tender devotion. Augustin, even before his baptism and conversion, tells us that he found much delight in Cicero's book, now lost, called Hortensius, which contained a beautiful pathetic exhortation to love and pursue wisdom, but adds, in this so great ardor one thing only displeased me, that I found not there the name of Christ. For this name, through thy mercy, O Lord, this name of my Savior thy Son, my tender heart had piously imbibed with my mother's milk, and deeply retained; and whatever wanted this name, how learned, how elegant, or instructive soever it might be, did not perfectly satisfy me.[51] Many will say they feel nothing of this sweetness and delight; this may sometimes be an effect of an interior trial of spiritual dryness or desolation of the soul; but to many we may answer: How should they be delighted or comforted with this name who have no feelings of love, and are all coldness and indifference towards him, whose hearts are even enslaved to criminal passions, and full of irregular desires of worldly honor, riches, and pleasure. Ah! Bring one of those souls that love their crucified Jesus, and she will feel and understand what is here said.

Our devout countryman, St. Aelred, in his preface to his book on spiritual friendship, tells us that after he had once tasted the sweetness of this holy Name, the eloquence of Tully, with which he had been formerly much delighted, became dry and insipid to him, because he could relish nothing where he did not meet with that adorable name of Jesus, or something which called it to his mind. St. Jerome remarks that St. Paul repeats often the name of his dear Redeemer, even where it is superfluous, and sometimes where it rather renders the sense of the text embarrassed; he would name him whom he loved, even needlessly, and out of place, which the attentive reader may observe in all his epistles, without remarking it, says he. St. Bonaventure writes in his life of St. Francis that this seraphic

---

51. *Conf.* 1.iii. C.4.

lover recited the psalms with great devotion of spirit, and when the name of God occurred in them, he showed in his accent and features an inexpressible sweetness which his heart felt in that word, out of tender love and veneration: He once persuaded his brethren to pick up and lay in some decent place all written papers found on the ground, lest the name of God should occur in them and be trampled on. When he pronounced and heard the holy name of Jesus, he was filled interiorly with jubilee of heart, so as to appear altered exteriorly in his body as if ravished with some sweet sound or taste. St. Francis of Sales, exhorting a superior of a nunnery never to leave Jesus alone in spirit, because he makes it his delight to be with us and to have us present: To him, he adds, the breasts of the sweet Jesus are full of delicious milk, and are, as it were, painful unless some spiritual babe present itself to receive the delicious juice of his love. This we do by amorously invoking his Name, at least in spirit, and uniting ourselves with him in heart and affection. The same tender lover of Jesus writing to a devout widow, begins thus his letter: I have no time to write and write only the great name of salvation, Jesus; O could, O could we once pronounce this holy Name of salvation from our hearts, what sweetness would it diffuse to our souls. How happy should we be, had we nothing in our understanding or mind but Jesus; nothing in our will but Jesus; nothing in our memory but Jesus; nothing in our imagination but Jesus. In all things Jesus would be to us, and we should be in all things to him. But alas! I cannot express what I mean by pronouncing this holy name. To speak of it, or to express it, we ought to have a tongue of fire.[52] St. Paulinus in elegant verse cries out, O God, O Christ, thou art all sweetness, all love, thou canst rather fill than satiate, thou communicatest thyself to us, yet art the more thirsted after thou art received by our souls, yet love not sated.[53] St Bernard writes, I take to myself his example from his humanity, and succor

---

52. L. ii. Ep. 27. and l.viii. Ep. 10.
53. Carm. De celso Puero.

from his omnipotence; of these I make up a sovereign healing composition, the like of which no one among the physicians could ever make. This electuary, thou hast, my soul, laid up in a little vessel of his name, most powerful to heal every pestilence in thee. Let it be always in thy breast, always in thy hand, that all thy thoughts, desires and actions, may be directed to him. In the same place he compares the name of the spouse to oil, for as oil furnishes warmth, healing physic and food, so this name enlightens and warms the soul, feeds and cherishes the affections of the heart, heals its sores, and assuages its pains. Art not thou comforted and strengthened, says he, so often as thou callest it to mind? What so fills the soul with sweetness and spiritual joy! What so recruits the wearied spirits and senses, repairs inward strength, gives vigor to virtue, cherishes pure affections? All food of the soul is dry if this oil be not poured upon it. It is insipid unless seasoned with this salt. If thou writest, it does not relish to me unless I read there Jesus. If thou disputest or holdest a conversation, it does not relish to me unless the sound of the name of Jesus be heard there. Jesus is honey in the mouth, music in the ear, jubilation in this heart. This name is also the sovereign healer: Is any one among us overwhelmed with sorrow? Let Jesus come into his heart, and thence into his mouth; and behold at the light of this Name, all clouds are scattered, peace and joy appear, etc.[54] Devotion to the holy name of Jesus is a mark of the love which a soul bears him, and thus may it be called a badge of the predestinated. The saints in heaven bear it written on their foreheads, by the marks which they wear in their glory, that whatsoever they are or possess is derived from him. The whiteness of their robes, the luster of their crowns, the dazzling rays of the glory which surrounds them, their joy, their immortality, are his gifts; and of this they wear in their glory the shining ensigns, which proclaim loudly to all creatures his glory, grace, and victory, in all their virtues. This is that new name which no one knoweth but

---

54. See section on St. Bernard.

himself.[55] The saints on earth, and the whole Church militant, are also marked with this seal, and by it acknowledge that they belong to the Lamb, and receive from him all their spiritual beauty and advantages. The name of Jesus expresses the excess of love which he bears us; also his infinite mercy in which he has healed all our wounds, procured preservatives and remedies against all vices, delivered us from the power of the devil, reconciled us to his Father, satisfied his justice, canceled all our debts, and removed all the obstacles of our salvation. This name, whenever we repeat it, must awake in our breasts our most tender love, in return for his infinite love; it must excite in us the strongest sentiments of gratitude and devotion, and an ardent desire to dedicate our souls with our whole strength to his love and service, and to draw others to the same. Thus St. Paul repeated this holy name so often, because his language was the effusion of his heart, which tasted in it the sweetness and felt the ardor of his love. In these sentiments he labored so much to make this adorable name known to all men, had it so frequently in his mouth and continually in his heart: such must be the devotion of our heart whenever we pronounce it. Thus it will be at once an act of faith, hope, charity, compunction, supplication, and entire oblation and sacrifice of ourselves to God. In these sentiments we cannot repeat it too often especially in temptations, dangers and tribulations. Jesus! Jesus! Jesus! be to me a Jesus, show mercy and save me: no one speaks it thus but he who loves, says St. Augustine.[56] It is likewise a homage of adoration and praise to our Redeemer.

Jesus is a name of triumph and glory, given him to be the title of honor which he bears to eternity, and which expresses his glorious victory over sin and hell. A victory in its object, manner, advantages, and all its circumstances, the most astonishing mystery, the most incomprehensible in itself, the most adorable to all creatures, and the most honorable to the Deity, to which it procures a homage

55. Apoc. 19:12.
56. Tr. 4 in Joan.

equal to his immensity. This name of the glory of our Redeemer ought to be most venerable to all who love him, or have the least spark of zeal for his honor. We are obliged to honor this name, not only out of duty and gratitude, but also by obedience to his father, who, to honor his son with him, has commanded that every knee in heaven and on earth, in religious awe and devotion, and in hell, by constraint and fear, should bend to adore him at the sound of his religious name. It is an ancient law and custom of the church, that all the faithful testify their veneration for the holy name of Jesus by bowing their head whenever they pronounce or hear it. This ecclesiastical precept is confirmed by the general council of Lyons, recorded in the body of canon law. Many Protestants of the church of England observe this pious custom, both in public worship and elsewhere; and many of their learned prelates and theologians have proved against the rigid Calvinist, that it is a wholesome act of religion, conformable to the divine precept of honoring this name.

The councils of Avignon for that province, and of Bezieres for that diocese, granted in the fourteenth century, an indulgence of ten days to those, who in dispositions of sincere contrition for their sins, devoutly bow their head in pronouncing the holy name of Jesus. Pope Sixtus V gave an indulgence of twenty days for the whole church on the same condition. Every faithful lover and faithful adorer of our crucified Redeemer Jesus, is struck with horror to hear his holy name, at the sound of which angels adore with awe and love, and devils tremble, impiously profaned, filling up impious exclamations and idle unmeaning discourses, and the most horrible oaths, execrations and blasphemies; such horrible impiety kindles in our breasts an ardent zeal to repair his honor by making all amends in our power by compunction and the most fervent homages of adoration, praise and love.

Against the impious custom of swearing, a pious confraternity was erected by Pius IV, and confirmed by St. Pius V, and Urban VIII, with the grant of a plenary indulgence, on the feast of the Circumcision of our Lord, and of one hundred days each time, for hindering a rash oath, or blasphemy in another. Every member is obliged to correct or pray for a person who swears rashly in their hearing. It is their first salutation, when they meet any one on the road to address them in the doxology; "praised be God," or "praised be Jesus!" which practice is recommended by an indulgence given to persons in the confraternity every time they devoutly use this salutation, or answer it by crying "Amen!" This is extended by other concessions to all the faithful: for Sixtus V in 1587, granted to all Christians an indulgence of fifty days, every time a person salutes another with these words, either in Latin or in any vulgar language: "praised be Jesus Christ!" and as many to him who shall answer "Amen," or "forever," or "through all ages." An indulgence of twenty-five days to those who shall pronounce with reverence and devotion the name of Jesus, or that of Mary, with a plenary indulgence of the article of death; if having made this salutation their habitual practice, they shall then piously invoke Jesus in their hearts, if they are not able to do so with their lips, and an indulgence of three hundred days each time, for piously reciting the litany of Jesus, two hundred for that of the Blessed Virgin Mary. These indulgences were confirmed by Benedict XIII in 1728.[57]

If we are bound never to mingle the adorable name of Jesus in profane discourse, but to honor it with exterior respect in our words and behavior, we ought to be solicitous to accompany this with great sentiments of interior veneration, awe and devotion, and never to pronounce it but with hearts penetrated with holy dread and respect, and animated with love and confidence by the Holy Ghost. Thus we shall always find it a name of sweetness, love, and heavenly comfort; a name of sanctity, and all virtues; truly a name of salvation. Jesus is to us all our good, our Savior, our King, the spouse

---

57. Indulgences are a way of quantifying the value of any given spiritual act. The effects of such acts can be applied to the souls in Purgatory to relieve their suffering and hasten their entry into heaven. They can also be applied to the benefit of the individual who "earns" them.

of our souls, our physician, our protector, our advocate, our light, our strength, our comfort, our joy, our only God, our only sovereign and eternal happiness. To unite ourselves to him in heart and spirit under all these characters, and to consecrate ourselves to his love, and implore his continual succor, we ought often to repeat to him in our hearts, with the most feeling sentiments of devotion; "Jesus, Jesus, my Jesus, and my all!"[58] Through him we must offer all our devotions to the adorable Trinity. In his name we must perform all our actions: whatever you do in word or in work, do all things in the name of our Lord Jesus Christ.[59] Our greatest happiness must be ever to engage him to bless the beginning, the process, and the end of all our undertakings, and all our actions; to be animated more and more perfectly in all we do with the Holy Spirit, and always to bear him in our hearts by his divine love. But in sentiments of profound adoration, love, praise, compunction, humility, confidence, and earnest supplication, we ought to bear this sacred name in our heart, and at prayer to have it often in our mouth, especially in all distresses and agonies of death; and lest we should not then be able to pronounce it, let us do this with all possible devotion in our daily evening prayers for our last hour. He says to every one of us, *"put me as a signet upon thy heart, as a signet upon thy arm"* (Song of Sol. 8:6); we must prepare and open our hearts to him, that he may engrave on them his name in indelible characters of love, in order to inflame all our affections; likewise in our minds, that we may make him the most noble and the darling object of our thoughts. We must also engrave it on our arm, making him the beginning and end of every thing we do, that he may heal our irregular desires, strengthen our weakness, banish sloth, inconstancy, and pusillanimity, and enable us to execute the good resolution with which he inspired us; that thus all our senses and actions be invariably directed to him and his love. The same love and zeal ought to

---

58. St. Ambrose, l. de Viror.
59. Col. 3:17.

engage us to do all that lies in us to contribute to the propagation of the glory of Jesus, of the kingdom of his love, and of the veneration of his name. O that all men would be induced to pay him their homages, that all tongues were employed in singing his praise, and in proclaiming aloud the sweetness of his love, the excellence of his perfections, and the power of his name. O that amongst men, whom he so mercifully redeemed, every knee on earth would bend at its sacred sound, as without exception do all, not only in heaven, but also in hell. O divine Jesus! cries out a devout servant of God, on thee depends my happiness, my life, and my death; whatever I do shall be done under the patronage, and in thy name: if I watch, Jesus shall be before my eyes; if I sleep, I will close my breathing his pure love, if I walk, it shall be in the sweet company of Jesus; if I sit, Jesus shall be at my side; if I study, Jesus shall be my master; if I write, Jesus shall conduct my hand and pen. It shall be my highest pleasure to write his holy name. If I pray, Jesus shall form and animate my prayers; if I am fatigued, Jesus shall be my rest; if I am sick, Jesus shall be my physician and comforter; if I die, it is in the bosom of Jesus, who is my life; and I hope to die. Jesus shall be my tomb, and his name and cross my epitaph. To live united in spirit with Jesus, will be the best means of living every day more and more perfectly by his spirit, and of being sanctified by him in all our actions, thoughts, and words. By adoring and invoking Jesus so frequently in the day, that we may do it in desire and virtually in every action, we make our whole lives a perpetual sacrifice of praise and love to him, in the perpetual adoration of his divine majesty, in acknowledgment of his infinite power and sovereignty, and of all his mercies and benefits, especially of his sacred incarnation and death. The Emperor Justinian gives the reason for this practice among all Christians, because says he, we never can return due thanks and praise for the infinite benefit of his incarnation. By the same practice we consecrate to God, and sanctify all our actions and thoughts through our Redeemer. The same Emperor says in his Code to the Roman Law, we always proceed in all deliberations and all actions in the name of our Lord Jesus Christ. And he begins his Institutes by this solemn prayer: "In the name of our Lord Jesus Christ." He begins also particular laws by the same, or by this which is equivalent, and which our English municipal law retains in the ordinary form or style of wills: "In the name of God, Amen."[60] The primitive Christians expressed it by the sign of the cross before every action. And we may make this sign with our thumb on our breast, or at least repeat this invocation by a single fervent humble thought, without the danger of any one perceiving or taking notice of it. This agrees even with the style and practice of the heathen Greeks and Romans borrowed from the people of God. In that city, which in beginning and undertaking any manner of affairs, has recourse to the gods, says the great historian of Rome.[61] The Greeks opened all their councils by a sacrifice.[62] Hence the custom of their poets to begin every composition by the invocation of some divinity, which even Lucretius observed. What the first principles of reason or the law of nature ingrafted in all hearts taught the heathens in the midst of the darkest ignorance and spiritual blindness, and degeneracy of manners: what the divine precept, promulgated by the Apostle inculcates: sentiments of religion, love and gratitude, and duty to our God and Redeemer, ought to make us find our principal comfort and happiness in, as well as our constant obligation and great eternal interest.

The perpetual union of our souls with God, in Jesus Christ, will be the sacrifice of our whole lives to him, and the most easy and perfect means of our sanctification in all our actions and moments. We want no other prompter and incentive to it than a sincere and ardent love. This will render it not only easy, but even the greatest and uninterrupted joy of our lives. We shall soon find by experience,

---

60. Justin. *Code.* 1. I, tit. 27, leg. 2.

61. Livy, and Cicero Orat. *Pro Muraena initio.,* Plin. *Panegyr. Initio,* etc.

62. Cf. Aristophanes and Taylor in his *Elements of the Civil Law, Let. On Justice.*

and feel in the innermost powers of our souls, how sweet God is to those who love him, and who seek him with their whole hearts, and that his conversation has no bitterness, nor his company any tediousness, but joy and gladness.

Besides such assiduous aspirations, we ought to have regular hours and devotions, to honor Jesus at leisure, and with greater recollection in our closets, or at the foot of the altar, in presence of the adorable sacrament. We may recite with singular devotion, at certain times every day before Mass, or so often every week, the litany of the name of Jesus, recommended by an indulgence of 300 days, each time a person in the state of grace recites it. We may have, at least, set days for the short office of the incarnation, compiled by the devout Henry Suso, or that by Cardinal Berulle; the litany of the name of Jesus, or other devotions in honor of the mystery in Blosius, etc. Nothing will more contribute to stir up and entertain in our souls the most fervent love of Jesus and the most ardent devotion to his holy name, than frequent devout meditation on his holy life and adorable mysteries, at least a quarter of an hour a day may be set apart for such an exercise; or we may read with interruptions, so as to dwell on pious aspirations and resolutions, some part of the Gospel, or in the meditations on the life of Crist by Lewis de Puente; or those by F. Lewis of Granada; or at least, a short Lecture in the Life of our Lord Jesus Christ by F. Neveu; or in F. St. Jur's Armour de Connoisance de J. C. Every Friday ought to be consecrated by some extraordinary mortification and devotion, in honor of the sufferings of Christ, and every day, at least, by some short prayer: and if at any time we hear the holy name of God, or of Jesus, profaned by a blasphemy or rash oath, our heart should be ready to burst asunder with bitter grief. If we were not able to prevent, or correct such horrible sacrileges, as persons who are not under our jurisdiction, we ought in spirit to cover our heads with ashes, and make what amends we are able by an interior act of humiliation, adoration, and praise, saying, with the blessed in heaven, "Hallowed be thy name," or with Habakkuk (3:18), "I will rejoice in the Lord, and exult in God my Jesus or Savior." By aspirations and devotions, and love, praise and thanksgiving, we ought to return incessant thanks to God, for this incomprehensible mystery of the incarnation, and death of the Son of God. In this spirit we cannot too often repeat the Canticles of Praise which the Holy Ghost has dictated in the divine scriptures as the Canticle of Zachary, or the Benedictus, that of the Blessed Virgin, called "the Magnificat," etc. In this spirit, St. Dominic instituted The Rosary, to teach the most ignorant, an easy method of devoutly entertaining themselves on the principal points of the incomprehensible mystery of the incarnation, by which all our devotions are rendered acceptable to God, and for which our whole lives ought to be one perpetual sacrifice of gratitude and praise. In a transport of lively faith and thanksgiving, the devout Jewess in the gospel, pronounced "the womb blessed which had born him, and the breasts which had given him suck." The Hail Mary" is repeated ten times in the Rosary, that the mind by dwelling longer on the same great mystery, may be enlightened the better to understand it, and the heart more inflamed with love in praising God for it.[63] If the blessed Virgin is pronounced Blessed, it is through her divine Son, and he is praised as infinitely blessed, and worthy of all homages, as the heavenly choirs sing in the Revelations of St. John. In honor of this mystery was the triple angelical Salutation called the *Angelus* instituted to be said morning, noon, and evening, by Pope John XXII, in 1316, introduced into France under Lewis XI, in 1472. A Plenary indulgence is granted to all,

---

63. Those who take offence at the "Hail Mary" or its frequent repetition, certainly do not reflect that it is a doxology in honor of the incarnation, the most adorable and incomprehensible of all the divine mysteries and benefits, for which we can never return sufficient homages of thanksgiving and praise, though we devote to it all our powers and faculties, and all our moments. These forms of words ought to be most unexceptionable, being dictated by the Holy Ghost and recorded in Scripture by his special inspiration, for the comfort, edification, and instruction of the Faithful, through all ages, to the end of the world, and to serve to nourish their piety and devotion.

who having been at confession and communion on any day in the month, at their choice, shall say on their knees the *Angelus* at morning, noon, and evening, when the bell rings, and 100 days, as Benedict XIII declares in his Indult dated September 14, 1724. The same Pope, by a brief, dated the December 5· 1727, extended these indulgences to those religious persons who being hindered at that hour, shall recite it afterwards when at liberty. Benedict XIV confirmed these indulgences on the April 20, 1742, adding that during the whole Paschal time, the anthem with its verses and prayer, *Regina coeli*, is to be said standing, in place of the *Angelus*. Yet the indulgences are equally gained by those who not knowing the *Regina coeli*, shall say the Angelus, but this is to be said standing all the Paschal time and on all Sundays. The Church expressed her devotion to the holy name of Jesus, on the feast of the Circumcision, which is most remarkable in the old English Liturgy, both that in use before the Conqueror, and that of Sarum. St. Bernadin of Sienna, preaching penance in the chief cities of Italy, to exhort the Faithful to the love and service of our divine Redeemer, used at the end of his Sermons, to show the holy name of Jesus surrounded with rays of glory, painted on a board. Some found fault with this practice as a novelty; and by the Pope's ordering, the cause was discussed in solemn conference, or disputation in the Vatican church in 1427. St John Capistrano zealously defended the practice of his colleague, as proper to excite the devotion of the Faithful, with precautions to prevent all danger of superstition, so that it was approved by the holy see. A particular office in honor of Christ, in memory of his sacred name, was composed by F. Bernardin de Bustis, a frior minor, and some time after allowed by Clement VIII to the Franciscan order in 1430, to be said on January 14. It was extended to the Carthusians in 1643, on the second Sunday after epiphany, as appears from their breviary printed that year at Lyons; afterwards to the Spanish dominions; and lastly, by Innocent XIII in 1721, to the whole church on the second Sunday after Epiphany.

A Note on the "Hail Mary"[1]

IN THE HAIL MARY we are above all, not to pass over as insignificant those words of the evangelist, "And the name of the virgin was Mary" (Luke 1:28). For her very name is not without a mystery and ought to be to us a most amiable, sweet, and awful. "Of such virtue and excellency is this name that the heavens exult, the earth rejoices, and the angels sound forth hymns of praise when Mary is named," says St. Bernard. She is truly the star which arose from Jacob, and which, being placed above this wide, tempestuous sea, shines forth by the merits and examples of her life. "Oh! You who find yourself tossed in the tempests of this world, turn not your eyes from the brightness of this star if you would not be overwhelmed by storms. If the winds of temptations rise; if you fall among the rocks of tribulations, look up at the star, call on Mary. If you are tossed by the waves of pride, ambition, detraction, jealousy, or envy, look up at the star, call on Mary. If anger, covetousness, or lust beat on the vessel of your soul, look up to Mary. If you begin to sink in the gulf of melancholy and despair, think of Mary. In dangers, in distresses, in perplexities, think of Mary, call on Mary; let her not depart from your lips; let her not depart from your heart; and that you may obtain the suffrage of her prayers, never depart from the example of her conversation. Whilst you follow her, you never go astray; whilst you implore her aid, you never sink in despair; when you think on

---

1.   This passage is taken from Father Michael Muller's *The Devotion of the Rosary and Five Scapulars,* originally published by Benzinger Brothers in 1878, and more recently republished by Preserving Christian Publications, P.O. Box 6129, Albany, N.Y., 12206.3.

her, you never wander; under her patronage you never fall; under her protection you need not fear; she being your guide, you are not weary." Such are the sentiments of confidence, devotion and respect with which the name of Mary ought always to inspire us.

Next to this holy name the words of salutation come to be considered. "Hail" is a word of salutation, congratulation, and joy. The archangel addressed it with profound reverence and awe to this incomparable and glorious virgin. It was anciently an extraordinary thing if an angel appeared to one of the patriarchs or prophets, and then he was received with great veneration and honor, being by nature and grace exalted above them; but when the Archangel Gabriel visited Mary, he was struck at her exalted dignity and preeminence, and approached and saluted her with admiration and respect. He was accustomed to the luster of the highest heavenly bodies, but was amazed and dazzled at the dignity and spiritual glory of her whom he came to salute Mother of God, whilst the attention of the whole heavenly court was fixed with ravishment upon her. With what humility ought we, worms of the earth and base sinners, to address her in the same salutation. The devout Thomas a Kempis gives the following paraphrase of the Angelic Salutation: "With awe, reverence, devotion, and humble confidence do I suppliantly approach you, bearing on my lips the salutation of the angel, humbly to offer you. I joyfully present it to you, with my head bowed out of reverence to your sacred person, and with my arms expanded through excessive affection of devotion; and I beg the same may be repeated by all the heavenly spirits for me a hundred thousand times and much oftener; for I know not what I can bring more worthy of your transcendent greatness, or more sweet to us who recite it. Let the pious lover of your holy name listen and attend. The heavens rejoice, and all the earth ought to stand amazed when I say 'Hail Mary.' Satan and hell tremble when I repeat 'Hail Mary.' Sorrow is banished, and a new joy fills my soul when I say 'Hail Mary.' My languid affection is strengthened in God and my soul is refreshed when I repeat 'Hail Mary.' So great is the sweetness of this blessed salutation that it is not to be expressed in words, but remains deepeer in the heart than can be fathomed. Wherefore again I most humbly bend my knees to you, O most holy Virgin, and say: 'Hail Mary full of grace.' Oh! That, to satisfy my desire of honoring and saluting you with all the powers of my soul, all my members were converted into tongues and into voices of fire, that I might glorify you, O mother of God, without ceasing! And now, prostrate in your presence, invited by sincere devotion of heart and all inflamed with veneration for your sweet name, I represent to you the joy of that salutation when the Archangel Gabriel, sent by god, entered your secret closet, and honored you with a salutation unheard from the beginning of the world, saying 'Hail, full of grace, the Lord is with thee'; which I desire to repeat, were it possible with lips pure as gold and with a burning affection, and I desire that all creatures now say with me, *Hail*."

In like sentiments of profound respect and congratulation with the angel, we style her full of grace. Though she is descended of the royal blood of David, her illustrious pre-eminence is not derived from her birth or any other temporal advantages, but from that pre-rogative in which alone true excellency consists, the grace of God, in which she surpasses all other mere creatures. To others, God deals out portions of his grace according to an inferior measure; but Mary was to be prepared to become the mother of the Author of grace. To her, therefore, God gave every grace and every virtue in an eminent degree of excellency and perfection. "Mary was filled with the ocean of the Holy Ghost poured upon her," says Venerable Bede (in Mt. C. 1). It was just that the nearer she approached to the fountain of grace, the more abundantly she should be enriched by it; and, as God was pleased to make choice of her for his Mother, nothing less than a supereminent portion of grace could match her transcendent dignity. The Church therefore applies to her that of the Canticles: "Thou art all fair, and there is no spot in thee" (Song of Sol. 4:7).

In the words "the Lord is with thee" we repeat with the angel another eulogium, consequent of the former. God, by his immensity and omnipotence, is with all creatures, because in him all creatures have their being. He is much more intimate with all his just, inasmuch as he dwells in them by his grace, and manifests in them the most gracious effects of his goodness and power; but the Blessed Virgin, being full of grace and most agreeable in his eyes above all other mere creatures, having also the closest union with Christ as his Mother, and burning with more than seraphic divinity, she is his most beloved tabernacle, and he favors her with the special effects of his extraordinary presence, displaying in her his boundless munificence, power, and love.

The following praise was given to her in the same words both by the Archangel Gabriel and St. Elizabeth: "Blessed art thou amongst women." Mary is truly called blessed above all other women, she having been herself always preserved from the least stain of sin, and having been the happy instrument of God in converting the maledictions laid on all mankind into blessings. When Judith had delivered Besthulia from temporal destruction, Ozias, the prince of the people, said to her; "Blessed art thou, daughter, above all women upon the face of the earth" (Judith 13:23). And "the people all blessed her with one voice, saying: thou art the glory of Jerusalem, thou are the joy of Israel, thou are the honor of our people." How much more emphatically shall we, from our hearts, pronounce her blessed above all women who brought forth Him who is the author of all manner of spiritual and eternal blessings to us. She most justly said of herself, in the deepest sense of gratitude to the divine goodness, "Behold, from henceforth, all generations shall call me blessed" (Luke 1:48).

By bestowing these praises on Mary, we offer principally to God a profound homage of praise for the great mystery of the Incarnation. The pious women mentioned in the Gospel who, upon hearing the divine doctrine of our Redeemer, cried out with admiration, "Blessed is the womb that bore thee, and blessed are the breasts which gave thee suck" (Luke 11:27), meant chiefly to commend the Son. In like manner, the praises we address to Mary in the

Angelical Salutation are reflected in the first place on her divine Son, from whom and by whom alone she is entitled to them: for it is for his gifts and graces and for his sake that we praise and honor her. On this account, the prayer is chiefly an excellent doxology for the great mystery of the Incarnation. Whence, having styled the Mother blessed above all women, we pronounce the Son infinitely more blessed, saying "And blessed is the fruit of thy womb." He is the source and author of all her graces and blessings; she derives them only from him; and to him we refer whatever we admire and praise in her. Therefore, in an infinitely higher sense of praise, love, and honor, and in a manner infinitely superior to her, we call him blessed forever by God, angels and men: by God, as his well beloved Son, and in his divinity coequal and coeternal with the Father; by the angels, as the author of their being, grace, and glory, inasmuch as he is their God; by men, in his Incarnation as the repairer of their losses and their Redeemer. We, considering attentively the infinite evils from which he has delivered us, the pains and labors which he sustained for us, the ransom which he has paid with his precious blood to redeem us, the everlasting and infinite advantages which he has purchased for us with the boundless felicity of heaven, the excess of his goodness, love, and mercy, and his infinite majesty and perfection—we, I say, bearing all this in mind, ought in a spirit of love and praise ever to call her blessed through whom we receive so great a Savior; but him infinitely more blessed, both for his own adorable sanctity and for all the graces of which he is the source.

The most holy and glorious name of Jesus, which is added to this doxology, is a name of unspeakable sweetness and grace—a name most confortable and delightful to every loving soul, terrible to the wicked spirits, and adorable with respect to all creatures. So that at its very sound every knee in heaven, on earth, and in hell shall bend, and every creature be filled with religious awe and profound veneration and respect.

The last part of the prayer is a supplication. The prayer of the blessed spirits in heaven consists chiefly in acts of adoration, love, praise, thanksgiving, and the like. We, in this vale of tears and miseries, join sighs even to our hymns of praise and adoration. So extreme are our spiritual wants and trials, that we never present ourselves in prayer before Almighty God without imploring his mercy and graces with the greatest earnestness possible and the deepest sense of our needs. It is in this sincere feeling of our necessities and the most humble and earnest cry of our heart that the fervor and very soul of our prayer consist. God knows, and with infinite tenderness compassionates, the depth of our wounds and the whole extent of our numberless and boundless spiritual miseries. But our insensibility under them provokes his indignation. He will have us sincerely feel and acknowledge the weight of our evils; our extreme spiritual poverty and total insufficiency, the baseness of our guilt, the rigor of his judgements, the frightful torments of an unhappy eternity which we deserve for our sins, and the dangers from ourselves and the invisible enemies with which we are surrounded. He requires that we confess the abyss of miseries in which we are sunk, and out of it raise our voice to him with tears and groans, owning our total dependence on his infinite mercy and goodness. If a beggar ask an alms of us, his wants make him eloquent—he sums them all up to move us to compassion; sickness, pains, hunger, anguish of mind, distress of a whole family, and whatever else can set off his miseries in the most moving manner. In like manner, when we pray we must feel and lay open before our Heavenly Father our deep wounds, our universal indigence, inability, and weakness, and with all possible earnestness implore his merciful aid. We must beg that God himself will be pleased to form in our hearts and sustain such sincere desires, that he inspire us with a deep sense of our wretchedness, and teach us to lay this before him in such a manner as will most powerfully move him to pity and relieve us.

We have recourse to the angels and saints to beg their joint intercession for us. For this we address ourselves in the first place to the Blessed Virgin, as a refuge of the afflicted and of sinners. In this prayer we repeat her holy name to excite ourselves to reverence and devotion. By calling her Mother of God, we express her most exalted dignity, and stir up our confidence in her patronage. For what can she not obtain for us of God, who was pleased to be born of her! We at the same time remember that she is also spiritually our *Mother*, for, by adoption, we are brothers and coheirs of Christ. She is to us a mother of more than maternal tenderness:; incomparably more sensible of our poverty and weakness, and more ready to procure for us all mercy and assistance, than mothers according to the flesh can be, as in charity she surpasses all other mere creatures. But to call her mother, and to deserve her compassion, we must sincerely renounce and put an end to our disorders, by which we have too often trampled upon the blood of her Son.

These words, "Holy Mary, Mother of God," are a kind of preface to our petition, in which we humbly entreat her to pray for us. We do not ask her to give us grace; we know this to be the most precious gift of God, who alone can bestow it on us. We only desire her to ask it for us of her Son, and to join her powerful intercession with our unworthy prayers. We mention our quality of sinners to humble ourselves in the deepest sentiments of compunction, and to excite her compassion by laying our extreme miseries and wants before her, which this epithet of sinners expresses beyond what any created understanding can fathom. Mary, from her fuller and more distinct knowledge of the evil of sin, and the spiritual needs of a soul infested with it, forms a much clearer and more exact idea of the abyss of our evils than we can possibly do and, in proportion to them and to the measure of her charity, is moved to compassionate us under them. But we must mention our sins with sincere sentiments of contrition and regret; for the will which still adheres to sin provokes indignation, not compassion, in God and in all the saints, who love his sanctity and justice above all things. We must, therefore, mention our guilt with the most profound sentiments of confusion and compunction. In proportion to their sincerity and fervor, we shall excite the pity and mercy of God and the tender compassion of his Mother Mary, having borne in her womb the Author of grace and mercy, has put on the bowels of the most tender compassion for sinners. By this mention of our quality of sinners, we sufficiently express what it is that we beg of God—namely, the grace of a sincere repentance, the remission of all our sins, and the strength to resist all temptation to sin. We ask also for all graces and virtues, especially that of divine charity. All this is sufficiently understood by the very nature of our request without being expressed; for what else ought we to ask of God through the intercession of her who is the Mother of the Author of grace? We beg this abundance of all graces, both *at present*, because we stand in need of it every moment of our lives, and for the hour of our death, that great and most dreadful moment, which must be a principal object of all our prayers. The whole life of a Christian ought to be nothing else than a constant preparation for that tremendous hour which will decide our eternal lot, and in which the devil will assail us with the utmost effort of his fury; and our own weakness in mind and body, the lively remembrance of our past sins, and other alarming circumstances and difficulties, will make us stand in need of the strongest assistance of divine grace and the special patronage of her who is the protectress of all in distress, particularly of her devout clients in their last and most dangerous conflict.

Amen, or so be it, expresses an earnest repetition of our supplication and praise. As the heart in the ardor of its affections, easily goes far beyond what words can express, so neither is it confined by them in the extent and variety of its acts. In one word it often comprises perfect acts of faith, hope and charity, adoration, praise and other such virtues. Thus by amen it repeats with ardor all the petitions and acts of the Lord's Prayer and the Angelical Salutation. Some devout persons have made this short but energetic and comprehensive word one of their most frequent aspirations to God during the course of the day—meaning thereby to assent to, confirm, and repeat, with all possible ardor and humility, all the hymns and perfect acts of profound adoration, humility, love, praise, zeal, thanksgiving, oblation of themselves, total resignation, confidence in God, and all other virtues, which all the heavenly spirits offer to God, with all their power and strength, and with the utmost purity of affection, without intermission to eternity. In these acts we join by the word Amen, and desire to repeat them all with infinite fervor, were it possible, for ever, and with them we join the most sincere sentiments and acts of compassion and a particular humility, condemning ourselves as infinitely unworthy to join the heavenly choirs or faithful servants of God in offering him a tribute of praise; most unworthy even to pronounce his most holy name or mention any of his adorable perfections, which defiled lips and faint divided affections rather profane and depreciate than praise and honor.

Such are the sentiments of faith, hope, charity, gratitude, humility, and sorrow which we express in reciting the Hail Mary: such are the graces and favors which we ask in a few words of which the Hail Mary is composed. Were we to say the prayers of all prayer books we could not express deeper sentiments of religion than we do in the Hail Mary, nor ask for greater favors than we pray for in the Angelic Salutation. No wonder, therefore, that all good Christians always delighted in repeating most frequently the Our Father and the Hail Mary.

APPENDIX

The Hesychast Prayer
in the Orthodox Church [1]

THE PROBLEM OF methodology in the Hesychast Prayer cannot be separated from that of prayer in general as understood by the Eastern Orthodox tradition. Nor can one speak of prayer as something isolated from the totality of the spiritual life. I shall therefore start by situating Orthodox teaching about prayer in the broader context of the spiritual life. Let us start by discussing the concept of [the soul's] union with God—of necessity in a brief manner—as understood in the Eastern Orthodox Tradition, and then discuss the means of achieving this union.

I will refrain from making comparisons or drawing parallels with non-Christian traditions, principally because I do not have the necessary knowledge. I will however point out certain equivalents with the Western Church's tradition because most of us have our roots in this tradition and this will perhaps allow some of you to better situate what I have to say because of being able to see their connection with concepts more familiar to you.

---

1. Originally published in *Connaissance des Religions* and translated by the editor. Published with permission of the editors of *Connaissance des Religions*. The author at times exaggerates the differences between the Eastern and Western churches and many of the Church Fathers he quotes are a common heritage of both churches.

1 - UNION WITH GOD IN THE EASTERN ORTHODOX TRADITION

1) For everyone connected with this tradition which derives primarily from the Greek Fathers—though the Latin Fathers are certainly not excluded—*Union with God is conceived of as a veritable deification* which the spiritual writers, following the Fathers of the Church readily express by means of metaphors which express a true compenetration of the divine and the human: metaphors such as that of red-hot iron or iron penetrated by fire, like iron which while remaining iron, nevertheless acquires luminosity and warmth which are the properties of fire. Or again by analogies such as a burning coal or a crystal penetrated by light.

Consider the following statement taken from St. Maximus the Confessor who is one of the Fathers who has in a most penetrating manner written about the doctrine of the union of man and God: "Deified man no longer himself wishes anything: he is like the air, completely illuminated by the sun, or iron completely penetrated by fire. This is what Christ the Savior said to the Father, realizing in himself the type, model or exemplar of what we should become: *Not as I will, but as Thou wilt.* And after him the admirable Apostle St. Paul said, as if denying himself and no longer knowing if he had any life in himself: *if I live, it is not I, but Christ who lives in me.* And thus, there is in such situations, only one and the same common energy between God and those who are like God. (The term "energy" is here used in the sense of the pouring forth or radiation of being, of the profound effulgence which is the nature of being.) I repeat, there is thus only one and the same common energy between God and those who are like God, or rather, the energy which is uniquely God's and which compenetrates those who are like him in accordance with His goodness."

This text alludes to a doctrine which is more or less fundamental in Eastern Orthodox tradition: the distinction in God between

His essence and His energy. With regard to all these realities, we naturally express ourselves within the limits of human ability and hence always in a less than perfect manner. What the Fathers however wished to tell us is that there is in God a mysterious kernel which is beyond all knowledge and all communication; and also an effulgence which is truly divine, which is "something of God" if one may so express it, and which constitutes the eternal life of the [three] divine Persons, and which can be communicated to man. This deification is brought about in some manner (always one must express things with our human limitations) by a kind of penetration, or compenetration of man by this divine energy, by this effulgence of the divinity.

2) This immediately leads us to ask the following question: is the *deification of man* which would seem to be the ultimate purpose of all the spiritual life, *the becoming aware of something that already exists*, or is it *the result of a progressive transformation.?* For the Eastern Christian tradition, both statements are true. In effect, to some degree, it is a question of becoming aware of something that already exists, of something which is a given, and which is given in a certain way from the very beginning. The Orthodox tradition distinguishes in man—not all the Fathers do so explicitly, but expressing things in this way in no way distorts their thought— there is in man, as an initial gift of God, a sort of deiformity, a conformity of human nature in itself with God, which each man possesses from the moment of his creation, and hence from the beginning of his spiritual life. But this conformity of nature with God is conceived of as a point of departure, which the individual must build on in order to develop himself. And in order to achieve this development, two conditions are necessary: on the one hand a further gift from God, a gift which is gratuitous and which in no way depends upon man; and this immediately demands of man an attitude of openness and dependency, an attitude of welcoming the other, excluding all dependence on himself, all feelings of satisfaction with himself, and, if I may so express it, all temptation to take refuge in himself. On

the other hand, it requires the cooperation of human liberty. One can then say that there are three stages or steps in this conformity of man with God:

There is the fundamental conformity of human nature, a sort of point of departure which is present in each man, and which finds itself carried to the point of incandescence by the gift of the Holy Spirit. This gift, for the entire Christian tradition, is normally linked to the individual's entrance into the Church through Baptism, Baptism and Confirmation (the gift of the Holy Spirit, and the sacramental gift of the Holy Spirit) are not separable. These are the normal means for the participation of man with the Holy Spirit.[2]

What follows is the whole process of the development of the spiritual life by the cooperation, or as the Fathers say, by the *synergy* (*syn-ergie*), the constant cooperation between divine grace, the gratuitous gift of God, and human liberty which welcomes this gift in order to allow it to transform her and come to fruition in her. The Fathers often point to the distinction between these two fundamental steps, the initial phase and the phase of fuller development, which is the fruit of the cooperation between divine Grace and human liberty, by the two terms "image" and "likeness." These two terms are taken from the story of creation in Genesis where it is said that *God created man in his image and likeness.* For a certain number of the Fathers of the early Church (and this distinction has generally been preserved in the Eastern Orthodox tradition), the *image* corresponds to the initial phase of conformity between man and God, the fruit of the gift of grace, but also of the innate conformity of human nature with God—that predisposition of human nature which is made for God—and *likeness* corresponds to the full achievement of union with God or conformity to God. And the text of St. Maximus which I have just read to you concerns this last stage where man is entirely penetrated with God precisely because all

---

2. In the Eastern Orthodox Church, Baptism and Confirmation are often given simultaneously.

exercise of his own separate will, all self-will has disappeared, and the divine energy, the divine light is truly able to diffuse itself through and in him without encountering any obstacle.

3) *In this union with God*, as described, *man remains a person who is aware.* There is no complete absorption of man in God, but man remains, to use Christian terminology, a person, or to use the Greek, a *hypostasis*, though no longer an individual. In our every day experience we cannot conceive of a difference between people other than on the level of individual distinctions. We consider it as a axiomatic that no being can be distinguished from others except to the degree that it is something *other*, or insofar as there is something definable about it that, if I can so express it, makes it distinct and in so doing makes it different than the others. As Christians understand the Trinity, the Father, Son and the Holy Spirit are the same reality; they are one and the same thing, while at the same time they are three distinct persons. Once again, our word three is quite inadequate precisely because it is borrowed from our experience which is only accessible to individual perception. But there is something in this, I believe, that is terribly important: it is that the latter reality of the person is an essentially communicable reality, because in God the divine essence, the very being of God, is possessed in common by all three. Spiritual progress leads man to despoil himself of everything of an individual nature, to detach himself from his natural condition and all that he is, in order to enter in a total communion with God and with the others. Such however can only be approached in a completely antinomic fashion, because we are obliged at one and the same time to maintain an element of distinction, but a distinction in the bosom of a communion where every individual element that clings to our natural condition tends to efface itself. This then is, in a highly abbreviated form, how the Eastern Orthodox tradition conceives of the union of man and God.

II - HOW IS ONE TO ACHIEVE THIS UNION WITH GOD?

How, and by what means, is this union with God to be achieved? In what manner? Once again, one could say that it is realized in an antinomic fashion, at one and the same time by a going beyond one-self, by an *ecstasy*—I use the term ecstasy not in the sense of a psychological experience, but in the etymological sense of the word which is a going out of one-self, a leaving of one's "I" behind, and—by implication as I am about to explain—of an *enstasy* or a re-entry into oneself. And once again, we have here two antinomic situations, but it is essential that the distinction between the one and the other be maintained.

1) First of all it is necessary to go out of oneself. It is an absolutely fundamental principle taught by the entire Christian tradition that God, because of His transcendence, cannot in reality be reached by means of sensible perceptions or images, nor consequently by feelings that the individual is able to awake in himself by his own efforts; nor can He be attained by means of concepts of a rational nature. Only by means of what the Fathers call the "divine sense," a sort of new faculty, which if you like, is injected into man; only this divine sense can attain to God.

Here is what St. Gregory Palamas, a fourteenth-century saint of the Greek Church has to say upon the matter:[3]

> Men cannot unite themselves with this divine and incomprehensible light and see it unless they purify themselves by the fulfillment of the commandments and consecrate themselves to spiritual and

---

3. John Meyendorff, *A Study of Gregory Palamas* (London: The Faith Press, 1964); *The One Hundred and Fifty Chapters*, translated by Robert E. Sinkewicz (Pontifical Institute of Mediaeval Studies, 1988).

purifying prayer in order to receive the supernatural power of contemplation.

(It is this supernatural power of contemplation which is, as we shall see, the divine sense which alone can perceive God.)

How can we describe this power which depends neither on the activity of the senses nor on that of the intelligence? Certainly not otherwise than did Solomon.

(In the Book of *Proverbs*—utilizing a translation by Origin of the Hebrew which somewhat varies from that given in current versions of Scripture.)

In any event we will appeal to no less an authority than Solomon who was more greatly endowed with wisdom than any of his predecessors and who said: *it is both an intellectual and a divine awareness* (sensation). In coupling these two adjectives, he persuades his listener to consider it as neither a sensation nor an intellection. This "intellectual sensation" is thus different than either of these two entities.

(What he wishes to tell us is that this divine awareness which permits us to perceive our divine object has at one and the same time the character of an intellectual perception—but that is far more, because it is neither a concept nor something explicit—and on the other hand it has a quality of immediacy, of warmth, of experience, and of something felt. But it is neither a sensation nor an intellection. It is something beyond either of these.)

"One should then speak of it in this manner, or better still, following the great Denis" (Denis the Areopagite, the "pseudo-Denis")

One should call it a union, but not a knowledge: "it is necessary to know," he says, "that our intellect on

223

the one hand possesses an intellectual power which permits it to see intelligibles, and that, on the other hand, union which surpasses the nature of intelligence, links it to that which is transcendent.

(What St. Denis wishes to tell is that there are two faculties in us that can attain to what is spiritual: on the one hand, our intelligence in its natural function, but which allows us to attain to intelligibles by means of concepts in a knowledge which is expressible and can be formulated in concepts and notions; and then another part, which he calls union which is rather an awareness or perception of the presence of the divine, but which is superior and beyond all conceptional or notional perception.)

Or again: "the intellectual faculties as well as sensations become superfluous when the soul, having become deiform, surrenders to the rays of inaccessible light in an unknown union or blind flight.

(What he wishes to say here is that we are in a state of unknowing; when we attain to God, we are, as it were, blind to our natural faculties. Once again, it is neither by sensations, a sensible perception, nor by intellectual knowledge that can be formulated in concepts that we really attain to God. This is not to say that all the formulations about God are without any value: they all partake of truth, but they do not actually and vitally encompass God. As a famous author of the fourth or fifth century known under the name of Macarius of Egypt put it: "the ideas of God, the words by means of which we desire to express the divine realities, are like a glass of water painted on a wall. It can faithfully represent the reality but it does not quench the thirst.")[4]

---

4. *Fifty Spiritual Homilies of St. Macarius the Great* along with a brief life by Prof. Ivan Michailovich Kontzevich can be obtained from Eastern Orthodox Books, P.O. Box 302, Willits, California, 95490.

St. Gregory Palamas continues: "As for me, I consider that our holy faith is also, in a certain fashion, a vision of our heart which goes beyond all sensation and all intellection, for it transcends all the faculties of our soul."

(This is an extremely interesting statement because it shows us that there is a continuity between simple faith, which is to say, adhesion to the Word of God, the fact of believing, of believing what God has told us. We read in the Gospel that *no one has ever seen God*, but that *it is the Son who has revealed Him*, and that by adhering to this word of Christ beyond all that we can comprehend, sense, or perceive, we have a real knowledge of God. The faith, the simple faith, the mere adhesion to the word of God—responding to a profound instinct of our heart, one moreover placed there by the Holy Spirit, allows us to go beyond sensation and intellection. The faith already is truly proportionate to that which God is, but in a manner which is still obscure, which must be deepened. The "divine sense," the divine sensation about which St. Gregory Palamas speaks to us in connection with this initial faith, is in the last analysis only a development. It is the faith becoming conscious of its object, realizing it by a sort of interior instinct developed in us under the action of the Holy Spirit.)

> As for me, I consider that our simple faith is also a vision of our heart which goes beyond all sensation and intellection, that it transcends all the intellectual and sensible faculties of our soul. It remains thus a vision and an understanding of the heart which goes beyond all intellectual activities. By means of the true faith we have already left reason behind. Thus it is that one does not possess God by acquiring a knowledge of beings in one's heart. It is not by means of philosophy or by means of profane science. One *possesses God* by believing in one's heart that *Jesus is the Lord*, a belief established

within the individual who believes by means of simplicity of the faith.

In this text St. Gregory Palamas seems to approach the Western spiritual writers, notably St. John of the Cross who stresses very strongly—and I believe that it is almost the key to his entire doctrine—that the faith—in giving this word "faith" its full meaning, the inner sense that leads us to first of all go to the word of God, a faith which becomes more and more aware of its object, in the great awareness of presence—St. John of the Cross lays down, at the foundation of his spiritual synthesis, the principle that only the faith is proportionate to God, that only the faith allows us to truly approach God. It is in this sense that one can say that our perception, our experience of God and our deification, implies a going out of our selves while on the other hand, even though it seems paradoxical, union with God requires an entering into our-Selves.

2) If union with God is expressed in terms of a going out of one-self, of an ecstasy (ex-stasy), in so far as this implies the soul must strip off its normal manner of feeling, knowing, and also of loving—insofar as it implies a total renouncing, not only moral, but ontological on the level of the individual, a renouncing of one-self and of all things created —*union with God should be formulated in terms of an interiorization, of a return to one's true-Self*

> Consider the following text of St. Basil which so clearly stresses this: " The soul which is neither dispersed among exterior objects, nor distracted by the world of the senses, returns to its self and climbs by itself to the contemplation of God. Burning and resplendent with the divine beauty, it finds that it has forgotten of its own nature.

This text of St. Basil—a Greek text dating from the fourth century—synthesizes these two components, for it shows us that man, in reentering into him-self, at the same time depasses himself. This is because what he finds in him-self is precisely this presence of God, of the divine energy which transfigures him interiorly to the degree that he is open to it.

In order to better understand this, it is necessary to consider the statements of the Fathers of the Church—and also those of many Western spiritual writers, especially St. John of the Cross and those from Germany and Holland during the fourteenth century. These authors conceive of the spiritual path towards God according to the neo-Platonic schema of an emanation and return, of the going forth from God in some way by creation, and of the return to God by means of union with God. But if the schema is neo-Platonic, it nevertheless obscures these realities which despite this manner of formulation, do not conform exactly to the neo-Platonic doctrine. The neo-Platonic doctrine has been profoundly transformed by Christianity. In accord with this conception, as St. Maximus the Confessor said, "man exists in God from all eternity in so far as he is the *logos*," the *logos* being the uncreated thought of God. Moreover, for St. Maximus and the Orthodox Tradition, this uncreated thought or mind of God is not in the divine essence, but precisely at the core of the divine energies or, if you like, of the thought-will of God. Man is eternally thought by God and each man, and at the same time humanity as a whole, as the community of all human persons, and thus [each individual] man, for all eternity, exists in God as, if one can so express it, as an uncreated archetype. The projection, the image of each of us, exists in God from all eternity, and this idea, this thought-will of God with regard to each human being, is evidently that of divinized man. In the beginning God did not desire that man, like nature, should be sufficient unto himself in the order of nature, and so it came about that He added a gift, entirely gratuitously, of divinization, of deification. God, from all eternity, thought of man in accordance with the destiny that He had endowed him with, to be truly deified in Him. In creating man, God conferred on him—once again, it is very difficult to give expression to these things—an existence distinct from himself; but to say distinct from himself is not to say out of harmony with himself. Between man and God there is not, I will say, a reality which is partaken of in common. God and man are not two in a series of numbers which are linked by a common term.

Finding himself in existence, man is not yet divinized, but he is called to divinize himself. A the heart of his being, in that which the Fathers call the "*nous*," which is to say, in the superior part of the soul (which the Western spiritual writers call the "fine point of the soul" or "the most profound part of the soul," the "summit of the soul" or to use the phrase of St. John of the Cross, "the substance of the soul") in the deepest part of his being, is inscribed an innate instinct, a desire for God, for union with Him, which is in some way a constitutive part of his being. This is what is expressed in the oft quoted formula of St. Augustine—and which is therefore of Western origin—which corresponds so well with the thought of the Fathers with regard to the image of God in man: "You have made us for Yourself and our heart is not content until it rests in Thee."
It is in this intimate center of the soul that the action of grace comes and inserts itself by the action of the Holy Spirit. The presence of the Holy Spirit comes and inserts itself in order to give essential dynamism to this thrust, to this tendency which is at the heart of every being, inserting at the same time a supernatural quality through the very presence of the energy and efficacy of the Holy Spirit. And the progress of the soul will consist in its becoming aware of this essential desire, of this profound tendency towards God inscribed within her both by her nature and by the Holy Spirit. And this progress will involve, not only the discovery of this tendency, but also the consenting to it, and the adhering to it with one's free will.

This adherence will more and more take the form, not of a succession of deliberate acts (this will undoubtedly be necessary in the beginning, every time that the soul finds it necessary), but essentially of a *state* of welcoming of the gift with all one's being. This state, or if you wish, this gift of abandoning oneself to God, to this profound dynamism, on the part of the "essence of the soul," corresponds precisely to what deliberate acts are with regard to our faculties. When we perform an act, when we use our will to do something, this act of the will expresses itself by a distinct formal and expressible act. When we use our intellect, when we understand something, it is also an act which can be situated in time, an entirely formal act of our intelligence. As opposed to this, that to which we are called is more profound, it is a state, which is to say, a constant disposition, but it is something above and beyond distinct and deliberated acts. It is a kind of "consenting," if I can so express it, to a vital instinct. And it is this which will constitute the profound movement of the being. We will come back to this shortly.

As a result, the spiritual life of man who has already to some degree realized this deification, will be a profound consenting to an instinct, to a movement inscribed within him, taking support from his nature, but inscribed in him by the Holy Spirit which is present within him. This is why one can truly say that from this moment on, it is not the man himself who tends towards God, but rather the Holy Spirit within him. In a certain manner, when man enters into this divine eternal life, in the bosom of the Trinity where the Father loves the Son through the energy of the Holy Spirit, the Son also loves the Father by this same energy which re-ascends towards Him, and man is truly taken up, and introduced into this intra-divine life which is expanding in him by means of the action of the Holy Spirit. And St. Gregory Palamas particularly stresses this in saying that in the bosom of the Trinity—it is one of those rare Orthodox texts which give expression to it, but which is entirely accepted by this tradition—that the Holy Spirit, but not Holy Spirit in so far as it is a *hypostasis*—and here one finds a difference between Orthodox and Latin theology derived from St. Augustine and classical medieval thought—the Holy Spirit in so far as it is *energy*, the divine energy communicated by the person of the Holy Spirit, is a mysterious love which the Son uses with regard to the Father. The mysterious love of the Father for the Word mysteriously engendered, and which the Word, the well-beloved Son of the Father, himself uses towards the Father who engendered him. And it is this same energy of the Holy Spirit which man uses in order to love God, and also to love all his brothers and all of creation.[5]

III - NOW WE COME TO THE PATH TOWARDS UNION WITH GOD OR THE WAY WHICH LEADS MAN TO UNION WITH GOD.

1) It is certain that on this path towards unity with God, *the most important thing is prayer*, precisely because man cannot do anything without the help of God. Once again, man cannot approach God by means of his own strength, by means of his own faculties or his own means. It is necessary that God give him His Spirit in order to awaken in his heart this spiritual concern, this faculty for communion which renders union possible. And in the whole of spiritual warfare, throughout the entire struggle where victory is at stake—if one can speak of it in terms of a "victory"—perhaps a "welcoming" or the reception of the gift of God would be more appropriate, prayer will be the constant and indispensable weapon.

Here for example is what we read in *The Way of a Russian Pilgrim*, a book written in the last century and available in many pocket-book editions:[6]

---

5. It may not be without value to observe that theological differences between the Orthodox and Latin traditions are not to be viewed as contradictory or irreconcilable, but rather as representative of two main tendencies within Christianity which may perhaps be best described as complementary. In any case, let not these differences prevent Western Christians from savoring the high teachings of the Eastern Church and deriving benefit therefrom.

6. *The Way of a Pilgrim* and *The Pilgrim Continues His Way*, the translation by French and available from Harper and Row is recommended.

The Apostle Paul speaks in this manner about prayer: *I beg you before everything else to pray,* he says. Many good works are asked of the Christian, but the work of prayer is more important than all the others, for without it nothing good can be accomplished. Without frequent prayer one cannot find the joy which leads to God, one cannot know the truth, one cannot crucify the flesh with its passions and desires, one cannot be illuminated in the heart by the light of Christ and unite oneself with Him in salvation. I say frequent because the perfection and the accuracy of our prayer does not depend on us. As the Apostle Paul says: *We do not know what we must ask.* The only thing that lies within our power as a means to achieve purity in prayer which is the mother of all spiritual benefits, is frequency. "Grasp the mother and you will become a descendent" says St. Isaac the Syrian, teaching us in these words that in order to practice the virtues, one must first of all acquire the habit of prayer.[7]

And much closer to our times, Father Joseph the Hesychast almost a contemporary and one of the greatest of the spiritual fathers of Mount Athos, a man who has only recently passed away and who still has numerous followers on the Holy Mountain, said the following to Father Ephrem—who is currently one of the best known spiritual directors on Mt. Athos and in the Greek Orthodox world—I quote Father Ephrem:

---

7. *The Ascetical Homilies of Saint Isaac the Syrian* (Boston: The Holy Transfiguration Monastery, 1984).

My venerable teacher, Father Joseph, has often told this humble servant: if God conducts some souls between his hands, the indication of this is one thing: prayer. Prayer in turn teaches them everything else and sanctifies them. The prayer which my holy teacher had in mind is the meditative and uninterrupted prayer, the prayer of Jesus which he himself said throughout his entire life from the moment that he discovered it. He was so deeply absorbed in this prayer that he could go without eating, but never without the prayer.

Certainly, this in no way excludes the entire spectrum of activities associated with the spiritual life. *Prayer is not the only activity, but it is the most fundamental.* Moreover, it is in prayer that union with God is realized: once one arrives at a certain state, prayer itself will be the mode of realization of unity with God.

2) But the life of prayer itself leads to knowledge, as a result of which there is a complete development which corresponds to that growth of the spiritual life of which I spoke above: the full accomplishment of the passage from *image* to *likeness*. And here once again we meet with a given which is completely traditional, and which is accepted in Western Christianity as much as in the Orthodox tradition, namely the recognition of *a distinction between these two fundamental stages*. Granted, this is not an air-tight division—every distinction is by the nature of things a little artificial, yet despite this, there are two fundamental stages *of prayer*.

Here for example, for the West—this will perhaps provide you with a way of understanding what the Orthodox writers wish to convey—here is what a Western author, Father Marie Eugene of the Infant Jesus, says with regard to the Carmelite conception derived from St. John of the Cross and St. Teresa of Ávila, on the development of the life of prayer. He tells us that there are two quite distinct phases in spiritual knowledge.

In the first phase, God assures the soul of his ordinary grace, or general help, and leaves him to direct and initiate the spiritual life. In the second phase God intervenes progressively in the life of the soul by an assistance which is called special or particular, which becomes more and more powerful, lifting the initiative from the soul, and imposing on it submission and abandon until at last, the perfect reign of God is established, and the soul becomes the true son of God, being renewed by the Spirit of God.

We effectively find this distinction between the two phases of the spiritual life throughout the Orthodox Tradition. But once again, one cannot establish a strictly chronological succession between them. There is rather a sort of compenetration between the two phases. The one does not absolutely exclude the other.

Here for example is what a contemporaneous author, Monseigneur Kallistos Ware, an Orthodox Bishop in England writes. Summarizing the doctrine of the Orthodox Fathers he says:

The prayer of the heart takes two distinct forms. One, these are the very words of Theophane the Recluse (A famous Russian spiritual author from the last century): 'the one is difficult. The individual forces himself to achieve it by himself. The other is spontaneous as when the prayer exists and acts by itself. In the first stage the prayer is still something that man offers by his own conscious effort, naturally assisted by the grace of God. In the second the prayer arises spontaneously by itself. It is given to the man as a gift. It appears to him as if he were taken by the hand and forcibly led from one chamber to another. It is no longer the man who prays, but the Spirit of God which prays in him. Such a prayer which is bestowed as a gift, can only occur occasionally.

(Once again we see the coexistence of these two modes or forms of prayer.)

On the other hand, it can also be continuous. In the second case, the prayer follows no matter what one does, whether one speaks or writes. It prolongs itself in dreams and awakens the man in the morning.

(St. Isaac the Syrian tells us that the movements of a purified heart are like an incessant psalm raising towards the invisible.)

Prayer is no longer a series of acts, it becomes a state.

(This is what we have said above: a sort of state of permanent consenting, an interior instinct which expresses itself in all aspects of life and all the person's actions.)

Prayer is no longer a series of acts, it becomes a state. And then one discovers how to accomplish the commandment of Paul to *pray without ceasing*. According to the instructions of Isaac the Syrian: 'When the Spirit makes its home in a man, that person cannot cease to pray, for the Spirit constantly prays in him. Then, whether he be awake or asleep, the prayer never stops in his soul, whether he eats or drinks, whether he is lying down or working, and even when he is in the deepest sleep, the perfume of the prayer breathes spontaneously in his heart.

Fundamentally, the prayer has truly become an instinctive condition, the profound movement of the entire being.

We have then presented in a synthetic manner the two phases of prayer such as tradition reveals to us.

3) *The Active phase of prayer*, that in which we truly make an effort, a conscious effort, a succession of acts in order to pray.

In the Orthodox tradition—and at this point it diverges from the Western tradition such as it developed after the middle ages and in the sixteenth century—this active phase of the life of prayer, of the spiritual life, will be characterized not by what the Western writers call discursive meditation, but by vocal prayer; by concentrated vocal prayer. You know that in the West methods of prayer were developed which utilized the discursive intelligence, reflection, even feelings and the imagination. Certainly, little by little the entire process became simplified in order to arrive at a prayer which was truly contemplative. But the Western tradition, more or less according to the school of spirituality, very much insisted—again, we note, after the middle ages—on the need for discursive meditation, reflection accompanied by feelings or "affections" as they are called, in the practice of prayer. The Eastern tradition is much more reserved with regard to this and the normal form of prayer for man, as long as he is in this first phase of his spiritual life, will be the vocal prayer said with concentration. And this is extremely important: it is necessary, according to an expression constantly repeated by the Orthodox writers, an expression taken from St. John Climacus—perhaps the greatest spiritual writer of the Greek Church in the seventh century—"it is necessary to imprison the intellect in words." Which is to say that when one prays, it is necessary to be entirely concentrated on what one says, but without "reflection" on what one says, and without going beyond that in order to produce in oneself any feelings, more or less forced which one constructs oneself in one way or another.

An author who published a rather good book on Russian monasticism, Father Victor Arminjon, summarizes in the following manner the teaching of a famous Russian spiritual director of the last century, the bishop Ignace Briantchaninov, whose principal writings are about to be published in the collection "Spiritualite Oriental" by the Abbey of Bellefontaine under the title: *Approaches to the Prayer of Jesus.*[8] It is a very remarkable book, one full of great wisdom while at the same time being extremely practical. And here is how one can summarize the teaching of Bishop Ignace Briantchaninov with regard to the prayer of beginners—it being well understood that one remains a beginner in the spiritual life for a long period of time:

> Bishop Ignace Briantchaninov shows himself entirely skeptical with regard to so-called personal prayer that finds its food in the imagination, in self love poorly camouflaged, and in insuffiently controlled feelings. To a monk, returning to his cell after having conscientiously fulfilled his obligations of public and official prayer (by the offices and chants of the Church), the Bishop proposes another office of individual prayer to be recited by him in solitude.

(And the prayer of the monk—but also that of any Christian—which can become a fervent spiritual prayer, resembles very much the prayer of the Church, and because of that, a liturgical prayer, and this by usage of established texts and formulas.)

> He insists that one be faithful to this. He affirms that the repetition of traditional prayers, elaborated by skilled and knowledgeable masters, immersed and nourished by Patristic and Scriptural sources, and indeed, delineated by the Fathers of the Church and Holy Scripture, have a much greater value than anything that the individ-

---

8. *On the Prayer of Jesus*, translated by Father Lazarus (London: Watkins, 1964).

ual can come up with by himself. Canonical prayers, even when used in private, have been polished and refined by monks over the ages, and as a result, they offer a richness of expression and a poetic rhythm which in no way prevents the person who recites them from deriving a legitimate sense of pleasure. But, in the opinion of bishop Ignace Briantchaninov, the quality of the person's attention and the tranquility of recitation, is far more important than the number of pages read or prayers recited.

Another contemporary author, Tito Colliander, author of an excellent short treatise also published in the Bellefontaine "Collection of Eastern Orthodox Spiritual Writers" (*Spiritualite orientale*) says much the same thing in another manner: with regard to the prayer formulas that the person starting out on the spiritual path is invited to use he tells us:

> These prayers are the fruit of the Church's experience culled over the centuries. By means of them we join the vast community of the people of God in prayer. You are not alone, but rather a cell in the body of the Church which is the Body of Christ. The recitation of these formulas will also gain for you the necessary patience which not only the body, but also the heart and the soul require in order to strengthen your faith. When the heart and soul unite with the words spoken, true prayer results. Thus attention or concentration is indispensable. Do not allow your thoughts to wander about. Each time that you find yourself distracted, bring yourself back to that place where you are. You can recite the Psalms in the same way. And in

this manner, you will learn to practice perseverance
and vigilance in prayer.

What is recommended here is to have a text of prayer and, simply to enclose one's soul in it, to be attentive to God in one's faith and to say to God what is in the words off the text; to refuse to allow the soul to turn away and engage in useless and strange thoughts, but simply, without embroiling oneself in reflecting on what one is saying, or trying to reproduce in oneself sentiments and emotions of some kind or another. I shall come back to this point shortly.

When we come down to practical practice, personal prayer involves two things; short prayers which are texts that are somewhat elaborated, and which the monk willingly uses for prayers in his cell; and then the *prayer of Jesus*.

The prayer of Jesus consists of this very short invocation which is founded on the Gospel texts themselves: "Lord Jesus Christ, Son of God, have pity on me." or " have pity on me, a sinner." And the greater part of the personal prayer of the monk, or simply of the layperson who wishes to deepen his spiritual life, will consist of unceasingly repeating this prayer of Jesus. This in two different fashions: on the one hand by consecrating a certain amount of time each day, a time which is exclusively given over to this prayer; and on the other hand, throughout the entire day of repeating it every time one can let the soul express itself, no matter what one is engaged in doing. But, according to circumstances, this can be done in a completely interior manner, even such a small act as the simple glance of the soul raising itself towards God.

And the repetition of this prayer of Jesus, this very simple formula, according to the Orthodox tradition, has a three-fold benefit:

1) A certain *impoverishment of the discursive intelligence*. It is in point of fact an extremely short prayer, the content of which is, from a certain point of view, conceptually minimal. At the same time, if I can so express myself, it contains everything. But in no way does it encourage the mind to deliberate or to be distracted, not

even with regard to spiritual or religious subjects. It is the simple supplication of the soul before Christ, in the presence of God. Thus it is a prayer which from the start incorporates a very great simplification of mental and intellectual activity, and which at the same time places the individual on the path of discovery of that profound instinct inscribed in us, in the very depth of our hearts by the Spirit which is the very essence of prayer.

2) On the other hand, the recitation of this prayer in a rhythmic manner, or simply with the rhythm of respiration—saying the larger half with inspiration, and the remainder with expiration, with a short pause, is certainly *a factor leading towards interior unification,* a means of struggling against distractions and against all wandering about of the mind. It is something which is highly productive of peace on the most profound level of our being. In the fourteenth century, the great hesychastes of Mt. Athos elaborated an integrated method which is more complex, and which is still described for us in *The Way of a Pilgrim* (in French, *Recits d'un pelerin russe*), which instructs us to fix our attention on the location of the heart and specifies certain conditions for the accomplishment of this prayer.[9] But it is necessary to say that this method, in all its rigor, can only be practiced under the direction of a spiritual master who has used it for a long period of time, and that it is not without its dangers. In our days, the monastic settings where it is still used in this manner are quite rare. In general, the spiritual fathers currently available, think that it suffices to say the prayer slowly, calmly, and in accordance with the pattern of one's respiration; and in accordance with the expression I have used above, to enclose oneself in the spirit of the words. Tranquility in recitation, the monotony of repetition and the simple attention given to the meaning of the words is a great means of recollection. It is as if one were seated before the Lord, like a beggar or supplicant at the side of the road, and crying out one's

---

9. *Athos, the Holy Mountain*, Philip Sherrard (New York: Overlook Press, 1985).

desire, one's appeal to passersby from time to time. Today, the psycho-physical Hesychast method of the fourteenth century is hardly practiced anywhere, even on the Sacred Mountain. I have nowhere personally met with its current usage. I do not say with certainty that it is no longer used in certain caves or hermetical retreats in the southern part of Mt. Athos where an elder with some disciples may live. Such is possible, but little is known of this and all in all, even in the most well-known Hesychast centers, this ancient method is no longer practiced. On the other hand, however, these centers strongly insist upon the need to use the prayer for extended periods of time, and of the need to enclose one's soul within the words of the prayer with a great deal of concentration. There are a certain number of cells in a place called Katounakia *on the southernmost tip of Mt. Athos* where a number of ancient sages surrounded by disciples live. Among them—still living, is a most remarkable spiritual father with five or six disciples who said to me that "it is necessary for me to be extremely gentle with the youth of the modern world. One can no longer demand of them the penances and ascetical rigors that one formerly could. They have physical needs that are much greater than that of our ancestors, and hence one cannot impose on them the same amount of fasting or even the same deprivation in their exterior surroundings." (This gentleness is called in Greek the "*economy*," or the adaptation required of a person.) "But," he added, "on the other hand, when it comes to need for attention in prayer, one cannot allow for any economy, or any condescension." Consider for a moment the amount of time given to prayer among such individuals (it is relatively restricted in many of the semi-hermetical groups on Mt. Athos): the monks do not say the canonical office, the divine office every day. They replace it during the week with the prayer of Jesus. And the monks in this small community of five or six mentioned above spend a little less than three hours every day in their cells saying the prayer of Jesus in place of the divine office; some of it in the morning and some in the evening. In addition, during the night, as a rule, at least one hour of personal prayer is added to these three hours. And so it is that they spend a total of four hours every day reciting with great peace this prayer of Jesus in a very simple rhythmic manner. And, needless to say, this is always under the direction of the spiritual father to whom each renders an account of his spiritual progress.

In some of the other monasteries on Mt. Athos the amount of time consecrated to this prayer is longer. Indeed, there is the group of monks under the direction of Joseph the Hesychast, the monk of whom I spoke to you a short time ago, a group committed to the semi-hermetical life who consecrate almost the entire night, a period of at least six hours at a stretch, to the recitation of the prayer of Jesus. Saying only this prayer, peacefully, calmly, in their cells, all alone and in darkness. And then, each day, at the end of the night, they gather to recite together in unison some prayers in preparation for Holy Communion and in order to celebrate the Eucharistic liturgy. For, in these Hesychast groups the daily celebration of the Mass is very common as is the almost daily practice of communicating. Because these monks, these groups have so greatly increased in number and have once again filled several large monasteries with the cenobitic life in common, they have been obliged on Mt. Athos to adopt a somewhat different kind of life, one especially characterized by the daily celebration of the entire liturgical office, the office of the Church. This has led to some shortening of the time for prayer in the cells; but nevertheless, a greater part of the night is consecrated to this prayer—at least three or four hours each night. In general the monks sleep for a short time in the evening, then follows three or four hours of prayer in their cells, followed by going to the Church for the canonical offices and then once again a short period for sleep in the morning. There is, throughout the entire Hesychast spiritual tradition, a great insistence on this nocturnal prayer. Certainly the night is the most suitable and propitious time for prayer. Not only is the first part of the divine office, Matins, celebrated while it is still night, but above all the prayer in the solitude of one's cell, personal prayer, takes place at night. And it is generally preferable for the monk to sleep a little in the morning and a little in the evening in order to leave free the most important part of the night in order that it might be consecrated to prayer. But here the manner of doing so varies a little from place to place and according to the direction of the various spiritual fathers. And this is indeed quite normal. There are other monasteries where one insists less exclusively on the prayer of Jesus, and perhaps more, for example, on the recitation of the psalms in a calm and peaceful manner— something which moreover allows for the better listening to the psalms read during the office—and still other prayers; or time consecrated to the reading of the Word of God, a practice which incidentally always has a place in monastic life. There also exists in England a small monastery that follows the Athonite tradition, and which is under the direction of the spiritual Father Sophrony.[10] This Father Sophrony is a disciple of Silouane. You perhaps are familiar with the staretz (spiritual director) Silouane whose writings have been published in an abridged manner by the Bellefontaine collection of "Eastern Orthodox Spiritual Writers" ("*Spiritualite orientale,*") as well as in a large volume accompanied by the commentary of Father Sophrony in the collection "*Presence.*" This is one of the most fundamental works which provide access to the Orthodox tradition of prayer.

Father Sophrony has founded a small monastery where during the week the divine office or canonical office as it is called in the West, is not celebrated, but replaced by the prayer of Jesus recited in common. The monks first of all say some prayers which are simply called initial prayers (prayers which follow classical formulations which are somewhat equivalent to the prayer "Come Holy Ghost" as used in the West, and which includes the Our Father.) followed

---

10. *Wisdom from Mount Athos* (Actually the writings of the Staretz Silouane who died in 1938) presented by Archimandrite Sophrony, Crestwood, N.Y.: St. Vladimir's Press, 1973); *His Life is Mine* (London: Mobrays, 1977).

immediately by the slow recitation in rotation of the prayer of Jesus on a rosary of one hundred beads for two to two and a half hours, both morning and evening. For a somewhat shorter period of time during the evening for Vespers. The formula used is that which I have already given you: "Lord Jesus Christ, Son of God, have pity on me a sinner," but this formula can be more or less varied. St. Seraphin moreover said so himself when he gave some instructions on this subject: one can for example say "Lord Jesus Christ, Son of God, by the intercession of your most Holy Mother (the Virgin Mary) have pity on me" or again, "have pity on us." Father Sophrony uses a formula which does not sound very musical in French, but which is very beautiful with regard to its content: "Lord Jesus Christ, Son of God, have pity on your world," the world which belongs to you, the world which is yours. One can also insert the name of the saint of the day, and he also does this. For example, the disciples of Father Sophrony always carry a rosary of one hundred beads on which the prayer used is formulated: "Lord Jesus Christ, Son of God, by the intercession of your holy father so and so . . . such as St. Benedict, or St. Theodore, have pity on us." And the divine office is recited in this manner. In general, those who have made a retreat in this monastery, and who have participated in this, derive a great deal of spiritual benefit from it. You see then that there are many possible formulas, but all of them are essentially similar.

3) Moreover, in this monotonous repetition of the prayer, it is necessary to add that at the heart of the prayer of Jesus *is the Name of Jesus.*

The Name of Jesus is for the Orthodox tradition a little like a verbal icon. You know that in the Orthodox churches there are what are called icons, which are representations, be it of Christ, or a saint. These icons are by no means merely ways of decorating a house or a church. Nor are they meant to simply recall to mind a person or past event. Rather they are a sort of real presence. Two of the greatest theologians, two of the greatest fathers of the Greek Church have very much insisted on this fact because the icon is a bond with the person of Christ, with the Mother of God, and with the saints. The icon becomes, as it were, a relay station of a presence, a relay station of the action of a saint on us. Of course, the icon is in itself only a piece of wood; there is nothing about it that is divine as such. But the fact is that it represents a person who has truly entered into the mystery of God, if it is not Jesus Christ who is God Himself incarnated. And when it is the Mother of God or the saints who are depicted, the icon represents persons who have realized the plenitude of deification. And indeed, as a result, by means of the intermediation of the icon, we are the benefactors of the energy, of the spiritual radiation of these persons. Similarly, in the prayer of Jesus, the Name of Jesus itself is, in a way, an icon of Christ. By means of the Name of Jesus, even though it is pronounced in its substance by a human person, the divinizing energy of Christ reaches us. It is a kind of *sacramental*, a sensible reality which is completely penetrated with the acting presence of Christ. It is from this that the power of the Name of Jesus, of the Name of Christ is derived when it is invoked.

We see this by referring to the Acts of the Apostles where St. Peter, in his discourse after the healing of the lame beggar at the gate of the Temple says: *There is no other Name by which we can be saved.* The invocation of the Name seems to be a privileged manner of entering into contact with the divinizing and deifying energy of Christ.

This is why the monks consecrate some of their time exclusively to this prayer, be it in their cells, or in certain cases in common. (But this is relatively rare; such is the situation in the monastery of Father Sophrony and of some other groups on Mt Athos, but most of the time it is said alone in the cell.) And then, throughout the day, at all times, while engaged in their occupations, whether the monks are working alone or in a monastic group. They can even continue to say it in a low voice. For example, in the monastery in which a disciple of Father Joseph is actually the higoumene, the superior, it is common to see the monks digging in the garden, or painting the wood on the shutters of the monastery windows, etc., while saying in a low voice, with great sweetness, the prayer of Jesus, throughout the day. But once again, one can say it silently in one's heart, when in a bus or on the subway, when in a train, while traveling, and under every circumstance. This is not strictly speaking continual prayer. It remains an intermittent prayer, a succession of acts, which has as its purpose to awaken in us, to conduct us, to a state of continual prayer, a state which is beyond this. This latter is a state, a condition in which it is no longer necessary to formulate any acts.

Once again, this teaching on active prayer which one finds with the Fathers very much insists upon the need to exclude all images, all sensations, all representations. I have already told you this, but I think it is a point which must be stressed. And here is how Bishop Callistos Ware summarizes the teaching of the Russian spiritual masters of the last century, who themselves in turn are only handing down to us what was taught to them.

> According to the teaching of Eastern Christianity, the faculty of the imagination by means of which we form more or less living images according to our aptitude, has only a very limited place in the work of prayer, and many, among which is included Theophane the Recluse, affirm that it has no place at all. "In prayer," according to Theophane, "one should never allow an image to interpose itself between the intellect and God. It is essential to remain in God. This implies before everything else, the awareness and ever present conviction that God is in us as He is in all things; that we live in the firm assurance that He sees everything in us and that He knows us better than we know ourselves. This certitude that the eye of God is always fixed on our interior being should never be accompanied by any visual concept, but should be

limited to the simple conviction or sentiment that such is the case. Never allow any concept, or any visual image. Eject from your intellect all images. In prayer, the simple rule is to never form an image of any kind whatsoever." Such is the common teaching of the eastern Fathers. As it is said among them: "He who sees noting in prayer, sees God." Our minds, habitually dispersed in a great diversity of thoughts and ideas should be unified, brought back from multiplicity to simplicity and emptiness; from diversity to sobriety. It should be purified of all mental images and all intellectual concepts until it is no longer conscious of anything other than the presence of God, invisible and incomprehensible.

The Orthodox writers speak of a state of "pure prayer." Pure not only from all evil thoughts, but from all thinking. One can find something in the West which is partially equivalent in what is sometimes called "the prayer of simple regard" or the "prayer of loving attention."

4) By the practice of active prayer, understood in this manner, a prayer which is however very simplified and which excludes all discursive activity of the mind and all activity of the imagination, man can come slowly to *a more and more profound experience of God*. Here for example is how a Russian monk of the last century briefly bears witness to this in a description of his spiritual journey which he left for his spiritual children:

> After I had spent many years practicing the continual prayer (But not the continual prayer in the strict sense, but rather this prayer of Jesus repeated constantly during the day), this prayer began to penetrate more deeply in my heart. Still later, in the

hermitage of Pokrov, the Lord visited me thanks to the intercession of Father Platon (who was his spiritual director). An inexpressible joy developed in my soul and the interior prayer began to operate. It filled me with a sweetness which was ineffable such that I could not sleep. I slept for one hour in the sitting position and then awoke freshened and alert as if I had never slept; And even when I was asleep, my heart was awake. And this contemplation started to bear fruit. This is indeed true, my son: the Kingdom of Heaven is within us. An inexpressible love towards all, accompanied by tears came to birth within me. If I wanted to, I could cry without stopping. And the Holy Scriptures, especially the Gospels and Psalms, is full of so great a sweetness for me that I can never be satiated with reading them. Each word of them fills me with admiration and leads me to pour forth tears.

(This spiritual understanding of Scripture, this meeting with God through Holy Scripture, is one of the forms of this superior aspect of prayer.)

Often, he continued, in the evening, when I am about to read the psalms or to say the prayer of Jesus, I am ravished, drawn outside of myself, I know not where, as Paul said, *whether in the body or outside of the body, God knows,* and when I return to myself, it is day.

In this manner the entire night passes in this state of possession with God. And as Father Callinique said—he was one of the great contemporary Hesychasts on Mt Athos who died in 1930 before the second world war—it sometimes happens that he was so ravished by the presence of God that he remained in this state for eight days without eating and without any awareness of what was going on around him.

And here is another witness which is more ancient, but there are still today certain spiritual fathers, certain great monks, especially on Mt. Athos, in Roumania, of which such things can be said. This is the attestation of St. Maximus of Cavsocalyvite, the burner of huts who founded the skite (hermitage) of Cavsokalyvia in the South of Athos. He was a monk who when he felt he was beginning to feel to much at home in his hermitage, would set it on fire and move some distance away. We have a very beautiful text which tells of his meeting with St. Gregory the Sinaite. Gregory was a monk who originally lived in the Sinai Desert and who spent some time on Cyprus. (It was during the time of the Arab invasions, the Arabs and the Persians having greatly disturbed the peace of the middle east.) Gregory arrived at Athos and met Maxumus the Cavsocalyvite and we have a contemporary text describing their meeting.

> St. Gregory said to Maximus: "May God grant me the ravishments which you know, most venerable Father! Let me ask you further: when your spirit is in God in this manner, what is it that you see with your spiritual eyes? And during such times do prayers rise to God from the depth of your heart? Maximus answered: "No, at such times such is impossible. As soon as the grace of the Holy Spirit descends on man by means of the prayer, it imposes silence. For the soul sees itself so completely invested by the grace of the Holy Spirit that it is no longer able to dispose of its own faculties. It completely submits itself to the Holy Spirit and the Holy Spirit leads it where it will: either to the immaterial heaven of divine light, or to the depth of some inexpressible contemplation, or again, as has sometimes happened to me, to a dialogue with

God. In summary, the Paraclete, the Holy Spirit, comforts his servant in accordance with his wishes, and gives him grace according to his needs. Anyone can confirm what I have said by referring to the Prophets and the Apostles who have been judged worthy of contemplation, even though men imagine that it is a power of the devil, or believe them drunkards, or turn away in derision.

(Referring to the episode in the Acts of the Apostles where the people, on seeing these men truly possessed by the Holy Spirit, imagined they were drunk.)

It is thus that the Prophet Isaias saw the Most High Lord on a throne surrounded by the Seraphims. And thus Stephen, the first martyr contemplated heaven open with the Lord Jesus seated on the right hand of the Father. In the same way, the servants of Christ are today still favored with similar visions.

(But these are no longer visions on the level of the unreformed imagination.)

There are in this, I know, those unbelievers who see here temptations and illusions. Their attitude stupefies me and their blindness astonishes me. How is it possible that they cannot see and cannot believe what the God of Truth has proclaimed through the mouth of the prophet Joel: *I shall pour forth my spirit on all flesh, your sons and your daughters will prophesy.* It is the grace of God which has descended on his disciples and which even today is given to them and which He will give them eternally as He promised. The man on whom the grace of the Holy Spirit descends perceives things in a very different manner than the sensible world habitually reveals itself to him.

(Or at least, he discovers by means of the sensible world, the true reality.)

These are realities which he never contemplated and which are far beyond anything that he could imagine. And then the Holy Spirit instructs his soul about supernatural and hidden mysteries about which the holy Apostle Paul said: *eye has not seen nor ear heard, neither hath it entered into the heart of man what things God hath prepared for them that love him.*

5) One thing about which it is also very important to insist, as much for the mature monk who has reached this spiritual level—one should remember that all this is not a prerogative of monastic life and lay people have also been blessed in this manner—as well as for those starting out on this path, is that this prayer should *always be accompanied* by a sentiment which the fathers call *compunction of the heart*: repentance for one sins, not just the feeling of guilt as such, but a profound nostalgia for God and a feeling of being distanced from Him, of being actually separated from Him by one's own fault. Bishop Ignace Briantchaninov speaks to us about this.

> Until the energies of the Spirit come to reside in the heart (which refers to what we have just described and the texts which I have read to you), the subtle influence of the blood (the natural activity of the non transformed *ego*) remains in man. As long as one is not purified and renewed by the Spirit, prudence consists of refusing to recognize as valid any sensation, any feeling of the heart, except the sense of repentance and salutary sorrow for one's sin mixed with hope in the mercy of God. From our fallen nature, God only accepts a single offering of the heart, a single sentiment, a single condition. *The sacrifice which He finds acceptable is*

that of a broken spirit, a bruised and humble heart.
This God will never scorn.

This attitude of the heart is one of the constant elements of the spiritual life in the Orthodox tradition.

6) Finally, to finish up, allow me to say a few more words about this approach to contemplation: on the necessity of not rushing ahead too fast. As I have just said, the essential thing in the spiritual life is prayer. Nevertheless, this prayer should be accompanied with a spiritual effort that involves all areas of action, and especially the most fundamental recommendation to in no way seek to achieve the superior states of prayer too early, and above all, before a profound purification of the entire being. To do so is to open the door to every possible illusion and to risk confusing sensations that seem to be spiritual which in reality they are not, with a true experience of God.

Ignace Briantchaninov once again tells us:

> This gift of true prayer (the veritable experience of God) is given to the person who is meek and humble before the magnitude of this favor. This gift is bestowed on one who has renounced his own self will and has given himself over to the will of God. This gift is given to the person who has mortified and overcome the flesh and the blood, who has mortified and overcome in himself wisdom of the flesh by means of the commandments of the Gospel. His life is resplendent in proportion to the degree that it is mortified.

(Mortification is conceived of here as a dying to oneself, not as an afflictive practice which is a little artificial and but only a gross and sensible way of conceiving it.)

> It comes about suddenly, entirely by benevolence;
> as life develops and comes to fruition, mortification

starts voluntarily. Those who seek with imprudence the higher states of prayer, especially if they are obstinate and guided by a spirit of presumption and the pride and of self sufficiency, are always marked with the seal of exclusion in accord with the dispositions of the spiritual law of the Gospel.

(He is making allusion here to the parable of those invited to the feast where the Lord excluded those who were not dressed in a wedding garment, this nuptial robe for coming to feast of union with God being the profound purification of all our tendencies.)

It is very difficult, and in most cases even impossible, to break this seal.

(I would almost say that the principal obstacle to the spiritual life is the wish to rush ahead too fast, because this involves a subtle pride, a presumption which results in the fact that one can never in the last analysis do more than imitate the spiritual life, and never actually come to the meeting with God.)

For what reason? This is why: Pride and presumption result in spiritual blindness and leads one to enter into relation with the demons and to submit oneself to them. We are hindered from seeing the falsity of our situation, not allowed to see our deplorable relations with these demons nor our terrible enslavement to them. "First the leaves sprout forth, and when God ordains, you will also produce fruits" say the Fathers.

(These leaves are this mortification, this active death to ourselves, and the fruits become the true meeting with God.)

Learn to start with the attentive prayer. A person who is first of all purified and prepared by attentive prayer, he who is formed and strengthened by the commandments in the Gospel and who is established on them, to him God, the God of mercy will give, at the moment when He wishes, by means of grace, the prayer of silence.

And this expression: "to practice the commandments," summarizes in the spiritual tradition all that activity involving the death to oneself in order to permit the grace of God to strengthen its control in us. Concretely, all this spiritual activity is translated, in the life of a monk, on the one hand into austerity by fasting—to which the Orthodox tradition always attaches great importance: fasting of which the norms are moreover defined by the traditions of the Church, and which are always practiced in their rigor, at least in the monasteries, but often by the laity who are leading a spiritual life—great insistence being placed on obedience. For the essential purpose of all this is to acquire humility. But humility is not acquired by the sentiments of humility, but by practice. And this practice will be obedience—not only obedience to authority which is but one aspect of this, but an attitude of being properly disposed, of submission, of being open to all, the taking care to never impose one's own tastes and preferences on another, except when what is involved is a vital matter which goes beyond us. But normally, to have this attitude of submission with regard to everyone. Obedience thus understood, obedience to all, fundamentally summarizes the entire spiritual effort. It is in this that humility is incarnated. Humility does not consist of saying or thinking that one is inferior to everyone else, because one can become complacent with a great deal of illusion from doing this. But when one obeys others because one looks at everyone with this attitude of welcoming, of openness, of benevolence, never seeking to impose our self in any manner whatsoever, then humility will be realized in our soul.

Beyond this, another form of obedience is abandoning oneself to Providence, leaving things up to God, never trying to impose our own will, not only on persons, but also on situations. An attitude in essence of being well disposed, seeking to read the will of God in all things, in all events, and submitting to them. This moreover sometimes leads the monastic life in the context of orthodoxy, to have a somewhat disorganized aspect, a sort of letting things go, a kind of imprecision and lack of strictness. But in fact, it is simply a question of the desire to never impose oneself and to remain always in a state of very great disponibilite.

I have also spoken to you of the importance given to staying awake and nocturnal prayer which is at one and the same time an exercise of prayer and an exercise of asceticism, a renouncing of oneself, a renouncing of one's comfort, and a way of expressing all the alertness of the soul which waits on God.

Importance is also given to body prostrations, to "metanies," to body positions in prayer which have an aspect which is certainly against nature, against our still untransfigured nature, but which at the same time contributes to our symbolizing, to making us realize with all our being, our interior attitudes. And all this ought to conduct the monk to what the Orthodox spiritual tradition calls *apatheia*, which is not impassibility in the stoic sense of the word, not the absence of the passions, but the integration of the passions, the integration of all the tendencies of our being in order that they might be entirely penetrated with this instinct of the Spirit which, yet once again, ought to in consequence permeate the life of the Christian and the monk, to make of his entire life a prayer. His life should truly become a state of profound orientation of his being towards God and towards all things, by means of all things.

There are yet many other things that I could say, but I shall stop here because I believe that the essentials have been more or less completely covered.

— Archimandrite Placide Deseille